Comprehensive Multicultural Education in the 21st Century

Increasing Access in the Age of Retrenchment

A Volume in
Contemporary Perspectives on Access, Equity, and Achievement

Series Editors

Chance W. Lewis
University of North Carolina at Charlotte

Contemporary Perspectives on
Access, Equity, and Achievement
Chance W. Lewis, Editor

(List continues on next page)

Comprehensive Multicultural Education in the 21st Century

Increasing Access in the Age of Retrenchment

edited by

Brandi N. Hinnant-Crawford
Western Carolina University

C. Spencer Platt
University of South Carolina

Christopher B. Newman
Azusa Pacific University

Adriel Hilton
Seton Hill University

INFORMATION AGE PUBLISHING, INC.
Charlotte, NC • www.infoagepub.com

Library of Congress Cataloging-in-Publication Data

CIP record for this book is available from the Library of Congress
http://www.loc.gov

ISBNs: 978-1-64113-629-7 (Paperback)

        978-1-64113-630-3 (Hardcover)

        978-1-64113-631-0 (ebook)

Printed in the United States of America

DEDICATION

This volume is dedicated to contributor C. Vandyke Goings, whose work and life illustrated the necessity for caring relationships in high quality education. May we all care as he did and cultivate other educators who do likewise.

C. Vandyke Goings
June 15, 1967– March 20, 2018

CONTENTS

INTRODUCTION

NATIONALISM, TERRORISM, AND THE RETRENCHMENT OF MULTICULTURALISM

The Challenge of Multicultural Education in the 21st Century

Brandi N. Hinnant-Crawford
Western Carolina University

C. Spencer Platt
University of South Carolina

Christopher B. Newman
Azusa Pacific University

Adriel Hilton
Seton Hill University

This current generation of scholars has been fortunate to operate during the "age of Obama." The age of Obama is reflected often upon as an era when women, people of color, the LBGTQ community and other under-

Comprehensive Multicultural Education in the 21st Century:
Increasing Access in the Age of Retrenchment, pp. xi–xvii
Copyright © 2019 by Information Age Publishing
All rights of reproduction in any form reserved.

represented populations have been able to make remarkable gains in social, political, and economic arenas. Many believed this nation would continue to build upon the legacy of past president of the United States of America Barack Obama with regards to the progress of people of color and women.

However, the age of Obama was simultaneously a time that came with significant challenges including: the shooting and/or killing of unarmed (mostly Black) citizens; the threat of deportation for DREAMERS, undocumented students and their family members; and the twin problems of the skyrocketing cost of a college education and the student loan crisis, to name a few. There is yet another challenge that has come with the Obama presidency: backlash against multiculturalism, social justice, and diversity. This came at a time when some were openly wondering if America had entered a new, postracial age, where race and ethnicity no longer limited people's life chances, after all, the President of the United States was Black. They did need to not wonder for long. We are currently less than a year removed from Obama's departure of the White House and notions of a postracial America now seem quaint and naïve.

On one fateful November night in 2016, with the election of Donald Trump, the realities that many of the advocates of multiculturalism, diversity, and social justice had grown accustomed to all shifted. Trump's surprising rise to the presidency emboldened many who oppose social justice and multiculturalism. Many students, teachers, staff, administrators, and professors who felt affirmed, validated, and valued now feel vulnerable and threatened.

It is important to consider what is occurring in the United States in an international context. The challenges multiculturalism and multicultural education face in the 21st century are not unique to the United States. Throughout the Western world there has been a retreat from multicultural values, evidenced by the rise of rightist populist movements throughout Europe. It is important to note that populist movements are not bound by ideology, and exist across the political spectrum. Judis (2016) describes an important distinction between leftist and rightest populist movements which multiculturalist cannot ignore:

> Leftwing populists champion the people against an elite or an establish-ment.... Rightwing populists champion the people against an elite that they accuse of coddling a third group, which can consist, for instance, of immigrants, Islamists, or African American militants. Leftwing populism is dyadic. Rightwing populism and triadic. (p. 15)

While rightist populist movements are receiving more press in recent election cycles, as a result of candidates running for high-profile positions, it is important to realize that these ideas are not as fresh as the awareness of these movements. Because of many European multiparty systems, they have been present in parliamentary branches for decades but in smaller numbers. What is of importance now is that their popularity is growing. Norris (2017) argued that the average share of the vote for rightwing populist parties has "more than doubled since the 1960s ... [and] their share of seats [in parliamentary branches] has tripled, from 3.8 percent to 12.8 percent" (para. 12). The advance of rightist populist movements is reactive and correlated with economic uncertainty and increased immigration (CNN Staff, 2017).

During the financial post-World War II boom, Europe welcomed immigrants from previously colonized countries, particularly in the Middle East and North Africa. As the economy changed, juxtaposed with a shift in mindset from socialist democratic values to neoliberalism, immigrants were viewed as competition for jobs and moochers of social welfare programs (Judis, 2016). Judis (2016) argues, "the most immediate factor in the [rightwing populist] parties' rise was the way they tied themselves to the growing popular disapproval of non-European immigrants and asylum seekers" (p. 99). This strategy of pitting the dominant majority against the marginalized will be one of the greatest challenges of multicultural educators in this New World Order.

These rightwing populist parties in the U.S. and abroad are antimulticulturalism and vocal about being so. Geert Wilders's, of the Freedom Party in the Netherlands, campaign website begins with the assertion, "The Netherlands Ours Again!" and an 11 point agenda, of which the first priority is to de-Islamize the Netherlands (Wilders, 2016). In Denmark, the Party Program of the Danish People's Party states preserving Danish culture and heritage as a priority. The platform goes on to explicitly state, "Denmark is not an immigrant-country and never has been. Thus we will not accept transformation to a multiethnic society" (Dahl, 2002, para. 7). In France, presidential candidate for the National Front party, Marie Le Pen, stated "Multiculturalism is the soft weapon of Islamic fundamentalists, which is allowed by useful idiots under the guise of tolerance" (Moore, 2019, para. 3). Here, in the United States, Trump has advocated mass deportations of illegal immigrants and building a wall along the nation's border with Mexico to keep "criminals" and "rapists" out of this country. In the rhetoric of such movements, the advocates of multiculturalism are the elites that are coddling "outsiders" that threaten the status quo.

The rightwing populism plays on the fears of "the people" especially in this age of growing terrorism. McGhee (2008) explains in the British context, and we would argue European and U.S. contexts as well, "hostility to multiculturalism and the associated new integration discourses could not be examined without considering the impact of terrorism or more accurately the impact of the response to 'the terror threat' " (p. 145). McGhee's text,

End of Multiculturalism? Terrorism, Integration, and Human Rights, discusses the British state's backlash to terrorism in the wake of 9/11 (September 11, 2001, U.S. World Trade center attacks) and 7/7 (July 7, 2005, London Metro attacks). While focusing only on the United Kingdom, he illustrates the various voices in the debate against multiculturalism rising from the left and the right. McGhee goes onto say, this terrorist age has "ushered in a new ethics of inhospitality and an even stronger sense of the precariousness and conditional nature of citizenship for certain communities" (p. 146). In this case, it is Islamic communities that bear the brunt of this burden. After surveying citizens in 10 European countries, Pew Research (Wike, Stokes, & Simmons, 2016) found between 40 and 76% of respondents thought the presence of refugees increase the likelihood of domestic terrorism, with the median for all 10 countries being 59%. Embracing multiculturalism in the face of terror is another key challenge for multicultural educators in the 21st century.

While some readers may take comfort in the fact that rightwing populist candidates like Geert Wilders and Marie La Pen did not win the top positions in their countries, their poisonous rhetoric and increased visibility has changed the political discourse in these countries. As Paauwe (2017) reports, in order to appeal to their voting base, the presence of Wilder required, "mainstream conservatives […] to mimic his populism … [and they] jumped on the train of conservative identify politics" (para. 2). Furthermore, extremist in their constituencies are propagating terror for marginalized groups and their supporters in many countries. The European Union's Agency for Fundamental Rights (2016) reports, "vigilante groups with ties to right-wing extremist groups violently attacked and harassed asylum seekers and migrants in Bulgaria, Finland, Greece, Hungary and Sweden" (p. 79). Additionally, in 2016 Member of Parliament Jo Cox was murdered as her assailant "uttered the words 'Britain first'" (Cobain, 2016, para. 2). Multiculturalists are challenged to remember discourse has consequences.

Where Do We Go From Here?

Globalism has forced once homogenous societies to interact as peers with diverse people, cultures, perspectives and ways of life or risk being left behind in the global marketplace. Despite the efforts of the giants in our field, and nearly 50 years of work advancing the purpose and process of multicultural education we are in a moment on retrenchment. However, as we look to the future of multicultural education, we know the challenges of multiculturalism are not unique to Europe or the United States. In the age of terror and rightwing populist movements, all of us are required to be vigilant on one hand, while being compassionate and empathetic on the other hand. It is our responsibility to teach the undeniable value of each life—regardless of race, creed, sexuality, religion, or country of origin despite its decreasing popularity. Norris (2017) asserts:

> Triggered by globalism's economic and migratory earthquakes, and by a backlash against progressive culture shifts, populism has infected the center-right decimated the social democratic center-left and it is likely to continue to gain ground, even if experiencing occasional electoral setbacks and defeats, until the underlying conditions change. (para. 12)

Multicultural educators cannot predict the next economic downturn or civil war and natural disaster that will result in a wave of individuals seeking asylum. That is not the job or task of multicultural education. However, we can and must continue to expose pupils of all ages to content and pedagogy that requires them to think critically, examine structures of power, probe incidences of privilege, consider (and appreciate) difference, and excel academically.

The collected works in this text examine the many contributions multicultural education and approaches can have on the advancement of society, primarily through schooling. In the first chapter, Haley, Bertrand, and Mitchell outline the demographic shift facing public schooling in the United States and provide guidance for teacher education programs preparing preservice teachers to educate culturally, linguistically, and economically diverse students.

After considering the multiple ways teacher educators can prepare teachers to work with diverse populations, the following five chapters look at discipline specific multicultural pedagogical practices, designed to increase student access to literacy (Dwight & Cryer), civic learning (Hinnant-Crawford & Baptist), history (King), and mathematics (Goings). Furthermore, Bryan and Wright present *African American Male Pedagogy* for the readers' consideration.

Yet, this text does not only explore pedagogy and curricular matters, but it examines systems that contribute to and detract from opportunities to learn for students from marginalized groups. Rush and Robinson present ways to disrupt disproportionality in special education referrals; while, Sutton-Palmer, Coaxum, and Ingram illustrate strategies to enhance the transition process from special education to postsecondary education. Readers' perspectives about special education and inclusion are problematized, as Kalyanpur explores the difference between special education in the Global North and Global South.

In addition to pedagogical practice and system processes—several chapters also explore the role of the environment in creating opportunities to learn. Patterson and Moore explore the need for holistic learning spaces that understand the intersectionality of race and gender, and the particular needs of nonmonoracial students. Similarly, Hinnant-Crawford, Platt, and Wingard argue the need for multiculturalism to invade classroom management and disciplinary practices to ensure equitable access to opportunities to learn.

Last but not least, Windchief, LaVeau, Del Duca, and Aderholdt remind scholars who wish to engage in research concerning marginalized communities about the significance of researcher positionality and conducting research in solidarity with rather than on marginalized populations.

The purpose of this book is to bring a more open and honest discussion regarding multiculturalism, the intersection of multiple identities, and the sociopolitical realities of subaltern people contemporary society. Our vision in editing this book was to bring together both emerging and established scholars in ways that are beneficial to practitioners, teacher educators, community based activists, students, policymakers, social service agencies, church leaders, administrators and researchers alike. We see this as a timely and essentially vital text for those who are committed to the work of social justice, equity and multiculturalism in these challenging times.

Social science research will continue to have a critical role to play in shaping our current and future understandings of our lived experiences and diverse populations will need to continue to have an active voice at every stage of this research's construction and dissemination. Research is needed that crosses the arbitrary lines of our disciplines and meets the needs of communities, cities, states, our nation and the world. In addition to crossing disciplinary lines, we should cross methodological lines for there are certainly many ways that many of the most pressing questions of our time can be answered. Finally, we urge scholars to continue to challenge the damaging, outdated and deficit-oriented research and practices that continue to marginalize and limit the life chances of people of color, women and other underrepresented groups. Academicians, researchers, activists, and practitioners must investigate strategies for advancing multicultural education in the age of terror and rightwing populism. If, collectively, we do all of the above, eventually, then together we will live in a more just and equitable society.

REFERENCES

Cobain, I. (2016, November 14). Jo Cox killed in 'brutal, cowardly' and politically motivated murder, trial hears. *The Guardian*. Retrieved from https://www.theguardian.com/uk-news/2016/nov/14/jo-cox-killed-in-politically-motivated-murder-trial-thomas-mair-hears

CNN Staff. (2017, May 5). Will Europe ride the populist wave? A visual guide. *CNN*. Retrieved from http://www.cnn.com/2017/03/15/europe/populism-in-european-elections-visual-guide/index.html

Dahl, K. T. (2002). *The Party Program of the Danish People's Party*. Retrieved from https://www.danskfolkeparti.dk/The_Party_Program_of_the_Danish_Peoples_Party#

European Union Agency for Fundamental Rights. (2017). *Fundamental rights report 2017*. Luxembourg City, Luxembourg.

Judis, J. B. (2016). *The populist expansion: How the great recession transformed American and European politics*. New York, NY: Columbia Global Reports.

McGhee, D. (2008). *End of multiculturalism? Terrorism, integration and human rights*. Berkshire, England: Open University Press.

Moore, F. (2017, April 11). French presidential hopeful Le Pen brands multiculturalism a 'WEAPON' for jihadis.*Express*. Retrieved from http://www.express.co.uk/news/world/790396/marine-le-pen-french-election-multiculturalism-emmanuel-macron-islamic-extremism

Norris, P. (2017, May 17). So is the wave of populist nationalism finished? Hardly. *The Washington Post*. Retrieved from https://www.washingtonpost.com/news/monkey-cage/wp/2017/05/17/so-is-the-wave-of-populist-nationalism-finished-hardly/?utm_term=.19f0759e48e3

Paauwe, C. (2017, March 22). A pyrrhic victory: Don't be relieved by the Dutch election—it's done nothing to stop populism in Europe. *Quartz*. Retrieved from https://qz.com/938736/dutch-election-results-and-xenophobia-dont-be-relieved-by-the-dutch-election-its-done-nothing-to-stop-populism-in-europe/

Wike, R., Stokes, B., & Simmons, K. (2016). *Europeans fear wave of refugees will mean more terrorism, fewer jobs: Sharp ideological divides across EU on views about minorities, diversity and national identity*. Washington, DC: Pew Research Center.

Wilders, G. (2016). *Preliminary Election Program PVV 2017–2021*. Retrieved from https://www.geertwilders.nl/94-english/2007-preliminary-election-program-pvv-2017–2021

CHAPTER 1

SITUATING A REQUISITE *PURPLE RAIN* IN MULTICULTURAL EDUCATION

Marjorie Hall Haley
George Mason University in Fairfax, Virginia

Shamaine K. Bertrand
Illinois State University

Tiffany M. Mitchell
West Virginia University

INTRODUCTION

This chapter is the combined effort of three female educators—all women of color; one teaches at the elementary level; one teaches in a middle school; and one is a teacher educator in a graduate school of education. All three are located on the eastern seaboard of the United States. There are several unifying themes around which these three individuals' paths intersect. The most demonstrative is their commitment in their lived experiences to shaping and creating spaces for culturally, linguistically, and cognitively

Comprehensive Multicultural Education in the 21st Century:
Increasing Access in the Age of Retrenchment, pp. 1–17
Copyright © 2019 by Information Age Publishing

diverse learners to be able to "laugh in the purple rain." In other words, ensuring that *all* learners are taught by responsible, caring individuals who approach their work assured that every student is capable of succeeding. In this chapter we set out to examine the shifting demographics across U.S. K–12 public schools followed by recent trends in teacher preparation and their impact on multicultural education. We then shift to a closer of examination of teacher preparation in multicultural education and focus on two model programs that are specifically designed to approach teaching and learning through a more inclusive lens that both enhances and embraces dialogic inquiry and community partnerships with schools. Next we each share our "story" as meaningful pieces of the "Purple Rain" metaphor. Finally, we conclude with suggestions and recommendations that situate a purple rain in multicultural education with culturally, linguistically, and cognitively diverse learners.

Shifting Demographics in U.S. K–12 Public Schools

According to the U.S. Census (2012), minorities now 37% of the U.S. population are projected to comprise 57% of the population by 2060. The demographic shift has already begun in public schools. According to the Department of Education Pew Research report, in the fall of 2014, 50.3% of students in public schools were minority students and 49.7% were White students and in the years following the percentages are expected to increase for minorities and decrease for White students (Krogstad & Fry, 2014). The demographic shifts we are seeing in public schools largely stem from increases in Hispanic, Asian, and multiracial populations and a decrease in White student populations. Public school classrooms in urban centers have predominantly been populated with students of color. The current trends since 2014 suggest that diversity appears to be expanding into areas and school districts that were predominantly White. Maxwell (2014) suggests that although the projected diverse majority will remain concentrated in major urban areas and in a handful of historically diverse states such as California, Florida, New York, and Texas, it is by no means an exclusively big-city or big-state trend. Further, in most major American cities, most African American and Hispanic students attend public schools where a majority of their classmates qualify as poor or low-income (Brownstein & Boschma, 2016). Now many rural and suburban communities are becoming increasingly diverse across racial, ethnic, and socioeconomic lines as well. With the continued growth of diverse populations in public schools the need for fresh perspectives on multicultural education and teacher preparation is paramount to ensuring educational equity for all students.

As we explore the changing populations across public schools in the United States, close attention must be paid to the systemic barriers students of color face. Historically, attempts have been made to mitigate issues of racial inequality in education through government policy as a means to solve the problem of discrimination in the American school system (Rowley & Wright, 2011). Much of the research cites landmark decisions and legislation such as the *Brown v. Board of Education in* Topeka, Kansas, *Civil Rights Act of 1964, Elementary and Secondary Education Act of 1965* and *No Child Left Behind* (NCLB) as key education policy measures. In essence, the goals of the major education policies involved mitigating impediments to student success particularly among minority groups that were historically disenfranchised through integration, providing Title I funding and resources to schools in need, and accountability through testing. Based on the Natiional Assessent of Educational Progress (NAEP, 2012) *Long Term Trends in Academic Progress Report*, the gaps in reading and math between White and Black and White and Hispanic students have narrowed since the 1970s. Although, achievement gaps based on standardized tests have narrowed, they are still prevalent. This is important to reflect upon as we prepare for the demographic shifts in public schools. We must ensure that all students are achieving at high levels in public schools as these shifts continue to increase.

Roughly 83% of teachers in public schools are White (National Center for Education Statistics [NCES], 2013). As populations continue to shift, U.S. schools must acknowledge a teaching force that does not mirror image its students. Goldenberg (2014) suggests that there can be a clash of cultures that occurs in classrooms between students of color that are mostly from low-income households and their teachers who are predominantly White and middle class. The work of Gay and Howard (2000) refers to this as a demographic divide across race, cultural, linguistic and socioeconomic contexts between teachers (predominantly White) and K–12 students (increasingly from racial/ethnic groups of color and low income). This is not to suggest that White teachers cannot teach students of color successfully— quite the opposite. Examining teacher preparation programs is critical to ensuring that incoming teachers learn how to employ multicultural competencies and culturally relevant pedagogy. As scholars in the field of multicultural education and cultural relevancy (Gay & Howard, 2000; Ladson-Billings, 2009) have previously suggested White teachers must not only recognize their privilege but also value the cultural experiences and knowledge of students of color and find meaningful ways to incorporate that into the classroom. Exploring fresh multicultural perspectives for teacher preparation helps to build a knowledge base to assist programs with the development of future educators that will benefit all students in increasingly diverse public school classrooms. This begs the question: *how do we best prepare teachers for multicultural classrooms?*

Teacher Preparation and Multicultural Education

U.S. public policy is filled with opinions about what teacher preparation should include or exclude, and if teacher preparation is necessary (Berry, Hoke, & Hirsch, 2004; Cochran-Smith & Fries, 2001). Teacher education seems crucial to the preparation of teachers, especially as teachers are prepared to meet the needs of an increasingly diverse P–12 student population (Milner, 2010). Preparing teachers for diversity, equity, and social justice are perhaps the most challenging and daunting tasks facing the field of teacher education (Milner, 2010). In the 2011 Obama Administration Plan for Teacher Education Reform and Improvement, former U.S. Secretary of Education stated:

> Over the next ten years, 1.6 million teachers will retire, and 1.6 million new teachers will be needed to take their place. This poses both an enormous challenge and an extraordinary opportunity for our education system: if we succeed in recruiting, preparing, and retaining great teaching talent, we can transform public education in this country and finally begin to deliver an excellent education for every child. (U.S. Department of Education, 2011)

Furthermore, the pervasive inequities for culturally, linguistically, and cognitively diverse (CLCD) students are proliferated by teachers' unintentional dispositions and low expectations of CLCD learners (Castagno, 2008; Ortiz & Fránquiz, 2015). Race and class further separate the powerful from the powerless when we should be moving towards empowerment of the disenfranchised (Cookson, 2011). The divide between the privileged and the marginalized students creates an achievement gap that continues to widen in a culture of low expectations (Delpit, 2012).

The need for successful recruiting, preparing, and retaining of great teachers is important because of the growing number of minority students who are the new majority in public schools (NCES, 2014). Traditional teacher preparation programs can no longer conduct business as usual. These programs must begin to consider the racial, linguistic, and class differences of today's public school students.

In 2013, the National Council on Teacher Quality (NCTQ) shared a report of the nation's teacher preparation programs. This report brought attention to improving what is at best a mediocre teacher preparation system in the United States (NCTQ, 2014). The report highlighted how imperative it is that teachers are classroom-ready upon graduation. Since the publication of this report teacher preparation has become an agenda item for state school boards and legislatures (NCTQ, 2014). In 2014, a second review of the nation's teacher preparation programs was written and revealed how since the release of the 2013 review, several states have made significant changes in teacher preparation policy. However, one important factor has been left out of these programs and that is including courses and field experiences that include exposure to multicultural education and racially, linguistically, and economically diverse classroom settings.

One of the purposes of teacher preparation is to prepare teachers to connect and communicate with diverse learners (Darling-Hammond & Bransford, 2005). Most preservice teachers enter teacher education programs, bringing prior knowledge and experiences they acquired from their families, personal experiences, and K–12 schooling; therefore, their beliefs are often developed long before they enter teacher preparation programs (Bennett, 2013; Swartz, 2003). These beliefs are often understood by preservice teachers as reality and as a result, can be a challenge to influence.

In order to influence the beliefs of these preservice teachers, preparation programs need to group coursework with field experiences in diverse schools and provide a framework that will enhance the success of preservice teachers working in diverse communities that include students from different racially ethnic, class, and linguistic backgrounds. A survey study conducted with 92 students in a teacher education program found that most students in teacher education programs held biases towards culturally diverse populations including beliefs that assessments should not be modified to address various language difficulties, and felt moderately uncomfortable with people who spoke different dialects (Walker-Dalhous & Dalhouse 2006). Negative stereotypes and lack of knowledge how to work with students of various ethnic, linguistic, and economic backgrounds may impact the quality of teaching.

Banks (2002) states that multicultural education has been a prime factor in the development of contemporary curricula; in fact within the past 30 years, it has made its way into public schools and institutions of higher learning. While it is not the priority topic of instruction in colleges of education, it is a contributing factor to curriculum and instruction for classrooms. Many teacher education programs confine diversity preparation to a course, workshop, or module that students are mandated to complete for certification requirements (Bennett, 2013). Most multicultural education course(s) attempt to "help prospective and in-service teachers develop the knowledge, skills, and dispositions needed for successfully working with diverse student populations" (Ukpokodu, 2009, p. 1). Gorski (2009) administered a research study that examined 45 U.S. based multicultural teacher education course syllabi from colleges and universities across America. The syllabi were limited to courses focused explicitly on multicultural teacher education (Gorski, 2009). The majority (30 out of

45) of the syllabi analyzed were from undergraduate courses and 15 were from graduate levels courses (Gorski, 2009). Using qualitative content analysis and drawing on existing typologies for multicultural education, he analyzed the theories and philosophies underlying multicultural teacher education course designs. The researcher concluded, "Most of the syllabi did not appear to be designed to prepare teachers to practice authentic multicultural education, they did appear designed to meet the NCATE standard" (Gorski, 2009, p. 312). Teacher education programs must go beyond meeting just the standards of college accreditation standards and educate preservice teachers so they may enter diverse classrooms as effective highly qualified teachers.

Innovative Multicultural Perspectives for Teacher Preparation

Teacher preparation programs must help teachers examine their own cultural beliefs and practices, gain a repertoire of cultural practices relevant to their diverse students, and acquire pedagogical knowledge and skills about how to create spaces to connect these cultural practices to the curriculum and in their daily instruction (Li, 2013). The need for infusing multicultural education into teacher preparation has been widely recognized in the literature but many studies have indicated that this is hardly realized in teacher education programs (Bartolomé, 2004; Darling-Hammond & Bransford, 2005; Gorski, 2009). With the changing nature of public schools, it is imperative to explore innovative teacher preparation programs that are attempting to mitigate the demographic divide that is increasingly becoming more and more apparent. As this is a newer trend, two graduate level teacher preparation programs, University of California, Los Angeles (UCLA) Center X and George Mason University (GMU) concentration in transformative teaching will be examined. These programs bring fresh multicultural perspectives into teacher preparation programs providing glimmers of hope in the field of teacher education in a changing cultural landscape.

UCLA Center X began in 1994 with the mission of preparing teachers to teach successfully for social justice in urban school spaces through critical study of race and society, inequity as structural, activism if necessary with multiculturalism being central to the curriculum (Quartz, Olsen, & Duncan-Andrade, 2008). What makes UCLA unique is the way in which it not only foregrounds multicultural education through critical readings in the field including prominent scholars such as Freire (1970), Giroux (1992), Banks (1994), Hooks (1994), Nieto (1999), Oakes and Lipton (2003) but also, in the focus on dialogic inquiry in connection with communities through partnerships with urban schools in Los Angeles. Center

X strives to teach culturally relevant and collaborative pedagogy in practical ways that will potentially transform urban spaces by building bridges with students, parents and communities in which they will work.

In spite of the many successes, Center X is an innovative teacher preparation program that faces many challenges. One main challenge is building and sustaining university-community-school partnerships. Quartz et al. (2008) found that many Center X teachers reported a wide gap in separating university conceptions and Los Angeles school realities, finding it hard to build pedagogical bridges between them. Also long term retention of teachers in urban settings has also proved to be another hurdle. In a longitudinal study by Quartz et al. it was reported that Center X graduates stay in teaching at higher rates than the national average, but many do leave as only 69% of those who were in the first cohort have stayed in education for 6 years and remained in a high poverty school. Although there is still a lot work to be done in regards to teacher retention and sustaining partnerships, Center X provides practical strategies for integrating a multicultural, collaborative curriculum for preservice teachers entering spaces filled with predominantly students of color and/or high poverty schools. The social justice framework is an attempt to merge community, schools and university to blend research theory and practice and challenge traditional norms of school with a focus on educational equity showing tremendous promise for today's classrooms. Center X at UCLA provides us with a concrete example of an innovative teacher preparation program focused on social justice and extends the principles of multiculturalism to ensure all students succeed in public classrooms. The next program mode is designed to address experiences in multicultural education for experienced, in-service teachers.

The transformative teaching masters of education concentration is innovative on many levels as it is a hybrid online course targeting experienced teachers currently in the field. This is critical to providing in service teachers with opportunities to learn multicultural perspectives and influence their teaching practice. According to the website (https://gse.gmu.edu/transformative-teaching/), the transformative teaching concentration provides teachers with the opportunity to reflect upon their teaching practices, create empowering learning environments and become informed participants in the policy arenas. The program is primarily online to accommodate full time teachers but also includes a two weeklong intensive summer courses. The titles of the course work differ from traditional teacher education curriculum in that it focuses on inquiry, reflection, and empowerment. See Figure 1.1 for the MEd concentration in transformative teaching course work sequence.

Course work in sequence for the masters degree cohort program

Year 1

- EDUC 647: Critical Reflective Practice | 1.5 credits | (one week on-campus)
- EDUC 649: Critical Dialogue in Education | 1.5 credits
- EDUC 651: Critical Theories and Pedagogies | 3 credits
- EDUC 653: Technology and Learning | 3 credits
- EDUC 655: Teacher Research Methods | 3 credits
- EDUC 657: Teaching for Democracy and Social Justice | 3 credits

Year 2

- EDUC 659: Teacher Leadership | 1.5 credits | (one week on-campus)
- EDUC 661: Teacher Empowerment and Policy | 1.5 credits
- EDUC 663: Culturally Relevant Pedagogy | 3 credits
- EDUC 665: Teacher Inquiry in Practice I | 3 credits
- EDUC 667: Teacher Inquiry in Practice II | 3 credits
- EDUC 669: Teaching and Learning in Practice | 3 credits

Figure 1.1.   MEd concentration in transformative teaching course work sequence.

This program shows tremendous promise but research is limited on its impact in shifting the culture of schooling other than anecdotal responses located on the website. But what can be gleaned from both GMU transformative teaching and UCLA's Center X are promising strategies to revamp and create teacher preparation programs that focus on multicultural perspectives in a new manner that values the experiences of all students, is reflective and collaborative. Both model programs seek to challenge dominant paradigms of teaching by using a critical lens, theoretical frameworks, and multicultural readings throughout the teacher preparation program, and therefore not reducing multicultural education to one course. These innovative programs embed multiculturalism in each course throughout the teacher preparation program but this is often not the case nationwide. The examination of higher education policies in teacher preparation is critical to understanding potential barriers to infusing multiculturalism in teacher preparation programs.

Higher Education Policies in Teacher Preparation

In 1977, the National Council for Accreditation of Teacher Education (NCATE) mandated multicultural education to be integrated into all teacher preparation programs using the following requirement: "The (teacher preparation) institution gives evidence of planning for multi-cultural education in its teacher education curricula including both the general and professional studies components" (NCATE, 1977, as cited in Ramsey & Williams, 2003, p. 213). The 1990s version of this require-ment stated, "The unit ensures that teacher candidates acquire and learn to apply to professional and pedagogical knowledge and skills to become competent to work with all students" (NCATE, 1997, as cited in Ramsey & Williams, 2003, p. 13). By the mid-1990s, a focus on preparing teacher candidates to teach diverse student populations influenced accreditation standards, teacher certification requirements, program and curriculum development, and the position statements of professional organizations (Ramsey & Williams, 2003). While there has been a push for teacher prepa-ration programs to focus on preparing teacher candidates for diversity by NCATE, putting this into practice was found challenging.

In a national evaluation of teacher education programs, the National Council for Accreditation of Teacher Education's Blue Ribbon Committee (2010) recommended "a dramatic overhaul of how teachers are prepared" in order to meet the needs of public education's most disenfranchised groups (p. 2). NCATE drew attention to teacher candidate preparedness for diverse populations. NCATE (2008) Standard 4 required teacher edu-cation programs to design, implement, evaluate curriculum, and provide "experiences for candidates to acquire and demonstrate the knowledge, skills, and professional dispositions necessary to help all students learn" to obtain accreditation. NCATE was clearly stating that teacher candidates must demonstrate and apply cultural competency resulting from experi-ences with diverse populations. While NCATE's diversity mandate seems to be what is needed in teacher preparation programs to prepare teacher candidates, it has been criticized because it "stops far short of advocating critical pedagogy and *social reconstructionist* approach" (Ramsey & Williams, 2003, p. 214).

In 2013, the Teacher Education Accreditation Council (TEAC) and NCATE merged to become the Council for the Accreditation of Educator Preparation (CAEP) in order to raise the performance of teacher candi-dates as practitioners in the nation's P–12 schools and raise the stature of the profession, This new accrediting body has five CAEP standards that reflect the voice of the education field on what makes a quality educa-tor (CAEP, 2013). The five standards are: (1) Content and Pedagogical Knowledge; (2) Clinical Partnerships and Practice; (3) Candidate Quality, Recruitment, and Selectivity; (4) Program Impact; (5) Provider Quality, Continuous Improvement, and Capacity (CAEP, 2013).

The CAEP (2013) standards did not use the same approach as NCATE (2008). CAEP (2013) used diversity to express their plan for recruitment of diverse candidates who meet employment needs. Standard 3.1 reads:

> The provider presents plans and goals to recruit and support completion of high-quality candidates from a broad range of backgrounds and diverse populations to accomplish their mission. The admitted pool of candidates reflects the diversity of America's P–12 students. The provider demonstrates efforts to know and address community, state, national, regional, or local needs for hard-to-staff schools and shortage fields, currently, STEM, English-language learning, and students with disabilities. (CAEP, 2013)

While it is important to have "plans and goals to recruit and support completion of high-quality candidates from a broad range of backgrounds and diverse populations," it is equally important to make sure that all teacher candidates are equipped by the colleges of education they attend to teach in diverse educational settings. Recruiting diverse teachers is important, but so is content and pedagogical knowledge that does not include any rhetoric or implementation regarding diversity. CAEP Standard 1: Content and Pedagogical Knowledge states:

> The provider ensures that candidates develop a deep understanding of the critical concepts and principles of their discipline and, by completion, are able to use discipline-specific practices flexibly to advance the learning of all students toward attainment of college- and career-readiness standards. (2013)

Teacher knowledge and pedagogies for teacher preparation are important factors to consider in merging multicultural education with teacher preparation programs. Scholars (Banks et al., 2005; Hammerness & Darling-Hammond, 2005) express that it is important to bring teacher disposition, knowledge, and pedagogies together under a coherent vision of multicultural teacher preparation to prepare teacher candidates to teach diverse student populations more coherently. Banks et al. (2005) suggest that teacher education programs be designed with the goal of making "attention to diversity, equity, and social justice centrally important that all courses and filed experiences for prospective teachers are conducted with these goals in mind" (p. 274). In order for this goal to be accomplished policies and teacher education standards must commit to mandating that teacher preparation programs focus on preparing teachers for diverse backgrounds.

The three authors of this paper all have experiences with teacher preparation programs as well as the impact of multiculturalism on teaching and learning in today's society. In this section they each share their "purple rain stories."

Marjorie is a tenured full professor in a graduate school of education.

As a teacher educator and methods professor I am responsible for training prospective teachers. I use socio-cultural theories as a nexus for collaborative practices in teacher training. These theories situate my work as it relates to preparing begin-ning teachers to work with today's millennial learners, i.e., culturally, linguistically, and cognitively diverse learners. Each academic year starts with groups of students comprised of individuals who are pursuing teaching credentials. As a graduate program and given our geographic location, students range in age from twenty-two to seventy. Some are career switchers, retired civil servants, and others have edu-cated their own children and are now proclaiming, "It's my time!" And while this makes for a richly diverse classroom setting, it also presents challenges to reaching the needs of everyone. To address the varying profiles, I provide carefully designed collaborative field experiences in multicultural settings to give pre-service teachers a first-hand approach at connecting theory to practice and exposing them to multiple venues in diverse settings.

In my role as a teacher educator I face the challenge of training teachers who (will) go into classrooms and be responsible for providing instruction and assessment for students about whom they know very little and/or have anything in common. I must teach them to create various teaching strategies and assessment practices that allow teachers to differentiate instruction in ways that are pedagogically sound and culturally sensitive.

My students tell me that I set the bar high—that while I am demanding and exacting, they appreciate my genuine concern for each of them and my sincere goal to prepare them to be excellent practitioners. Training teachers is for me a privilege. I take it very seriously and feel honored to be part of a profession that has such a far-reaching impact. It is one of the most exciting times and spaces to be in—inspiring others to discover their passion and truly become agents of change.

Shamaine is an elementary teacher who works in a Title I school.

"You have no choice but to succeed!... Education is not a choice, it's what you need … I am not putting up with the drama today, get it together!" These were some of the many comments I heard walking down the hallways of the elementary school where I spent my first years in the teaching profession. This school had a predominantly Black teaching staff and the teachers treated the students like they were their own. While the students in this school were generally regarded as "unsuccessful" and "not likely to succeed," they beat the odds and succeeded academically.

My first years at this high minority, high poverty elementary school provided me with "real world" experience teaching culturally, linguistically, cognitively diverse, ethnic minority, and low-income students for which my teacher education program did <u>not</u> prepare me. When I look back on my first years in the classroom, I believe it was my experience growing up in a middle to low income Black community that helped me reach the students who were in my classroom. I could relate to their strug-gles and building relationships with them definitely made it easy for me to teach. After a few years, there was a change in the teaching demographics for various reasons and the teaching staff became more diverse.

It was at this moment that I realized that not all teachers know how to teach minority students from low-income backgrounds. Also, I noticed the effects of colleges of education not teaching prospective teachers how to teach diverse student populations—the ultimate impact. I believe that it is imperative for teacher preparation programs are preparing prospective teachers for the linguistically, ethnically, and socioeconomically diverse student populations they will teach.

Tiffany is a middle school civics teacher in a culturally diverse school setting.

As a minority student from a low socio-economic background, I felt that my history and culture were rarely reflected within K–12 classroom spaces. However, being reared by a single mother in a socially conscious home, I was taught in-depth about race, equality and social justice. Prompted by these experiences I became a history and civics teachers as a career switcher from public policy. I have taught in charter schools where the student populations were 100% minority and 100% from low socio-economic backgrounds to diverse public schools with a wide range of students from varying racial/ethnic groups and socio-economic classes. What I have learned from teaching in both settings is that multicultural education is beneficial for all students.

My teacher practice was largely influenced by my upbringing. I often supplement and teach outside of the curriculum in an effort to provide students with diverse perspectives of US History, Civics and Economics. As a teacher of color, my experiences allow me to understand systemic oppression and stories of triumph in communities of color on a deeper level. Those experiences equipped me with the knowledge to enrich a history curriculum that is largely dismissive of people of color. However, translating that to middle school students on a level they can grasp was a challenge that I learned to mitigate over time. Aside from a course or two my graduate teacher preparation program was largely devoid of ways to teach through a multicultural lens, critical readings that would be beneficial to that work or tools to implement culturally relevant instructional practices. I did not receive that until I entered the doctoral program. In my opinion, that is far too late. I didn't become a teacher through the traditional route and in some ways that was beneficial. In hindsight I wish I had known about Banks, Freire and Nieto earlier in my teaching career. Their work and our work in classrooms is critical. Teacher preparation programs can and should provide teachers with the tools and strategies for developing multiple layers for multicultural classroom instruction.

Recommendations

We readily acknowledge that there are numerous skills and strategies that can be useful tools for teaching culturally, linguistically, and cognitively diverse learners. For the most part, it simply comes down to "good teaching is good teaching." Teaching methodology is at best trendy and at worst systemic. We have experienced and witnessed open-spaced education to flipped classrooms. The advent of technology and its influences in our schools have permeated curricula content and information delivery systems. Perhaps when we once and for all abandon the notion that there is one way to teach and learn (one size fits all!), we can reshape and reconceptualize a paradigm in which we truly attend to the needs of *every* individual in myriad ways.

We offer the following list of recommendations that we feel may serve as a point of departure in teacher preparation for creating spaces for conversations and situating a requisite purple rain in multicultural education:

- Participate in a learning community
- Seek ways to incorporate students' cultural experiences
- Build a classroom culture that values differences
- Reach out to others to understand how to respond to your diverse students' attitudes, motivations, and behaviors
- Engage in self-reflection in order to identify your own cultural identities and the roles they play in classroom instruction

Conclusions

There are many teachers who believe that student learning can be greatly influenced by effective teaching. Those teachers who have confidence in their ability to teach persist longer in their teaching efforts, provide greater academic focus in the classroom, give different types of feedback, and ultimately improve student performance (Gibson & Dembo, 1984). Unfortunately, students marginalized based on their race, social class, ability, linguistic background, gender identity, or sexuality (and various intersections of these) in any demographic context regularly encounter school policies and practices that, by and large, culturally de-capitalize, devalue, and strip away aspects of their identity (Irzarry, 2011; Mayo, 2013; Valenzuela, 1999).

It is incumbent upon teacher educators to train teachers to learn about their students' cultural and social practices. They must also work with them to integrate cultural knowledge and practices into their everyday teaching to successfully engage in multicultural education. The preparation of teachers for diversity, especially in terms of building teacher capacity to become effective multicultural educators, is "imperative to ensure that demographic transition does not destabilize schools and that student performance, among all subgroups, reaches increasingly demanding benchmarks" (Frankenberg & Siegel-Hawley, 2008, p. 9). Translating cultural differences in instruction, therefore, is a demanding process that requires teacher reflection and inquiry, formal training and informal learning, and extensive support (Li, 2013).

In this chapter we set out to create a space for examining an array of multicultural perspectives for teacher education programs to consider when preparing prospective teachers who will work with culturally, linguistically, and cognitively diverse learners. While highlighting the shift in demographics in the United States, we hope to emphasize building teachers' ability to identify their own cultural practices and then figure out how to relate to those of their students. Two program models were used to demonstrate efforts underway to re-construct teacher education programs. These program models along with current policies that shape and inform teacher preparation are positive steps that provide impetus for enhancing the teacher workforce of the twenty-first century.

AUTHORS' NOTE

We feel the chapter title merits explanation. Music icon Prince passed in 2016 just as we began writing this chapter and as his music touched each of our lives at various stages, we felt compelled to honor his work and legacy by connecting his *Purple Rain* song lyrics to our ongoing work. The words and meanings embedded in the song resonate with our commitment to making a difference and empowering the disenfranchised, marginalized, and historically voiceless.

REFERENCES

Banks, J. (1994). *An introduction to multicultural education*. Needham Heights, MA: Allyn &Bacon.

Banks, J. A. (2002). An Introduction to multicultural education (3rd ed.). Boston, MA:Allyn & Bacon.

Banks, J. A., Cochran-Smith, M., Moll, L., Richert, A., Zeichner, K., LePage, P., ... McDonald, M. (2005). Teaching diverse learners. In L. Darling-Hammond & J. Bransford (Eds.), *Preparing teachers for a changing world* (pp. 232–274). San Francisco, CA: Jossey-Bass.

Bartolomé, L. I. (2004). Critical pedagogy and teacher education: Radicalizing prospective teachers. *Teacher Education Quarterly, 31*(1), 97–122.

Bennett, S. V. (2013). Effective facets of a field experience that contributed to eight preservice teachers' developing understandings about culturally responsive teaching. *Urban Education, 48*(3), 380–419.

Berry, B., Hoke, M., & Hirsch, E. (2004). NCLB: Highly qualified teachers-the search for highly qualified teachers. *Phi Delta Kappan, 85*(9), 684.

Brownstein, J. B., & Boschma, R. (2016, February 29). The concentration of poverty in American schools. *The Atlantic.* Retrieved from http://www.theatlantic.com/education/archive/2016/02/concentration-poverty-american-schools/471414/

Castagno, A. (2008). "I don't want to hear that!": Legitimating whiteness through silence in the schools. *Anthropology & Education Quarterly, 39*(3), 314–333.

Characteristics of public, private, and Bureau of Indian Education elementary and secondary school teachers in the United States: Results from the 2007–08 Schools and Staffing Survey. (n.d.). Retrieved June 1, 2016, from https://nces.ed.gov/pubs2009/2009324/tables/sass0708_2009324_t12n_02.asp

Children's Defense Fund. (2015). Ending Child Poverty Now Report. Retrieved June 2, 2016, from http://www.childrensdefense.org/newsroom/mediare-sources/ending-child-poverty-now.pdf

Cochran-Smith, M., & Fries, M. K. (2001). Sticks, stones, and ideology: The discourse of reform in teacher education. *Educational Eesearcher, 30*(8), 3–15.

Cookson, P. (2011). Madison was right: Why we urgently need a national vision for public education. *Teachers College Record.* Retrieved from http://www.tcrecord.org ID Number: 16392.

Council for the Accreditation of Teacher Education. (2013). CAEP 2013 Accreditation Standards and evidence. Retrieved from http://edsource.org/wp-content/uploads/commrpt.pdf

Darling-Hammond, L., & Bransford, J. (2005). *Preparing teachers for a changing world: What teachers should learn and be able to do.* San Francisco, CA: Jossey-Bass.

Delpit, L. (2012). *Multiplication is for white people: Raising expectations for other people's children.* New York, NY: The New Press.

Frankenberg, E., & Siegel-Hawley, G. (2008). *Are teachers prepared for America's diverse schools? Teachers describe their preparation, resources and practices for racially diverse schools.* Los Angeles, CA: Civil Rights Project/Proyecto Derechos Civiles.

Freire, P. (1970). *Pedagogy of the oppressed.* New York, NY: Seabury Press.

Gay, G., & Howard, T. C. (2000). Multicultural teacher education for the 21st century. *Teacher Educator, 36*(1), 1–16. http://doi.org/10.1080/08878730009555246

Gibson, S., & Dembo, M. H. (1984). Teacher efficacy: A construct validation. *Journal of Educational Psychology, 76,* 569-582.

Giroux, H. A. (1992). *Border crossings: Cultural workers and the politics of education.* New York, NY: Psychology Press.

Goldenberg, B. M. (2014). White teachers in urban classrooms embracing non-white students' cultural capital for better teaching and learning. *Urban Education, 49*(1), 111–144. http://doi.org/10.1177/0042085912472510

Gorski, P. C. (2009). What we're teaching teachers: An analysis of multicultural Teacher education coursework syllabi. *Teaching and Teacher Education, 25*(2), 309–318.

Hammerness, K., & Darling-Hammond, L. (2005). The design of teacher education programs. In L. Darling-Hammond & J. Bransford (Eds.), *Preparing teachers for a changing world* (pp. 390–441). San Francisco, CA: Jossey-Bass.

hooks, b. (1994). *Teaching to transgress: Education as the practice of freedom*. New York, NY: Routledge.

Irizarry, J. G. (2011). *The Latinization of U.S. Schools: Successful teaching & learning in shift in cultural contexts*. Boulder, CO: Pardigm.

Krogstad, J. M., & Fry, R. (2014). Dept. of Ed. projects public schools will be "majority-minority" this fall. Retrieved from http://www.pewresearch.org/fact-tank/2014/08/18/u-s-public-schools-expected-to-be-majority-minority-starting-this-fall/

Ladson-Billings, G. (2009). *The Dreamkeepers: Successful teachers of African American children* (2nd ed.). San Francisco, CA: Jossey-Bass.

Li, G. (2013). Promoting teachers of culturally and linguistically diverse (CLD) students as change agents: A cultural approach to professional learning. *Theory Into Practice*, *52*(2), 136–143.

Maxwell, L. A. (2014, August 20). U.S. school enrollment hits majority-minority milestone—Education Week. *Education Week*. Retrieved from http://www.edweek.org/ew/articles/2014/08/20/01demographics.h34.html

Mayo, C. (2013). *LGBTQ youth and education: Policies and practices*. New York, NY: Teachers College Press.

Milner, H. R. (2010). What does teacher education have to do with teaching? Implications for diversity studies. *Journal of Teacher Education*, *61*(1-2), 118–131.

NAEP. (n.d.). 2012 Long-term trends in academic progress. Retrieved May 31, 2016, from http://www.nationsreportcard.gov/ltt_2012/

National Center for Education Statistics. (2013). Characteristics of public and private elementary and secondary school teachers in the United States: Results from the 2011–2012 schools and staffing survey. *U.S. Department of Education*. Retrieved from https://nces.ed.gov/pubs2013/2013314.pdf

National Center for Education Statistics (2014). Projections of education statistics to 2022. *U.S. Department of Education*. Retrieved from https://nces.ed.gov/pubs2014/2014051.pdf

National Council for Teacher Quality (2014). 2014 Teacher Prep Review: A review of the nation's teacher preparation programs. Retrieved from http://www.nctq.org/dmsView/Teacher_Prep_Review_2014_Report

National Council for the Accreditation of Teacher Education (NCATE). (1977). *Standards for Accreditation of Teacher Education*. Washington, DC: Author.

National Council for the Accreditation of Teacher Education. (1997–2009). NCATE –Unit Standards. Retrieved May 30, 2016, from National Council for the Accreditation of Teacher Education Web site: http://www.ncate.org/public/unitStandardsRubrics.asp?ch=4#stnd4

National Council for the Accreditation of Teacher Education. (2010). Report of the Blue Ribbon Panel, Transforming teacher education through clinical practice: A national strategy to prepare effective teachers. Retrieved on June 1, 2016, from http://www.ncate.org/LinkClick.aspx?fileticket=zzeiB1OoqPk%3d&tabid=715

National Council for Accreditation of Teacher Education. (2008). *Professional standards for the accreditation of teacher preparation institutions*. Washington, DC: Author.

National Education Association (NEA). (2008). *English Learners Face Unique Challenges*. Retrieved on June 1, 2016, from http://www.nea.org/assets/docs/HE/ELL_Policy_Brief_Fall_08_(2).pdf

Nieto, S. (1999). What does it mean to affirm diversity? *School Administrator, 56*(6), 32–35.

Oakes, J., & Lipton, M. (2003). Schooling: Wrestling with history and tradition. *Teaching to Change the World*, 2–39.

Ortiz, A. A., & Franquíz, M. E. (2015). Coeditors' introduction: Cultural responsive practices in the preparation of teacher who serve emergent bilinguals. *Bilingual Research Journal, 38*(1), 1–5. doi:10.1080/15235882.2015.1027619

Quartz, K. H., Olsen, B., & Duncan-Andrade, J. (2008). The fragility of urban teaching: A longitudinal study of career development and activism. In F. P. Peterman (Ed.), *Partnering to prepare urban teachers: A call to activism* (pp. 225–247). New York, NY: Peter Lang.

Ramsey, P. G., & Williams, L. R. (2003). *Multicultural education: a source book*. New York, NY: Routledge.

Rowley, R. L., & Wright, W. D. (2011). No "white" child left behind: The academic achievement gap between black and white students. *The Journal of Negro Education, 80*(2), 93–107.

Swartz, E. (2003). Teaching white preservice teachers pedagogy for change. *Urban Education, 38*(3), 255–278.

Ukpokodu, O. N. (2009) Pedagogies that foster transformative learning in a multicultural education course: A reflection. *Journal of Praxis in Multicultural Education, 4*(1), 1–9.

U.S. Census Bureau, D. I. D. (2012.). Demographic and geographic estimates. Retrieved from https://www.census.gov/did/www/schooldistricts/index.html

U.S. Department of Education (2011, September). Our future, our teachers: The Obama administration's plan for teacher education reform and improvement. Retrieved from http://www.ed.gov/sites/default/files/our-future-our-teachers.pdf

U.S. Department of Education, National Center for Education Statistics (2014). *The Condition of Education 2014-083*. Washington, DC: U.S. Department of Education Office of Educational Research and Improvement. Retrieved from http://nces.ed.gov/pubs2014/2014083.pdf

Valenzuela, A. (1999). *Subtractive schooling: US-Mexican youth and the politics of caring*. Albany, NY: State University of New York Press.

Walker-Dalhouse, D., & Dalhouse, A. (2006). Investigating White preservice teachers' beliefs about teaching in culturally diverse classrooms. *The Negro Educational Review, 57*(1–2), 69–84.

CHAPTER 2

READING AS EMANCIPATION

Using the *Literacy as Access Framework* to Ensure Cultural Competency in Educators

Dwight C. Watson
Southwest Minnesota State University

James D. Cryer
University of Northern Iowa

"We must teach learners the functional, navigational skills so that they can have access to power."

—Lisa Delpit

At the 2013 National Reading Recovery and K–6 Classroom Literacy Conference, the lead author was asked to present a session titled Literacy as Access: Understanding Cultural Competency. This session was a part of the administrative strand and the purpose was to provide literacy leaders

Comprehensive Multicultural Education in the 21st Century:
Increasing Access in the Age of Retrenchment, pp. 19–36
Copyright © 2019 by Information Age Publishing
All rights of reproduction in any form reserved.

(administrators, lead teachers, literacy coaches) theoretical and applied information pertaining to diversity, equity, social justice, and inclusion through a literacy lens. The aspiration was that this presentation would enable literacy leaders to better incorporate tenets of cultural competency into their literacy programs, preschool programs, and literacy interventions in their school contexts. The session was crafted as a replicable professional development opportunity that could be rolled out by literacy leaders to their local constituency.

In crafting this chapter, we thought that the intent of the presentation could easily become guidelines for others who are responsible for shaping the pedagogical practices of educators; therefore, the purpose of this chapter is to amplify some of the practices that were discussed in the session to a wider audience and to showcase the functional utility of the *Literacy as Access Framework* (see Figure 2.1).

We titled our article "Reading as Emancipation" because we know that literacy educators must think boldly about the power of reading, and they should be provocateurs as they lead others on the journey to cultural competency. We believe that access to literacy is a democratic imperative and when teachers, principals, and other literacy leaders embrace reading as a functional, navigational skill that provides learners access to power, then they are conducting acts of emancipation. Our desire is that literacy leaders will be empowered to promote literacy and the liberating constructs of cultural competency in their schools to emancipate students' learning.

The organizational framework of the article focuses on critical components of cultural competency which are knowledge, skills, and dispositions. We believe that before one's knowledge can be enhanced, an educator must first be a fertile receptacle so that the knowledge can germinate and possess dispositional willingness. In the *Literacy as Access Framework*, this is Level III in which the educator must "Know Yourself" in order to create a literacy accessible environment.

We begin the chapter by amplifying the research context for why cultural competency is an imperative (Shor, 1992; Villegas & Lucas, 2002). The next section of the chapter focuses on creating a shared knowledge base so that literacy leaders and educators can communicate with consistent nomenclature and content (Lipman, 1995; Obidah & Howard, 2005). This section is followed by the skills component that delineates the *Literacy as Access Framework*. Once educators develop their dispositional stance and enhance their knowledge base, then they are capable of deconstructing their current instructional practices and reinventing them as culturally responsive practices that are inclusive of all learners (Moule & Higgins, 2007).

Literacy as Access for All Students

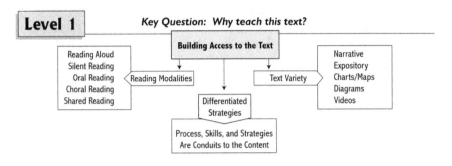

Level 1

Key Question: Why teach this text?

Building Access to the Text

Reading Aloud
Silent Reading
Oral Reading — Reading Modalities
Choral Reading
Shared Reading

Narrative
Expository
Charts/Maps — Text Variety
Diagrams
Videos

Differentiated
Strategies

Process, Skills, and Strategies
Are Conduits to the Content

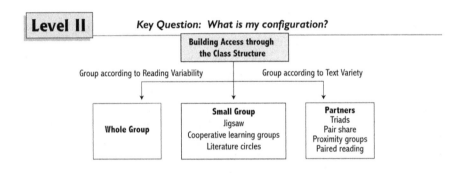

Level II

Key Question: What is my configuration?

**Building Access through
the Class Structure**

Group according to Reading Variability   Group according to Text Variety

Whole Group

Small Group
Jigsaw
Cooperative learning groups
Literature circles

Partners
Triads
Pair share
Proximity groups
Paired reading

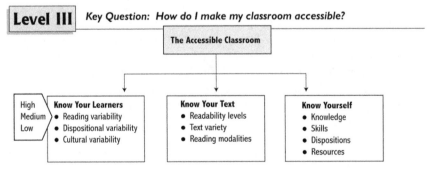

Level III

Key Question: How do I make my classroom accessible?

The Accessible Classroom

High
Medium
Low

Know Your Learners
• Reading variability
• Dispositional variability
• Cultural variability

Know Your Text
• Readability levels
• Text variety
• Reading modalities

Know Yourself
• Knowledge
• Skills
• Dispositions
• Resources

Created by Dr. Dwight C. Watson, 2006

Figure 2.1.

A CONTEXT FOR CULTURAL COMPETENCY

As Delpit (2006) stated, the purpose of literacy is to provide all learners access to opportunity. She commented that educators need to make sure that our learners are taught the functional, navigational skills so that they can have access to power. Embedded in this statement is that to learn to read is emancipatory and liberating; therefore, a democratic imperative. Teacher preparation should impact knowledge, dispositions, and skills for the redistribution of power (Gay, 2000; Irvine & Armento, 2001; Irvine & York, 1995; Ladson-Billings, 1994, 1995a, 1995b; Lipman, 1995). A role of literacy educators is the continuous development and preparation of learners; therefore, they should impress upon their learners the importance of reading as a conduit to the redistribution of power (Sleeter, 1993; Tatum, 2005; Tiezzi & Cross, 1997; Yeo, 1997). Continuous professional development for educators should be designed to include focused commentary about issues related to the broader concerns connected to diverse learners (Darling-Hammond & Bransford, 2005).

In the literature, the term culturally competency is also referred to as culturally responsive, culturally appropriate, culturally congruent, culturally relevant, and emancipatory (Gay, 2005, Irvine & Armento, 2001; Sleeter 2001). Characteristics often associated with culturally competent pedagogy include positive perspectives on parents and families; communication of high expectations; learning within the context of culture; student-centered instruction; reshaping the curriculum; and educators as facilitators (Ladson-Billings, 1994; Gay, 2000).

Culturally competent educators provide instruction that is culturally relevant. Cultural relevance is evident through the integration of cultural knowledge, prior experience, and performance styles of diverse learners to make learning more appropriate and effective for them; it teaches to and through the strengths of learners. Culturally relevant instruction integrates a wide variety of instructional strategies that are connected to different approaches to learning (Council of Chief State School Officers, 2013). Educators should know the research, nomenclature, and importance of cultural competency in order to affect change in instructional literacy practices in their classrooms. To change the instructional practices in the classroom, educators should focus on Level III of the *Literacy as Access Framework* in which they must not only be reflective practitioners by knowing themselves, "Know Yourself," but should also "Know Your Learners" and "Know Your Texts."

Because fewer people of color are entering the profession and the majority of practicing educators are not ethnically or racially diverse, it is imperative that those who are teaching possess the cultural competency to teach all students (Howard, 2006). If the educators did not acquire these practices in their teacher preparation program, then they must be provided access to these competencies through professional development opportunities. The administration must set the tone in order for these practices to be embedded in the schools' culture, climate, and classrooms (Brock, Moore, & Parks, 2007; Ladson-Billings, 2005).

DEVELOPING A SHARED KNOWLEDGE BASE: "KNOW YOUR LEARNERS" AND "KNOW YOURSELF"

One of the primary goals of educators is to have the dispositions and knowledge base to work with diverse readers (Allen, 2005). Before educators can embark on cultural competency integration, the literacy leaders must make sure that the educators understand the common constructs of cultural competency such as diversity, diverse learners, inclusive learning environments, social and racial justice, and linguistic competency.

Without a shared knowledge base, educators may not respond to learners as individuals in order to ensure equitable instruction for all learners. Thomas and Collier (2003) surmised that educators may view learners from diverse backgrounds with a deficit perspective. There may be a misconception that methods, strategies, and instructional frameworks can be taught and learned in a decontextualized manner apart from the contexts and learners within those contexts. The *Literacy as Access Framework* showcases that the learner, the text, the context, and the instruction are all integral to the literacy acquisition of diverse learners. The framework also embraces the actuality that educators must honor and respect diversity as inclusive of individual difference (e.g., personality, interests, learning modalities, and life experiences) and group differences (e.g., race, ethnicity, ability, gender, identity, gender expression, sexual orientation, nationality, language, religion, political affiliation, military status, regional origin, and socioeconomic background), (Pendakur, 2016).

Educators must be aware that diverse learners may have learning differences because of gender, language, cultural background, differing ability levels, disabilities, learning approaches, and/or socioeconomic status (Alli, Rajan, & Ratliff, 2016). Diverse learners may have academic needs that require varied instructional strategies to ensure their learning. Learning differences are manifested in such areas as differing rates of learning, motivation, attention, preferred learning modalities, complexity of reasoning, persistence, foundational knowledge and skills, and preferred learning and response modes (Banks & Banks, 1995; Council of Chief State School Officers, 2013; Stevenson, 2014).

Literacy leaders must prepare teachers to work in inclusive environments. Inclusive learning environments are welcoming and accepting of each and every learner including those who are vulnerable to marginalization and exclusion and those who traditionally have been left out of and excluded from appropriate educational and learning opportunities. Inclusive environments expand the concept of inclusion that is most frequently associated with equal access to general education for students with disabilities. Inclusive approaches embrace diversity; provide access to high-level knowledge, skills, and application for every student; adapt instruction to meet individual needs; encourage coteaching and collaboration among general and resource educators; foster collaboration with families and community members; maintain high expectations of all students; and support student achievement and growth (Carey, 2004; Council of Chief State School Officers, 2013; Stevenson, 2014).

Effective teachers must understand concepts such as privilege, access, equity, power, marginalization, disenfranchisement, and other terms pertaining to critical race theory and social justice. Literacy leaders should emphasize that the goal of cultural competency is to learn skills that will enable teachers to relate across cultural lines (Adams et al., 2013).

To understand the knowledge base of cultural competency, educators must also be cognizant of social and racial justice. Social and racial justice examines the microsocietal perspective regarding issues of oppression and social change and carefully considers how the macroperspective informs the micro moment in the classroom. A social and racial justice approach attends to seek change at the individual level, but sets its sights on changing the systems and structures that perpetuate inequality and inequity in society. Power and privilege are addressed along the lines of socially-constructed identities (Gay, 2005; Hackman, 2005; hooks,1994). Educators should understand that power is both individual, and more importantly tied to social identity group membership (Adam, Bell, & Griffin, 1997; Adams et al., 2013).

Another knowledge component of cultural competency is linguistic competency. Educators should have the knowledge, skills, and dispositions to understand and appreciate English language learners (ELL), be they children or adults. Educators must recognize that English language learners may not have command of English because English is not their first language, but may be their second, third, or fourth language (Thomas & Collier, 2003).

For instance, a learner from Cameron may know his indigenous language, his colonized language, as well as English. Do educators understand the nuances of the languages that this person has to navigate as a learner in the classroom or later as an adult in the work place? Do educators understand the term the *language of oppressors* and the sociopolitical context in which this intersect the lives of their learners? Educators who are linguistically competent understand the needs of English language learners as well as the social context in which language is used in the academic, formal, or informal register (Darling-Hammond & Bransford, 2005).

Another component of linguistic competency is the understanding and appreciating of the nuances of African American Vernacular English (AAVE). This English is derivative of Black peoples' historical, social, and racial context. A Black learner may pronounce a word differently during reading and a teacher must recognize whether to view this as a reading miscue when conducting a running record. The learner may see the word *brother*, but pronounce it *bruvver* (Delpit, 1995). The learner knows what this word means and can answer any questions pertaining to the text, but the educator may over emphasize the AAVE pronunciation at the expense of the comprehension. The educator then spends extensive time over correcting the learner to the point that the learner feels shameful of his or her home language pronunciation. Educators should hold themselves accountable to recognizing these differences and empower AAVE speakers to use their language during informal register times and when reading for understanding (Tatum, 2005).

But these learners should also be taught the functional, navigational tools that will give them access to power; therefore, they must learn *cash* language or the *language of commerce* and how to switch to the formal register—code switching (Kunjufu, 2002; Thomas & Collier, 2003). Educators must understand that linguistic competence is the system of linguistic knowledge possessed by native speakers of a language. It is in contrast to the concept of linguistic performance, the way the language system is used in communication (Cattani, 2002).

Before educators can attempt to apply cultural and linguistic competency in the classroom, they must have the knowledge base to understand the interconnectedness of concepts (diversity, cultural competency, inclusion, social justice, etc.). They must also understand the historical, theoretical, contextual, and pedagogical aspects of these concepts (Kelly-Jackson & Jackson, 2011). Through professional development, interactive dialogues, and courageous conversations, educators must challenge their assumptions and explore opportunities to connect with all learners (Darling-Hammond & Bransford, 2005).

LITERACY AS ACCESS FRAMEWORK: APPLYING THE SKILLS OF CULTURAL COMPETENCY

At the beginning of this chapter, readers were challenged to begin thinking boldly about the power of literacy and to look at reading as emancipation, or as a democratic imperative, that allows individuals access to power and opportunities typically associated with the dominate culture. It was the goal of the authors to help educators develop their own dispositional stance and to enhance their knowledge base in order that they might champion this message as they lead others on the journey to cultural competency. But the question is where to start? In the following discussion, three levels of understanding related to using the Literacy as Access

Framework are presented to help educators create culturally relevant environments within their schools and classrooms. The framework was created by the lead author as a schematic for educators to follow if they were to embrace the tenets of cultural competency in their literacy environments so that the teaching of reading was accessible to all learners and that all learners could see themselves reflected in the texts, context, practices, and configurations.

In order to create culturally relevant literacy environments, we must first understand what culturally relevant teaching means. According to Ladson-Billings (2009), culturally relevant teaching is a pedagogy that empowers students intellectually, socially, emotionally, and politically by using cultural referents to impart knowledge, skills, and attitudes. These cultural referents are not merely vehicles for bridging or explaining the dominant culture; they are aspects of the curriculum in their own right. This means educators must be extremely thoughtful and purposeful while planning lessons, developing implementation strategies, and organizing classroom configurations. The educator needs to insure a connection is created between the cultural identity and background each learner brings to the classroom and the content being taught. Thus, culturally relevant educators must have an ability to develop students academically, the willingness to nurture and support cultural competence, and the ability and desire to foster the development of a socio-political or critical consciousness (Ladson-Billings, 2009). The Literacy as Access Framework provides the model educators need to ensure culture competency in the classroom.

Level 1: Building Access to the Text: Why Teach This Text?

The most important element in creating a culturally relevant literacy classroom is the belief that all learners can become successful and effective readers. Before our students ever walk into the classroom, we, as educators, must see their brilliance and maintain this as the core reference point for all that we do in the classroom. So often in the belief that we are "being nice," we fail to realize the brilliance of our students and teach down to them, demanding little (Delpit, 2006). Without the belief that all learners (regardless of gender, disability, color of skin, or socioeconomic status) can succeed academically, socially, and emotionally, all efforts to truly help learners in the classroom will be superficial and bound to eventually fail.

After internalizing that all learners are brilliant and can learn, culturally competent educators need to make sure that all learners also gain access to basic skills. According to Delpit (2006) what we call basic skills are typically the linguistic conventions of middle-class society and the strategies successful people use to access new information. For example, punctuation, grammar, specialized subject vocabulary, mathematical operations, five-paragraph essays, and so forth are all conventions. Using phonetic cues to read words, knowing how to solve word problems, determining an author's purpose, and finding meaning in context are all strategies. In Level I of the *Literacy as Access Framework*, educators must intentionally build access to the text by using processes, skills, and strategies as conduits to the content. All learners need to know these basic skills because these are the skills that are emancipatory and lead to access to power and opportunity.

For example, the Core Curriculum State Standards for English/Language Arts indicates a basic skill that all first grade learners need is to be able to describe characters, settings, and major events in a story, using key details (CCSS.ELA-Literacy.RL.1.3.). The way in which this standard is taught, in a culturally relevant classroom is that educator must begin with a text that is familiar. A cultural competent educator would know that some learners struggle with too many new concepts at once so therefore the choice of literature and the modality (read-aloud, shared reading, independent reading, choral reading, etc.) in which the literature is shared should be familiar to the learners since the skill of identifying characters, setting, and major event may be new.

As stated in the standard, first grade learners are expected to be able to describe characters, setting, and major events in a story, using key details. To meet this standard, a culturally competent educator might choose a familiar classic like the Caldecott Medal-winning children's book *Where the Wild Things Are* by Maurice Sendak (1963) and ask the learners a variety of "wh" questions: Who is the main character of the story? Where did the story take place? Was there a problem and if so what was it? How was the problem solved? What did Max do when his mom sent him to his bedroom without supper? Why did Max do this? All of these are good questions and will help learners practice main idea, character development, and setting which are basic reading comprehension skills.

Once the learners have practiced the comprehension skills with a familiar text, a culturally competent teacher would continue to practice the skill, but would want to build affinity with learners from different cultures; therefore, instead of choosing another book written by a White male with a White male protagonist, the educator in a multicultural classroom working to create a culturally relevant classroom may choose to read a different Caldecott Medal-winning book, *The Snowy Day* by Ezra Jack Keats (1962), an African American writer with an African American male protagonist, to the learners. The educator could still ask similar "wh" questions, but by making an intentional choice to select a book that uses specific culture referents which will connect with African American learners, the educator will increase the reading engagement which will lead to basic reading skill attainment for all learners.

In addition to choosing various narrative style texts such as *The Snowy Day*, a culturally relevant classroom will also have a wide variety of other text types available for learners such as expository (informational) texts, charts/maps, diagrams, and videos. However, the goal for the teacher is to make sure these texts honor and respect the learner's home culture. In other words, a wide variety of text types, which represent the culture of all learners in the classroom, should be available to augment the required curricular choices. In a culturally relevant classroom, educators legitimize the learner's culture by making it a frame of reference for all texts (Ladson-Billings, 1992). For example, if an educator has Latino students in the classroom, then the educators should have books written and illustrated by Latino writers and illustrators such as *Papá and Me* written by Arthur Dorros and illustrated by Rudy Gutierrez (2008), *Going Home* written by Eve Bunting and illustrated by David Diaz (1996), and *Hispanic Scientists: Ellen Ochoa, Carlos A. Ramirez, Eloy Rodriguez, Lydia Villa-Komaroff, Maria Elena Zavala. (Capstone Short Biographies)* by Jetty St. John (1996). The more learners can identify their own culture and heritage in the texts they read, the more they appreciate and celebrate their identity as individuals and as members of a specific culture (Ladson-Billings, 1992).

In addition to choosing a variety of text types, culturally relevant educators should use a wide variety of reading modalities and strategies within their classrooms (McNair, 2012). Modalities are various ways in which the book can be presented to the learners. The learners can read the book independently as silent readers (sustained silent reading). The educator can read the book aloud to the learners (oral reading). The educator can have each learner read a section aloud to class (round robin oral reading) or ask all the learners to read a particular section together (choral reading). At every opportunity, a culturally relevant educator will use the cultural knowledge, prior experiences, and learning styles of their learners to inform the choice of which modality is the most engaging to culturally diverse learners in order to make learning more appropriate and effective for them (Gay, 2002). For example, African American and Hmong learners who grew up in an oral storytelling tradition may prefer the educator to read the text aloud to them, but other cultures may want to read silently and independently. The educator must be adroit in orchestrating the reading modalities and realize that the ultimate goal of reading is for learners to engage in sustained silent, independent reading with comprehension.

Whatever approach or methodology is implemented, however, one factor that is necessary for excellence is that learners are taught to think critically about what they are learning and about the world at large (Delpit, 2006). A major focus of the culturally relevant classroom is that learners are asked to compare their own experiences with what they read and to make assessments about the value of their reading (Ladson-Billings, 1992).

For example, in order to develop a heightened sociopolitical knowledge within their learners, in regards to experiences across the socioeconomic spectrum, a culturally relevant educator might choose to read the story *Those Shoes* by Maribeth Boelts (2007) and ask when reading, What do Jeremy and Antonio want so bad? How do some of the other children treat Jeremy and Antonio because they can't afford those shoes? Why can't all people afford to buy special shoes? Have you ever been treated badly because you couldn't afford to buy something? As Delpit (2006) states, when we teach appropriate conventions and strategies within the context of culture and critical thinking, we can produce learners who have keen understanding of their place in the world.

Level 2: Building Access Through the Class Structure: What Is My Configuration?

Not only is it important to use text variety, reading modalities, and differentiated strategies to help learners build access to literacy, but it is important also to consider the configurations of the classroom structure. It has been surmised that successful schools that serve low-income, African American learners should have an overwhelming sense of family, a sense of connectedness, and a sense of caring in order to ensure self-efficacy in the learners (Willis, 1995). Because of this, when entering a culturally relevant classroom, learners and educators can often be found working in cooperative, supportive classroom arrangements that resemble learners' home-living experiences more than typical school experience (Gay, 1975). For example, as a former principal, the coauthor enjoyed visiting one of his first grade teacher's classroom. In this classroom, at the start of the lesson, he would find the teacher sitting in a chair with all of her students sitting on a carpet area in front of her. During this time, the teacher would read aloud a "Big-Book" (An oversized book that has enlarged print and pictures that all the learners can see from afar. This Big Book is placed on an easel for easier viewing and handling.) to the student and there would be questions asked, thoughtful answers given, and conversations from both the teacher and learners about personal experiences associated with the events in the story. In addition, the teacher would use a Thinking Aloud strategy to help model different skills she was attempting to help her learners comprehend the story.

Following this whole group time, the teacher would dismiss her learners to a number of different reading centers placed around the classroom. At one center, learners would be grouped according to reading variability and work directly with the teacher on individual skills development. While the teacher worked with this group, another set of learners worked in a small cooperative learning group format at a different center to complete a specific literacy-related activity together that was related to the whole group reading. At another center, learners would be involved in reciprocal teaching or a literature circle where they each were assigned a role with specific expectations to complete and then to share their information. This might be accomplished by drawing, writing, or developing questions related to a supplemental reading piece. Finally, other learners were working as partners at a computer to read together, think together, and then share together their thoughts and impressions.

By using different classroom configurations, the teacher demonstrated to her students not only the importance of working together to solve problems, but also the social benefits of learning, teaching, and playing together as a community while respecting each other's feelings, thoughts, and actions in the process (Kelly-Jackson & Jackson, 2011). These are lifelong skills that will help the learners with current friend and family relationships and future partnered, community, and workplace relationships.

This teacher's classroom allowed learners to build access and more fully engage with the curriculum with an emphasis on feelings, acceptance, and emotional closeness by creating a caring community with and among her learners. This is an example of a culturally relevant classroom where educators share power with the learners because they understand that education is an empowering force for social change and personal growth (Shade, 1987).

Level 3: Building the Accessible Classroom: How Do I Make My Classroom Accessible?

Know Your Learners

Educators must know each learner as an individual and use the components of Levels 1 and 2 of the framework to tailor their teaching pedagogy, text selections, and classroom configurations to build a consistently accessible classroom for all learners. To accomplish this, an educator must believe in their learners' brilliance before the learners enter the classroom. Educators must take the time to discover their learners as people and understand what they are able to do outside of school—in church, at community centers, as caretakers for younger siblings—or what skills they may be able to display on the playground with their peers (Delpit, 2006). Educators must learn these other attributes of their learners from the learners themselves, their parents and community members, but also more importantly listening to their stories and experiences.

For example, early in his career as a principal, the coauthor and a few of his teachers (all White) had an eye-opening experience when they were invited to a funeral of a parent of one of their Black elementary students. At the church, in the heart of the Black community, they witnessed a much different funeral service than they were used to attending. They saw a few of their Black students playing instruments in the band and even one typically extremely shy student singing in the choir. This experience emphasizes that a culturally relevant pedagogy purports the notion of a teacher-student relations that is fluid and extends to interactions beyond the classroom (Kelly-Jackson & Jackson, 2011). Because of the time spent in the communities where his students lived, the coauthor was able to gain knowledge of what is valued in the culture and community. As a principal, he was then able to take this back to his school and use it as he worked with his teachers, their students, families, and community members.

In another example of working to create a stronger teacher-student relationship, the coauthor had the opportunity through his church to volunteer at a Vacation Bible School in a community church located in the heart of a neighborhood strongly affected by poverty. He was eager to interact with some of his elementary students and their parents outside of school, but when he arrived at the church he was taken back as he witnessed many of his upper elementary students traversing the dangerous and busy roadways with younger siblings following behind them. He was expecting to find parents leading children, but what he found were his students demonstrating adult-like care and responsibility for their younger brothers and sisters. Delpit (2006) explains, a lot of our youngsters in urban settings come to school with funds of knowledge, but the school is not able to connect that kind of knowledge to school problem-solving and advanced thinking. In a culturally relevant classroom, the educator would take the time to appreciate the home-life of each learner and become familiar with the learner's culture. This would enable the educator to discover the reading variability, dispositional variability, and cultural variability that exists among every learner in the classroom. By taking the time to get to know learners on a personal level, educators will create an atmosphere of trust among learners, parents, and community members. The accessible classroom is seen as an extended family.

A second way of building an accessible classroom is for educators to know the context and subject matter of the text they plan to use extremely well. When educators are choosing fiction stories they must know the characters, settings, plots, and themes of the text. However, they must also know the readability levels and age-appropriateness of the text. Educators need to be well versed in how to use the wide-variety of texts available and anticipate queries since they already know the uniqueness of each learner. For example, they would know beforehand which style of writing each child finds personally engaging and meaningful.

Finally, culturally relevant teachers need to understand the variety of text and which reading modalities best accompany the individual text. For example, an educator who worked with the coauthor epitomized cultural competency by using the story *Sophie* by Mem Fox (1989) when teaching about community and the special relationship between a Black girl and her grandfather—something many of the learners in the class, regardless of race, could appreciate and comprehend. The educator studied the text at great length, to determine how to discuss the sensitive topic of death and dying. She then read this story aloud to her learners during whole group time, knowing that a read aloud was the best modality to convey the sentiments of the text. But during reading center time, the educator made the book available for independent reading. The learners who read the book independently were asked to make text-to-self connections with the main character, Sophie. By taking this approach, the educator was intentional about making connections with the text and the learners in her class through a variety of modalities.

In a similar fashion, Delpit (2006) encourages educators to use familiar metaphors, analogies, and experiences from the learner's world to connect what they already know to school knowledge which allows them to better engage with the content. Ladson-Billings (1992) further suggests that educators need to know their texts in order to use literacy as a tool of liberation, both personally and culturally.

A third element in building an assessable classroom is for educators to take time to complete an honest reflection about their own cultural competency. Educators need to ask challenging questions about their own beliefs about race, socioeconomic status, gender, and disability. While many educators may believe they have the best intentions regarding their learners, their underlying hidden attitudes towards race, class, sex, and/or disability may actually cause them to treat learners and others who are different from themselves unequally and disrespectfully. Research has shown how oppression could arise out of warmth, friendliness, and concern through a lack of challenging curricula and evaluation (Massey, Scott, & Dornbusch, 1975). However, in a culturally relevant classroom many learners need and expect their teacher to push them (Delpit, 2006).

To set high expectations for all learners, culturally relevant educators are aware of the powerful role and responsibility they have as cultural brokers who have the opportunity to connect the familiar to the unknown and to be gatekeepers to social and political power. It is by taking the time to reflect on their own cultural competency, their strengths and biases, all educators will be able to meet the primary goal of culturally relevant teaching: to empower students to examine critically the society in which they live and to work for social change (Ladson-Billings, 1992).

Creating an accessible classroom that is culturally congruent is challenging and during the process mistakes will be made. However, if educators continue to believe that *all* learners are brilliant, and make intentional efforts to bring culturally relevant literature to life in their classrooms, they will make a lasting difference in the literacy emancipation of their learners.

Creating Culturally Competent Literacy Learning Environments

In conclusion, the authors want to reiterate the most salient points as a blueprint for creating culturally competent literacy learning environments. The chapter provided copious definitions of critical concepts that should be discussed and contextualized during professional development opportunities. Educators cannot teach what they do not know and they will feel more empowered when they can adroitly navigate the nomenclature and discourse of a discipline. The chapter also provided specific examples of how to be more linguistically and culturally competent. These described practices, anecdotes, and examples can be used to engage educators in reflecting on their own practices. Literacy leaders should encourage educators to deconstruct their current practices and reinvent them as culturally competent practices. Literacy leaders should then provide educators opportunities to share and model their instructional discoveries, successes, and problems-solutions. Through the various cases, definitions, examples, and described practices, our hope is that this chapter provided literacy leaders and educators the necessary tools to maximize their instructional potential.

We began the article with a quote from Lisa Delpit; therefore, we must end by coming full circle with another provocative statement. Delpit (2006) stated that we cannot prepare disenfranchised students to become the low level functionaries of our society by teaching them only the basics and not recognizing their brilliance. This statement is worthy of being touted in every school building across our nation as the mantra that can assist in transforming practices. If educators embrace *literacy as access to power* and *reading as emancipatory*, then they possess the dispositional stances that will enable them to become culturally competent and confident.

REFERENCES

Adams, M., Bell, L. A., & Griffin, P. (1997). *Teaching for diversity and social justice: A sourcebook*. New York, NY: Routledge.

Adams, M., Blumenfield, W., Castaneda, C., Hackman, H. W., Peters. M. L., & Zuniga, X. (2013). *Readings for diversity and social justice*. New York, NY: Routledge.

Allen, R. (2005). Promoting diverse leadership: Shared cultural backgrounds can strengthen bridges. *Education Update, 47*(3), 1–3 & 8.

Alli, N., Rajan, R., & Ratliff, G. (2016, March/April). How personalized learning unlocks student success. *Educase Review*, 12–21.

Banks, J. A., & Banks, C. A. M. (Eds.). (1995). *Handbook of research on multicultural education*. New York, NY: Macmillan.

Brock, C. H., Moore, D. K., & Parks, L. (2007). Exploring preservice teachers' literacy practices with children from diverse backgrounds: Implication for teacher educators. *Teaching and Teacher Education, 23*, 898–915.

Carey, K. (2004). The real value of teachers: Using new information about teacher effectiveness to close the achievement gap. *Thinking K–16: A Publication of the Education Trust, 8*(1), 3–42.

Cattani, D. H. (2002). *A classroom of her own: How new teachers develop instructional, professional, and cultural competence*. Thousand Oaks, CA: Corwin Press.

Council of Chief State School Officers. (2013). *Interstate Teacher Assessment and Support Consortium (InTASC): Model core teaching standards and learning progressions for teachers 1.0*. Washington, DC. Author.

Darling-Hammond, L., & Bransford, J. (2005). *Preparing teachers for a changing world: What teachers should learn and be able to do*. San Francisco, CA: Jossey-Bass.

Delpit, L. (1995). *Other people's children: Cultural conflict in the classroom*. New York, NY: The New Press.

Delpit, L. (2006). Lessons from teachers. *Journal of Teacher Education, 57*(3), 220–231.

Gay, G. (1975, October). Cultural differences important in the education of Black children. *Momentum*, 2–5.

Gay, G. (2000). *Culturally responsive teaching: Theory, research, and practice*. New York, NY: Teachers College Press.

Gay, G. (2002). Preparing for culturally responsive teaching. *Journal of Teacher Education, 53*(2), 106–116.

Gay, G. (2005). Politics of multicultural teacher education. *Journal of Teaching Education, 56*(10), 221–228.

Hackman, H. W. (2005). The five essentials components for social justice education. *Excellence in Education, 38*(2), 103–109.

hooks, b. (1994). *Teaching to transgress: Education as the practice of freedom*. New York, NY: Routledge.

Howard, G. (2006). *We can't teach what we don't know*. New York, NY: Teachers College Press.

Irvine, J., & Armando, B. (2001). *Culturally responsive teaching: Lesson planning for elementary and middle grades*. New York, NY: McGraw-Hill.

Irvine, J., & York, D. (1995). Learning styles and culturally diverse students: A literature review. In J. Banks & C. Banks (Eds.), *Handbook of research on multicultural education*. New York, NY: Macmillan.

Kelly-Jackson, C.P., & Jackson, T.O. (2011). Meeting their fullest potential: the beliefs and teachings of a culturally relevant science teacher. *Creative Education, 2(4)*, 408–413.

Kunjufu, J. (2002). *Black students, middle class teachers*. United States: African American Images.

Ladson-Billings, G. (1992). Reading between the lines and beyond the pages: A culturally relevant approach to literacy teaching. *Theory Into Practice, 31*(4), 312–320.

Ladson- Billings, G. (1994). *Dreamkeepers*. San Francisco, CA: Jossey-Bass.

Ladson-Billings, G. (1995a). But that's just good teaching: The case for culturally relevant pedagogy. *Theory Into Practice, 34*(3), 159–165.

Ladson-Billings, G. (1995b). Toward a theory of culturally relevant pedagogy. *American Educational Research Journal, 32*(3), 465–491.

Ladson-Billings, G. (2005). Is the team all right? Diversity and teacher education. *Journal of Teaching Education. 56*(10), 229–234.

Ladson-Billings, G. (2009). The Dreamkeepers: Successful teachers of African-American children (2nd ed.). San Francisco, CA: Jossey-Bass.

Lipman, P. (1995). Bring out the best in them: The contribution of culturally relevant teachers to educational reform. *Theory into Practice, 34*(3), 2002–2008.

Massey, G. C., Scott, M. V., & Dornbusch, S. M. (1975). Racism without racists: Institutional racism in urban schools. *The Black Soldier, 7*, 10–19.

McNair, J. C. (2012). "I never knew there were so many books about us" Parents and childre reading and responding to African American children's literature together. *Children's Literature in Education, 44*, 191–207.

Moule, J., & Higgins, K. M. (2007). The role of African American mentor teachers in preparing white preservice teachers for African American student populations. *Journal of Negro Education, 76*(4), 609–621.

Obidah, J., & Howard, T. (2005). Preparing teachers for 'Monday morning' in the urban school classroom: Reflecting on our pedagogies and practices as effective teacher educators. *Journal of Teacher Education, 56*(3), 248–255.

Shade, B. (1987). Ecological correlates of educative style of African American children. *Journal of Negro Education, 60*, 291–301.

Shor, I. (1992). *Empowering education: Critical teaching for social change*. Chicago, IL: University of Chicago Press.

Sleeter, C. (1993). How white teachers construct race. In C, McCarthy and W. Crichlow (Eds.), *Race identity and representation in education*, New York, NY: Routledge.

Sleeter, C. (2001). Preparing teachers for culturally diverse schools: Research and the overwhelming presence of whiteness. *Journal of Teacher Education, 52*(2), 94–101.

Stevenson, H. C. (2014*). Promoting racial literacy in schools: Differences that make a difference*. New York, NY: Teachers College Press.

Tatum, A. (2005). *Teaching reading to Black adolescent males: Closing the achievement gap*. Portland, ME: Stenhouse. Thomas, W. P., & Collier, V.P. (2003). Reforming education policies for English learners: Research evidence from U.S. schools. *The Multilingual Educator, 4*(1), 16–19.

Tiezzi, L., & Cross, B. (1997). Utilizing research on prospective teachers' beliefs to inform urban field experiences. *Urban Review, 29*(2), 113–125.

Villegas, A. M., & Lucas, T. (2002). Preparing culturally responsive teachers. *Journal of Teacher Education, 53*(1), 20–32.

Pendakur, V. (2016). *Closing the opportunity gap: Identity-conscious strategies for retention and student success*. Sterling, VA: Stylus.

Willis, M. (1995). *"We're family": Creating success in a public African American elementary school* (Unpublished doctoral dissertation). Georgia State University, Atlanta.

Yeo, F. (1997). Teacher preparation and inner-city schools: Sustaining educational failure. *The Urban Review, 29*(2), 127–143.

CHILDREN'S BOOKS CITED

Boelts, M. (2007). *Those shoes*. Somerville, MA: Candlewick Press.

Bunting, E. (1996). *Going home*. New York, NY: HarperCollins.

Dorros, A. (2008). *Papá and me*. New York, NY: HarperCollins.

Fox, M. (1989). *Sophie*. Voyager Books, Harcourt.

Keats, E. J. (1962). *The snowy day*. Viking Penguin.

Sendak, M. (1963). *Where the wild thing are*. New York, NY: HarperCollins.

St. John, J. (1996). *Hispanic scientists: Ellen Ochoa, Carlos A. Ramirez, Eloy Rodriguez, Lydia Villa-Komaroff, Maria Elena Zavala*. Mankato, MN: Capstone Press.

CHAPTER 3

BEYOND KNOWING YOUR HISTORY

Multicultural and Citizenship Education as Necessities for Democracy

Brandi N. Hinnant-Crawford
Western Carolina University

Najja K. Baptist
Howard University

Introduction

When examining the success or failure of educational institutions, one has to deal with the age-old question—What is the goal of education? Education has certainly been misused and abused, producing outcomes that are contrary to the ostensibly virtuous goals, particularly for children in the margins. In schools across the United States, we see children of color disproportionately placed in special education classes, while being underrepresented in gifted education. We see evidence of the school to prison

Comprehensive Multicultural Education in the 21st Century:
Increasing Access in the Age of Retrenchment, pp. 37–58
Copyright © 2019 by Information Age Publishing
All rights of reproduction in any form reserved.

pipeline, and we also see the persistent and pervasive gap in achievement between the rich and poor and between students of color and their White and Asian counterparts. When examining the outcomes of our current educational system, we have to ask what are the goals of state sponsored education for "other people's children."

In truth, the great experiment of public education began as a way to cultivate an educated citizenry ready to participate in the democratic process. This chapter puts forth, for your consideration, the role of multicultural education in preparing traditionally marginalized groups *and* traditionally dominant groups for active participation in democracy. The authors argue multicultural education is essential in cultivating the skills and dispositions necessary for citizenship.

This chapter will illustrate the extraordinary potential for advancing democracy when the citizenship and multicultural education are taught simultaneously and the dysfunction that can occur when such a coupling is absent. The chapter begins by defining citizenship and multicultural education and juxtaposing their similar goals. Following a discussion of the intentions of the two disciplines, the authors overview prominent approaches to teaching in each discipline—such as the C3 Framework in citizenship education and Culturally Relevant Pedagogy in multicultural education. The chapter also examines challenges faced by each discipline, such as Citizenship education's struggle for instructional time in era of accountability. Finally, we offer a contemporary illustration of the danger of a failure to acknowledge the significance of citizenship education and multicultural education using the activities associated with the 2016 US election cycle. We conclude that multicultural education is more than knowing one's history—but it is indeed a necessity for democracy. We begin with brief descriptions of citizenship education and multicultural education.

GOALS

Citizenship Education

The 2003 report, *The Civic Mission of Schools* argued that the goal of citizenship education should be to help young people acquire and learn the skills, knowledge and attitudes that will prepare them to be competent and responsible citizens throughout their lives. The Report goes on to outline four criteria for being a "competent and responsible" citizen. It states that such citizens:

1. are informed and thoughtful; have a grasp and an appreciation of history and the fundamental processes of American democracy; have an understanding and awareness of public and community is-

sues; and have the ability to obtain information, think critically and
enter into dialogue among others with different perspectives.
2. participate in their communities through membership in or con-
    tributions to organization working to address an array of cultural,
    social, political, and religious interests and beliefs.
3. act politically by having the skills, knowledge, and commitment
    needed to accomplish public purposes, such as group problem solv-
    ing, public speaking, petitioning and protesting, and voting.
4. have moral and civic virtues such as concern for the rights and wel-
    fare of others, social responsibility, tolerance and respect, and belief
    in the capacity to make a difference (Battistoni et al., 2003, p. 10).

In the 2006 report on citizenship education, titled *Developing Citizenship Competences from Kindergarten through Grade 12* (Torney-Purta & Lopez,
2006) citizenship education scholars and practitioners catalogue outcomes
of citizenship education and categorize them as knowledge, skills, dispositions, and motivations. The first domain of competence, knowledge, deals
with the acquisition of information—such as coursework around history and
civics that teach the components of democracy. The skills domain embod-
ies the ability to process new information. Dispositions and motivation,
much harder to teach, is the propensity for one to accept the responsibility
of his or her duty as a citizen.

The type of citizen an individual is, determines their responsibilities of
citizenship. Westheimer and Kahne (2004) put forth three types of citizens,
readily observable in the United States: the personally responsible citizen,
the participatory citizen, and the justice-oriented citizen. The personally
responsible citizen is one who "acts responsibly in his or her community
by, for example, picking up liter, giving blood, recycling, obeying laws, and
staying out of debt" (p. 3). The participatory citizen is one who, "actively
participates in civic affairs and the social life of the community at local,
state, and national levels" (p. 4). Last but not least is the justice-oriented
citizen, defined as individuals who "use rhetoric and analysis that calls
explicit attention to matters of injustice and to the importance of pursuing
social justice" (p. 4). Each type of citizen contributes in meaningful ways,
and individuals can be in more than one category. Citizenship education is
one formalized aspect of political socialization—and arguably the rationale
behind public schools.

Multicultural Education

Depending on which multicultural theorist one asks, the purpose and
tasks of multicultural education has nuanced differences. Nieto (2000)
describes multicultural education as transformative potential with a

primary purpose of "confronting issues of power and privilege in society" (p. 4). Whereas, Grant (2016) defines multicultural education as a "philosophical concept rooted in the principles of democracy, social justice, equity, and the affirmation of the value in human diversity" (p. 2). Gorski (2006) reassures while each scholar frames it differently, true multicultural education encompasses universal characteristics—it is political (not only pedagogical) and intentionally advances the causes of social justice, it identifies classroom practices but focuses on school and system reform as well, has the primary goal of eliminating educational inequality, and is good for everyone (p. 164). Intriguingly, Banks and Banks (2010) use terminology very similar to the goals of citizenship education when describing the goal of multicultural education; they explicate, "A major goal of multicultural education is to help students to develop the knowledge, attitudes, and skills needed to function within their own microcultures, the US macroculture, other microcultures, and the global community" (p. 25).

With an underlying principle of democracy, it seems multicultural education and citizenship education would be two sides of the same coin. Yet, somewhere a false bifurcation between multicultural and citizenship education was created. Indubitably, critics of multicultural education such as Schlesinger argued that the particularism would wear away the common culture—creating the premise that multiculturalism is antithetical to citizenship. Yet, when examining the stated purposes, one cannot dismiss the eerily similar goals. Furthermore, the bodies of work of noted scholars of multicultural education such as James Banks, Gloria Ladson-Billings, and Christine Sleeter contribute to both multicultural and citizenship education. For example, Sleeter (2014) argues:

> Multicultural education and citizenship education can be powerful together, but often are not. Diversity studies too often stress learning about the other rather than engaging with or learning to work in solidarity with diverse others. (p. 86)

In this chapter, we take Sleeter's notion a step further—not only can the two be powerful together, but they are insufficient when separate and disastrous when absent. In the following section, we describe the prominent approaches to teaching citizenship and multicultural education.

PROCESSES

Approaches to Citizenship Education

In 2003, the *Civic Mission of Schools* (Battistoni et al., 2003), outlined six promising approaches to civic education and tied them explicitly to the outcome they were most likely to impact. The six approaches were classroom instruction, discussion of current events, service-learning, extra-curricular activities, participation in student governance and simulations. The matrix (see Table 3.1) is a reproduction of the matrix in the *Civic Mission of Schools* illustrating the benefits of each approach.

Table 3.1.
Benefits of Different Approaches to Civic Education

		Citizenship Competencies				
		Civic and Political Knowledge	Civic and Political Skills	Civic Attitudes	Political Participation	Community Participation
Approach to Citizenship Education	Classroom Instruction	X	X		X	
	Discussion of Current Events	X	X	X	X	
	Service Learning		X	X		X
	Extra Curricular Activities		X		X	X
	Student Voice in Student Government		X	X		
	Simulations	X	X	X		

By the publication of *Guardian of Democracy* in 2011, the promising approaches have the empirical evidence to illustrate they are *proven strategies* for advancing civic outcomes (Gould, Jamieson, Levine, McConnell, & Smith, 2011). It should be noted, there are some reservations in the field about what actually are the best approaches to citizenship education. Geboers, Geijsel, Admiraal, and Dam's (2013) review of literature showed mixed results for the actual value-add of citizenship education and said it is important not to underestimate the role of the home and family in democratic socialization. On the other hand, Neundorf, Niemi, and Smets's (2015) empirical study found the citizenship education has compensation effects, particularly for children who have less politically involved families—showing citizenship education can play a role in cultivating civic equality.

In the United States, the National Council for Social Studies put forth the *C3 Framework: Guidance for Enhancing the Rigor of K–12 Civics, Economics, Geography, and History* in 2013. While not a specific set of standards, the framework serves as a foundation and an approach for the multiple disciplines that fall in the realm of social studies. The C3 Framework has 4 dimensions:

1. Developing questions and planning,
2. Applying disciplinary concepts and tools,
3. Evaluating sources and *using evidence*, and
4. Communicating conclusions and taking *informed* action [author emphasis].

The Framework gives suggestions of provocative questions that can serve as a basis for a lesson or unit. For instance, "Was the American Revolution revolutionary?" or "Was the Civil Rights Movement of the 1960s a success?" With such questions, the student then applies the disciplinary tools of history, economics, or civics to develop claims and counterclaims and uncover evidence to support or refute each. While the C3 Framework has been praised by citizenship education scholars, there is also skepticism regarding how widespread its implementation will be. Hahn (2016) explains:

> My own fear is that, like so often in the past, school districts with high-income families will implement this challenging, ambitious approach to teaching and learning [C3 Framework], but districts serving children in poverty, in rural and urban areas that have the least well-prepared teachers will not implement this challenging pedagogy. Rather, their teachers may continue to rely on lecture and recitation focusing on raising scores on multiple choice tests.

Hahn says that professional development for in-service teachers is critical for successful implementation of such a dynamic approach to citizenship education pedagogy; this is an assertion echoed by Thacker, Lee, and Friedman (2016) in their study of teacher implementation of C3.

Barr and associates (2015) conducted a randomized experiment assessing the effectiveness of professional development on teaching efficacy and student civic outcomes using the Facing History approach to citizenship education. Facing History is described as an interdisciplinary method that includes the examination of self-identity, group identity, and national identity and does not shy away for explicit exploration of discrimination, prejudice, and stereotyping. Teachers within the treatment group explored a historical case. The authors explicate:

> For this valuation, the historical content involved the failure of democracy in pre-World War II Germany, and specifically the steps leading up to the Holocaust. The case study examines hatred, racism, antisemitism, and examples of courage, care, and compassion. One central goal is for students to discover that historical events are not inevitable and that preventing injustice and preserving democracy requires citizens to be informed, ethically reflective, and active participants. (p. 5)

They found the professional development had substantial impacts on teacher efficacy to teach the material, and moderate impacts on student outcomes. These moderate impacts on students include statistically significant differences (and higher scores) on political tolerance, civic self-efficacy, engaging with civic matters, and overall understanding of history when having a teacher in the Facing History treatment group.

Kahne and associates (2016) argue citizenship education in the 21st century must also contend with the growing amount of participatory politics—especially if new age politics does not want to recreate the same disparities. Khane and associates define participatory politics as "interactive, peer-based acts through which individuals and groups seek to exert both voice and influence on issues of public concern" (p. 2). Conversely institutional politics is characterized by, "highly organized groups and institutional gatekeepers—political parties, government bureaucracies, news agencies, civic organizations, lobbyists, and special interest groups—[that] structure conversations about which issues serve attention and drive priorities of action" (p. 4). They make no qualms that social media has created a new terrain for participatory politics. Furthermore, they found 67% of youth engaged in participatory politics using social media or social networking compared to 39% of adults. Khane and colleagues point out in this new political environment, students continue to need the traditional knowledge, skills, and dispositions associated with citizenship education, but they must also be prepared to engage in the core practices of participatory politics:

1. investigation and research,
2. dialogue and feedback,
3. production and circulation, and
4. mobilizing for change.

While they caution educators to be savvy with how they use social media in the classroom, they do give explicit examples for how to embed these practices in coursework. They suggest: "[having students] collect data from members of their communities, carefully analyze community issues, present findings to authentic audiences, and interact with community leaders" which can increase agency and civic skill (p. 23). They also recommend that "youth can develop websites or public service announcements and share what they learned via YouTube or other social media" which aids in the development of student voice (p. 23).

There are volumes and volumes of texts on citizenship education. What is shared here is by no means exhaustive. The approaches examined above, including the C3 Framework and Facing History are exemplar approaches to citizenship education. It is unrealistic to believe that citizenship education works like this in every classroom. However, what is reviewed here is what scholars have put forth for how citizenship education should be approached to maximize its benefits to democracy.

Approaches to Multicultural Education

Multicultural education is unlike citizenship education in several ways. While it is an academic discipline, it is interdisciplinary. There is no set of standards that all multicultural education teachers adhere too; nor are there undergraduate majors or licensure areas in multicultural education. Teacher preparation programs have a multicultural education course or attempt to embed multicultural education principles in required coursework for preservice teachers.

Banks (1993) names five dimensions of multicultural education: content integration, knowledge construction, prejudice reduction, equity pedagogy, and empowering school and social structures. Each dimension is a part of achieving the objectives of multicultural education—but content integration, knowledge construction, and equity pedagogy are directly related to classroom practice. Banks and Banks (1995) define equity pedagogy as, "teaching strategies and classroom environments that help students from diverse racial, ethnic, and cultural groups attain knowledge, skills, and attitudes needed to function effectively within, and help create and perpetuate, a just, humane, and democratic society" (p. 152). With such a broad definition, a number of things could fall under the umbrella of equity pedagogy—including but not limited to culturally relevant and responsive pedagogies, bilingual education, and universal design for learning.

Culturally relevant pedagogy is one of the most well-known and lauded equity pedagogies. Ladson-Billings (1995) says the hallmark of culturally relevant pedagogy are students experiencing academic success, developing or maintaining cultural competence and developing a critical consciousness that allows them to challenge the social order. Again, possessing such a broad definition—culturally relevant pedagogy is applicable to a variety of academic disciplines. Since the birth of the concept, scholars have tried to operationalize what culturally relevant pedagogy looks like in practice. Ladson-Billings (2009) and others have painted portraits of equity pedagogy in case studies of exemplar teachers doing the work. Morrison, Robbins, and Rose's (2008) review of literature on classroom demonstrations of culturally relevant pedagogy takes Ladson-Billings' framework and defines practices related to each component (see Figure 3.1).

Academic Success	Cultural Competence	Critical Consciousness
• Scaffolding and Modeling • Using students strengths as starting points • Taking personal responsibility for student success • Creating cooperative environments • Holding high and explicit behavioral expectations	• Reshaping prescribed curriculum • Building on students funds of knowledge • Encouraging relationsips between communities and schools	• Facilite the development of critical literacy • Engage students in justice work • Make power dynamics in mainstream society explicit • Share power in the classroom

Source: Adapted from Morrison, Robbins, and Rose's (2008) "Operationalization of Culturally Relevant Pedagogy."

Figure 3.1.   Operationalizing culturally relevant pedagogy.

While Morrison and collaborators establish general practices, Morrell's (2008) text on critical literacy illustrates how these principles can play out in a high school English classroom. Building on student strengths, he bridged canonical texts with popular culture—reshaping the prescribed curriculum; one unit he presented was the Odyssey and the Godfather. Morrell explains that he paired the two because they both are pieces "that are larger than life; that portray the deeds of warriors and heroes; that reflect the ideals and values of a culture" (p. 94). In this unit, he melds high expectations and curricular rigor. He clarifies his intentions saying, "I wanted students to theorize the role of a hero in an epic. What characteristics are associated with heroism? What is the role of religion? What is the treatment of women? How is violence justified or glorified?" (p. 94). His assessment for the unit was modeled after the assessments he took as an undergraduate English major. The unit simultaneously allowed students to critique the values of their society—increasing sociopolitical consciousness—while they covered the difficult canonical text, *The Odyssey.*

Often practitioners think equity pedagogy is more applicable to social sciences and humanities than STEM content (Hinnant-Crawford, 2016). However, Gutstein (2003) gives examples of these principles applied to mathematics lessons as well. Using the Mathematics in Context curricula, he aims for his students to "use mathematics to understand—and potentially act on—their sociopolitical context" (p. 44). In his sample lessons he has two sets of goals—teaching for social justice goals and mathematics goals—one of which is changing the dispositions students have toward mathematics. Gutstein speaks in detail about how the work is grounded in the lives of the students and interdisciplinary, "Besides mathematics, all the projects include writing and interpreting data, graphs, pictures, maps, or texts (often newspaper articles) ...virtually every project related to and built upon my students' lived experiences as urban youth from immigrant, Latino, working-class families" (p. 47). Similar to C3 and the literacy coursework described by Morrell, his class project was inquiry based. Students were asked to determine whether or not racism impacted housing prices in a particular suburb. Students began the project by answering the following questions:

1. What mathematics would you use to answer the question?
2. How would you use mathematics?
3. If you could collect any data to answer the question, explain what data you would collect and why you would collect that data (Gutstein, 2003, p. 47).

Furthermore, students had to explain what types of data would provide evidence that racism impacted prices and what data would provide evidence to the contrary. After this initial portion of the project, they were required to evaluate the proposals of their peers—which distributes classroom power from being solely in the hands of the teacher. This approach acknowledges the expertise students bring to the classroom, maintains high expectations with rigor, and demonstrates an explicit intention to raise sociopolitical consciousness. In these disciplinary specific examples of multicultural education, it is evident that education embeds citizenship content. Morrell's lesson asked students to reflect on the values of society, which prompts students to be conscious of and critique the values of the society they live in—which is an exercise in citizenship. Similarly, Gutstein, had students to use mathematics as a tool to explore power relations in housing within their own community—another act of citizenship education.

While Morrell and Gutstein are elevated as examples here, they are not the only subject-specific scholars providing guidance on how to embed multicultural education across content areas. While there is not sufficient space to go through examples across the disciplines here, readers should note that literacy scholars (Johnson & Eubanks, 2015; Morrell, 2008; Winn & Johnson, 2011), mathematicians (Aguirre & del Rosario Zavala, 2013; Gutstein, 2003; Gustein & Peterson, 2006; Moses & Cobb, 2001), science educators (Lee & Buxton, 2010; Parsons, 2000, 2008), and citizenship scholars (Dilworth, 2004; Grant & Asimeng-Boahene, 2006; Pinckney & Faison, 2013) have written about exemplar teachers, sample lessons, and classroom processes that embody equity pedagogy.

Despite the operationalization put forth by Morrison and colleagues and an extraordinary number of the examples in the literature, Young's (2010) research shows that teachers have a limited understanding of what culturally relevant pedagogy actually is—focusing more on some aspects and completely ignoring others. In fact, Ladson-Billings (2014) even expressed concerns on the mutation of culturally relevant pedagogy from what it was meant to be. She details:

> My work on culturally relevant pedagogy has taken on a life of its own, and what I see in the literature and sometimes in practice is totally unrecognizable to me. What state departments, school districts, and individual teachers are now calling "culturally relevant pedagogy" is often a distortion and corruption of the central ideas I attempted to promulgate. The idea that adding some books about people of color, having a classroom Kwanzaa celebration, or posting "diverse" images makes one "culturally relevant" seem to be what the pedagogy has been reduced to. (pp. 81–82)

The failure to translate these great pedagogical strategies to common practice is one of many challenges faced by the fields of citizenship and multicultural education.

CHALLENGES

Despite the laudable goals and promising approaches to instruction, both multicultural education and citizenship education have experienced a number of challenges in recent years. The rise of accountability has hurt the proliferation of both within U.S. classrooms (Fitchett & Heafner, 2010; Morrison et al., 2008; Young, 2010). For example, in Young's (2010) study of culturally relevant pedagogy, one teacher argued, "You only have seventy minutes a day to teach math, and then they have to pass the test" (p. 254). Young rationalizes that the essence of the question was whether or not "the incorporation of culturally relevant pedagogy [would] impede students' mastery in math?" (p. 254). In a similar vein, Morrison et al. (2008) elucidate:

> Culturally relevant pedagogy is ultimately a constructivist pedagogy. Schools are currently set up to privilege the transmission theory of learn-

ing over the constructivist theory, and the rise of a standardized curriculum and high-stakes tests has only tipped the scales more toward this transmission theory. (p. 444)

Accountability has impacted citizenship education as well. McMurrer (2008) found that, post No Child Left Behind, 36% of districts decreased instructional time for social studies. On average, the time was decreased by 76 minutes per week. Fitchett and Heafner's (2010) analysis of national survey data over nearly a 20-year period found, "the neglect of social studies is not a new, but an accelerating trend" (p. 126). While once considered the primary purpose of schooling, the increased competition in the global market, has schools focusing time on other subjects.

In addition to the accountability challenge, citizenship education outcomes mirror those of math and language arts—students of color far underperform their peers on measures of knowledge. For instance, when examining NAEP Civics proficiency of high school seniors, African Americans, Latinos, and Native Americans are much more likely to score below proficient than their White and Asian peers (see Chart 1). Levinson (2007) designated this phenomenon as the "civic achievement gap." Khane and Middaugh (2008) speak more about a "civic opportunity gap" especially when it comes to high-impact civic learning opportunities. In their studies of students in California, they found African Americans were less likely to discuss social problems and current events, have civically oriented government courses, participate in simulations, have experiences with decisions making, and experience and open classroom environment than their White peers. Likewise, Latino students reported fewer opportunities for an open classroom climate, chances for simulations, and opportunities for service. Pickney's (2016) review of literature corroborates that one's access to high quality citizenship education is largely correlated to his or her race (see Figure 3.2).

While citizenship education is dealing with challenges in equitable access to instruction and securing instructional time in the context of high-stakes accountability, multicultural education has its own set of challenges—some of which stem from within the field. Gorski (2006) explicates that when he asks multicultural education professionals to define multicultural education what he most often hears is a response that is more of "a compassionate conservative consciousness than an allegiance to equity and justice" (p. 167). He goes on to espouse that multicultural educators have focused too much on "changing hearts to the disregard of transforming institutions" (p. 167). Similarly, Grant speaks of a co-optation of language and depoliticization of the language of multicultural education. He gives the example of Black Lives Matter, a political statement, being modified to All Lives Matter— removing the political message originally being championed.

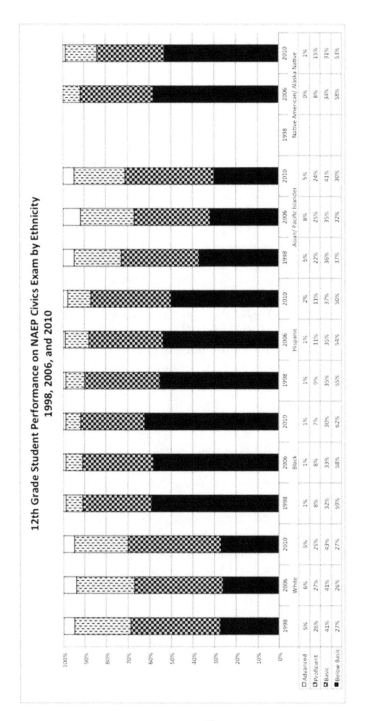

12th Grade Student Performance on NAEP Civics Exam by Ethnicity 1998, 2006, and 2010

Figure 3.2. Achievement disparities on NAEP Civics Exam.

Ladson-Billings (2014) explains some purported multiculturalists have taken a reductionist approach, implementing initiatives with narrow understanding of culture; furthermore, she argues "few have taken up the sociopolitical dimensions of the work, instead dulling it's critical edge or omitting it all together" (p. 77). In her early work on multicultural education and empowerment, Sleeter (1991) explained there are five approaches to multicultural education: (1) the human relations approach—getting along with the marginalized, (2) the teaching the culturally different approach—teaching the marginalized, cultural democracy approach—(3) redesigning schools and classrooms for the marginalized, the ethnic studies approach—(4) deep study about the history and conditions of a particular marginalized group, and (5) the multicultural and social reconstructionist approach. The fifth approach focuses on the development of critical consciousness so students can critique the world as it is and work to transform it. Multicultural education should be all of these things, but people have focused more on the human relations to the detriment of the others.

Multicultural and citizenship education both are challenged in the current context; the challenges they face do not negate their necessity. The recent election cycle demonstrates what happens when individuals do not acquire the knowledge, skills, dispositions, and values put forth in these two disciplines essential to democracy. Next we explain why this is the case.

OUTCOMES

Scholars could argue the 2016 election cycle is the outcome of inadequate citizenship and multicultural education. The low turnout, general lack of trust in government (Doherty, Kiley, Tyson, & Jameson, 2015), the proliferation of fake news (Higgins, McIntirye, & Dance, 2016; Sydell, 2016), and the divisive campaign rhetoric appear to be the perfect storm result when the knowledge, skills and dispositions of citizenship and the values of multiculturalism are not cultivated. This chapter elevates one current example that speaks to the impact of an inadequate focus on citizenship education and multicultural education.

The Normalcy of Whiteness, Maleness, and Heterosexuality in 2016 Election

Sonia Nieto argued years ago that multicultural education was not just for marginalized students. In fact, she explained:

Although the primary victims of biased education continue to be those who are invisible in the curriculum, those who figure prominently are victims as well. They receive only a partial education, which legitimates their cultural blinders. European American children, seeing only themselves, learn that they are the norm . . . the same is true for males. The children of the wealthy learn that only the wealthy and the powerful are the real makers of history. . .. Heterosexual students receive the message that gay and lesbian students should be ostracized because they are deviant and immoral. The humanity of all students is jeopardized as a result. (Nieto, 2000, p. 311)

In the U.S. 2016 election the dehumanization of persons who were not White, male, heterosexual, and Christian was widespread. Live on CNN, Steve King, a Republican US Representative from Iowa posed the question,

This "old white people" business does get a little tired ... I'd ask you to go back through history and figure out where are these contributions that have been made by these other categories of people that you are talking about? Where did any other subgroup of people contribute more to civilization. (Victor, 2016, para. 4)

While willful ignorance is real, one must ask what exposure Rep. King had to the contributions of other in his school curriculum.

When May and Sleeter (2010) spoke about the mission shift in multicultural education, they explained a new era has caused individuals to question the merits of diversity:

In the last decade, we have been a major retrenchment of the principles of multiculturalism ... despite emphasis on efforts to close the "achievement gap" multicultural education has all but disappeared. This move towards standardized curriculum was also framed within a wider growing skepticism of the merits of diversity per se, particularly, after 9/11. For many, ethnic, linguistic, and cultural diversity are no longer something to be celebrated, but feared. (p. 1)

Fear mongering was a strategy used in some political campaigns—advocating fear and distrust of the other. In President Trump's announcement of his candidacy, he painted an unpleasant picture of Mexicans:

The U.S. has become a dumping ground for everybody else's problems ... When Mexico sends its people, they're not sending their best. They're not sending you.... They're sending people that have lots of problems, and they're bringing those problems with us. They're bringing drugs. They're bringing crime. They're rapists. And some, I assume, are good people. (Delreal, 2015)

In the ordering of his remarks, the fact that *some* (or, we would argue a great majority) are good people seems to be an afterthought. As the campaign went on, President Trump was known for saying, "Build a Wall" on the southern border of the United States that Mexico will pay for. Similar disparaging remarks were made about people of the Islamic faith. In his announcement he argued, "Islamic terrorism is eating up the Middle East." Later, after a mass-shooting in San Bernadino, California, he called for a ban on all Islamic travel to the United States. Prior to this, he asked for surveillance on mosques and the establishment of a Muslim database (Diamond, 2015).

President Trump was recorded making comments where he bragged about sexually assaulting women and dismissed it as "locker room banter." Later he referred to his opponent as "such a nasty woman" in the middle of a live presidential debate. While not necessarily condoned by President Trump, it was common to see signs and t-shirts that said, "Trump that Bitch" referring to his opponent, Hillary Clinton, at rallies.

In addition to negatively casting Mexicans, Muslims, and using misogynistic rhetoric toward women—the presidential candidate Trump had unique ways of referring to individuals different than himself. While ostensibly comedic, throughout his campaign Donald Trump used the article "the" to describe different groups of people (Sanders, 2016). The gays, the Blacks, the Muslims. Linguist, Eric Acton, explained that beyond being odd, it, "is a way of highlighting the group's otherness from the speaker or his or her audience . . . there's a distancing effect, like they're over there" (Abadi, 2016, p. 1).

Donald Trump's campaign had an impact on citizenship education in schools. According to Costello (2017), who surveyed 2,000 teachers during the election, 40 percent were hesitant to teach about the election. While no candidate was named in the survey, in the open-ended responses, Trump was mentioned more than 1,000 times in 5,000 comments compared to all other candidates totaling 200 combined. She writes about what she has called the "Trump Effect" and argues it has undone some of the antibullying progress made within schools. She reports students from traditionally marginalized groups are terrified and students from dominant groups are emboldened. Cosetllo says, "Kids use the names of candidates as pejoratives to taunt each other" (p. 10). In the moments after the election, some teachers worked to ensure their students felt welcome, as pictures of signs in classrooms went viral. Particularly one (see Figure 3.3).

NECESSITY FOR DEMOCRACY

The 2016 election shows the education world what things may look like when people do not possess the skills, dispositions, and knowledge to be good

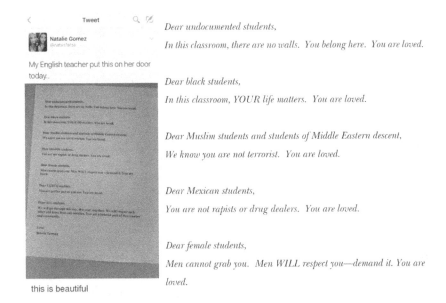

Figure 3.3.   Student tweets about teacher's inclusive response in hostile environment.

citizens. Contrary to Schlesinger's (1998) thesis, multicultural education does not disunite America; America can disunite on its own. Multicultural education does enable children to be American; it enables children to recognize the humanity in themselves and in individuals who are different. The goal of multicultural education is access and transformation—access to curricula, access to democracy, and access to the development of one's full potential and transformation of institutions and systems that render few powerful and many powerless. Multicultural education and citizenship education are both interdisciplinary and must be woven through each course to illustrate the utility of academic content to the lives of the students. To combat apathy in the nation's most vulnerable populations, we must incorporate both across the curriculum. Going forward, research on citizenship education must include longitudinal studies, broader definitions of success, and an emphasis on multiculturalism.

Without longitudinal studies, it is difficult to measure the success of citizenship education beyond collecting data on knowledge, attitudes, efficacy, and speculative constructs. Longitudinal research that connects classroom approaches to participatory behaviors in adulthood is what is necessary to truly evaluate the efficacy of citizenship education.

In addition to the need for longitudinal research, we also need to broaden the definition of success for citizenship education. Voting cannot be the primary outcome. As long as we consider voting a primary outcome of citizenship education, we have to narrowly focus on adult behavior as the major outcome. Broadening our understanding of the outcomes of citizenship education allows us to consider youth activities as valid expressions of citizenship. Success of citizenship education must be broadened when examining how citizenship is expressed in adulthood as well. Levinson (2010) writes a great deal about the "empowerment gap" and defines it as unequal distribution of political power in the United States (p. 332). She argues that individuals involved in traditional political behavior such as contributing to campaigns, voting and contacting politicians have the lion's share of political power in the United States. She acknowledges a narrow definition, "risks creating a circular and apparently deficit oriented argument in which I place certain groups at the bottom of a civic empowerment gap precisely because I discount forms of civic engagement in which they are particularly involved" (p. 6). She justifies her choice: first by explaining that these types of behaviors do exert influence and second by rationalizing political scholars have more accurate data traditional forms of participation. Yet, we argue new measures of tracking nontraditional behaviors should be developed and the definition of political empowerment broadened to include nontraditional behaviors. Take the Black Lives Matter movement that has swept the United States with demonstrations across the country as a response to police brutality and the shooting of unarmed African Americans. Frederick Harris explained that while Black Lives Matter did not catalyze a rise in Black or youth voting, the movement put criminal justice reform on political party platforms (Williams & Clement, 2016). That, too, is empowerment.

Beyond redefining our outcomes, we must redefine our methods. Multicultural approaches to citizenship cannot be optional. If civic knowledge is truly a precursor for later civic engagement, the incorporation of multicultural citizenship education could have consequences for the "civic achievement" and "civic empowerment." Particularly, if students are developing and maintaining cultural competence—group consciousness has been known to predict traditional forms of participation of African Americans (Leighley & Vedlitz, 1999; Shingles, 1981), Latinos (Stokes, 2003), and Asian Americans (Leighley & Vedlitz, 1999). While we consider the benefits for traditionally marginalized citizens, we cannot think about multicultural approaches to citizenship education as a solution for marginalized students. Only when students from dominant groups adopt the values of multiculturalism, and fully recognize the humanity of their ethnically, religiously, sexually, and linguistically diverse peers, will we begin to see political agendas that include the needs of everyone. The preamble of the

U.S. Constitution begins, "*We* the people, in order to form of more perfect union ..." Educators must understand that defining "we," as *all sectors of our population*, is as much a part of citizenship education as reading the Constitution. That is the challenge we faced in the 20th century and that we continue to face in the 21st century.

REFERENCES

Abadi, M. (2016, Oct. 17). 'The blacks,' 'the gays,' 'the Muslims'—Linguists explain one of Donald Trump's most unusual speech tics. Retrieved from http://www.businessinsider.com/donald-trump-the-blacks-the-gays-2016-10

Aguirre, J. M., & del Rosario Zavala, M. (2013). Making culturally responsive mathematics teaching explicit: A lesson analysis tool. *Pedagogies: An international journal, 8*(2), 163–190.

Banks, J. A. (1993). The canon debate, knowledge construction, and multicultural education. *Educational Researcher, 22*(5), 4–14.

Banks, J. A., & Banks, C. A. (2010). *Multicultural education: issues and perspectives.* Hoboken, NJ: Wiley.

Barr, D. J., Boulay, B., Selman, R. L., McCormick, R., Lowenstein, E., Gamse, B., ... & Leonard, M. B. (2015). A randomized controlled trial of professional development for interdisciplinary civic education: Impacts on humanities teachers and their students. *Teachers College Record, 117*(2), n2.

Battistoni, R., Berman, S. H., Bilig, S. H., Both, D., Fickling Brainard, A., Brown, N., & Carter, G. R. (2003). *The civic mission of schools.* New York, NY: Carnegie Corporation of New York.

Costello, M. B. (2017). *The Trump effect: The impact of the presidential campaign on our nation's schools.* Montgomery, AL: Southern Poverty Law Center.

Delreal, J. A. (2015, June 16). Donald Trump announces presidential bid. *The Washington Post.* Retrieved from https://www.washingtonpost.com/news/post-politics/wp/2015/06/16/donald-trump-to-announce-his-presidential-plans-today/?utm_term=.35d7da3ad085

Diamond, J. (2015, December 8). Donald Trump: Ban all Muslim travel to US. *CNN.* Retrieved from https://www.cnn.com/2015/12/07/politics/donald-trump-muslim-ban-immigration/index.html

Dilworth, P. P. (2004). Multicultural citizenship education: Case studies from social studies classrooms. *Theory & Research in Social Education, 32*(2), 153–186.

Doherty, C., Kiley, J., Tyson, A., & Jameson, B. (2015). *Beyond distrust: How Americans view their government.* Washington, DC: Pew Research Center.

Fitchett, P. G., & Heafner, T. L. (2010). A national perspective on the effects of high-stakes testing and standardization on elementary social studies marginalization. *Theory & Research in Social Education, 38*(1), 114–130.

Fitchett, P. G., Heafner, T. L., & VanFossen, P. (2014). An analysis of time prioritization for social studies in elementary school classrooms. *Journal of Curriculum and Instruction, 8*(2), 7–35.

Geboers, E., Geijsel, F., Admiraal, W., & ten Dam, G. (2013). Review of the effects of citizenship education. *Educational Research Review, 9*, 158–173.

Gorski, P. C. (2006). Complicity with conservatism: The de-politicizing of multicultural and intercultural education. *Intercultural Education, 17*(2), 163–177.

Gould, J., Jamieson, K. H., Levine, P., McConnell, T., & Smith, D. B. (Eds.). (2011). *Guardian of democracy: The civic mission of schools.* Lenore Annenberg Institute for Civics of the Annenberg Public Policy Center and the Campaign for the Civic Mission of Schools: Philadelphia, PA. Retrieved September 30, 2011, from https://www.carnegie.org/media/filer_public/ab/dd/abdda62e-6e84-47a4-a043-348d2f2085ae/ccny_grantee_2011_guardian.pdf

Grant, C. A. (2016). Depoliticization of the language of social justice, multiculturalism, and multicultural education. *Multicultural Education Review, 8*(1), 1–13.

Grant, C. A., & Asimeng-Boahene, L. (2006). Culturally responsive pedagogy in citizenship education: Using African proverbs as tools for teaching in urban schools. *Multicultural perspectives, 8*(4), 17–24.

Gutstein, E. (2003). Teaching and learning mathematics for social justice in an urban, Latino school. *Journal for Research in Mathematics Education,* 37–73.

Gutstein, E., & Peterson, B. (2006). *Rethinking mathematics: Teaching social justice by the numbers.* Milwaukee, WI: Rethinking Schools.

Hahn, C. L. (2016). Pedagogy in citizenship education research: A comparative perspective. *Citizenship Teaching & Learning, 11*(2), 121–137.

Higgins, A., McIntire, M., & Dance, G. J. X. (2016, November 25). Inside a fake news sausage factory: 'This is all about income.' *The New York Times.* Retrieved from https://www.nytimes.com/2016/11/25/world/europe/fake-news-donald-trump-hillary-clinton-georgia.html?_r=0

Hinnant-Crawford, B. N. (2016). Increasing access: the application of multicultural education to STEM. *Journal for Multicultural Education, 10*(3), 250–256.

Johnson, L. P., & Eubanks, E. (2015). Anthem or Nah? Culturally relevant writing instruction and community. *Voices from the Middle, 23*(2), 31.

Kahne, J., & Middaugh, E. (2008). Democracy for some: The civic opportunity gap in high school (Circle Working Paper 59). Medford, MA: Center for Information and Research on Civic Learning and Engagement (CIRCLE).

Kahne, J., Hodgin, E., & Eidman-Aadahl, E. (2016). Redesigning civic education for the digital age: Participatory politics and the pursuit of democratic engagement. *Theory & Research in Social Education, 44*(1), 1–35.

Ladson-Billings, G. (1995). But that's just good teaching! The case for culturally relevant pedagogy. *Theory Into Practice, 34*(3), 159–165.

Ladson-Billings, G. (2014). Culturally relevant pedagogy 2.0: Aka the remix. *Harvard Educational Review, 84*(1), 74–84.

Lee, O., & Buxton, C. A. (2010). *Diversity and equity in science education: research, policy, and practice.* New York, NY: Teachers College Press.

Leighley, J. E., & Vedlitz, A. (1999). Race, ethnicity, and political participation: Competing models and contrasting explanations. *The Journal of Politics, 61*(04), 1092–1114.

Levinson, M. (2007). *The Civic Achievement Gap* (CIRCLE Working Paper 51). Center for Information and Research on Civic Learning and Engagement (CIRCLE), University of Maryland, College Park, Maryland.

Levinson, M. (2010). The civic empowerment gap: Defining the problem and locating solutions. In L. Sherrod, C. Flanagan, J. Torney-Purta (Eds.), *Handbook of research on civic engagement in youth* (pp. 331–361). New York, NY: Wiley

May, S., & Sleeter, C. E. (2010). *Critical multiculturalism: Theory and praxis.* New York NY: Routledge.

McMurrer, J. (2008). NCLB Year 5: Instructional time in elementary schools. *Center on Education Policy Report.* Retrieved from https://www.cep-dc.org/displayDocument.cfm?DocumentID=309

Morrell, E. (2008). *Critical literacy and urban youth: Pedagogies of access, dissent, and liberation.* New York, NY: Routledge.

Morrison, K. A., Robbins, H. H., & Rose, D. G. (2008). Operationalizing culturally relevant pedagogy: A synthesis of classroom-based research. *Equity & Excellence in Education, 41*(4), 433–452.

Moses, R. P., & Cobb, C. E. (2001). *Radical equations: civil rights from Mississippi to the Algebra Project.* Boston, MA: Beacon Press.

National Council for the Social Studies. (2013). *The college, career, and civic life (C3) framework for social studies state standards: Guidance for enhancing the rigor of K–12 civics, economics, geography, and history.* Silver Spring, MD: Author.

Neundorf, A., Niemi, R. G., & Smets, K. (2015). The compensation effect of civic education on political engagement: how civics classes make up for missing parental socialization. *Political Behavior,* 1–29.

Nieto, S. (2000). *Affirming diversity: The sociopolitical context of multicultural education.* Boston, MA: Allyn and Bacon.

Parsons, E. C. (2000). Culturalizing science instruction: What is it, what does it look like and why do we need it? *Journal of Science Teacher Education, 11*(3), 207–219.

Parsons, E. C. (2008). Learning contexts, Black cultural ethos, and the science achievement of African American students in an urban middle school. *Journal of Research in Science Teaching, 45*(6), 665–683.

Pinkney, A. R. (2016). The role of schools in educating Black citizens: From the 1800s to the present. *Theory & Research in Social Education, 44*(1), 72–103.

Pinkney, A. R., & Faison, M. (2013). Critical citizens: Teaching the Civil Rights Movement in urban public schools. *The Ohio Social Studies Review, 50*(2).

Ross, E. W. (2006). The social studies curriculum: The purposes, problems and possibilities (3rd ed.). New York: State University of New York Press.

Sanders, S. (Host). (2016, June 8). #Meme of the week: Trump asked 'the gays' and got answers. [Radio broadcast episode]. Retrieved from http://www.npr.org/2016/06/18/482500360/-memeoftheweek-trump-asked-the-gays-and-got-some-answers

Schlesinger, A. M. (1998). *The disuniting of America: reflections on a multicultural society.* New York, NY: W.W. Norton.

Shingles, R. D. (1981). Black consciousness and political participation: The missing link. *American Political Science Review, 75*(01), 76–91.

Sleeter, C. E. (1991). *Empowerment through multicultural education.* Albany, NY: State University of New York Press.

Sleeter, C. E. (2014). Multiculturalism and education for citizenship in a context of neoliberalism. *Intercultural Education, 25*(2), 85–94.

Stokes, A. K. (2003). Latino group consciousness and political participation. *American Politics Research, 31*(4), 361–378.

Sydell, L. (Host). (2016, November 23). We tracked down a fake-news creator in the suburbs. Here's what we learned [Radio broadcast episode]. Retrieved from http://www.npr.org/sections/alltechconsidered/2016/11/23/503146770/npr-finds-the-head-of-a-covert-fake-news-operation-in-the-suburbs

Thacker, E. S., Lee, J. K., & Friedman, A. M. (2016). Teaching with the C3 Framework: Surveying teachers☐ beliefs and practices. *The Journal of Social Studies Research, 41*(2), 89–100.

Torney-Purta, J., & Lopez, S. V. (2006). Developing citizenship competencies from kindergarten through grade 12: A background paper for policymakers and educators. *Education Commission of the States (NJ3)*. Retrieved from https://eric.ed.gov/?id=ED493710

U.S. Department of Education. Institute for Educational Sciences, National Center for Education Statistics, National Assessment of Educational Progress (NAEP), 1998, 2006, and 2010 Civics Assessments.

Victor, D. (2016, July 18). What, congressman Steve King asks, have nonwhites done for civilization? *The New York Times.* Retrieved from https://www.nytimes.com/2016/07/19/us/politics/steve-king-nonwhite-subgroups.html

Westheimer, J., & Kahne, J. (2004). What kind of citizen? The politics of educating for democracy. *American educational research journal, 41*(2), 237–269.

Williams, V., & Clement, S. (2016, May 14). Despite black lives matter, young black Americans aren't voting in higher numbers. *The Washington Post.* Retrieved from https://www.washingtonpost.com/politics/despite-black-lives-matter-young-black-americans-arent-voting-in-higher-numbers/2016/05/14/e1780b3a-1176-11e6-93ae-50921721165d_story.html?utm_term=.d1b1f795a8f3

Winn, M. T., & Johnson, L. P. (2011). *Writing instruction in the culturally relevant classroom.* Urbana, IL: National Council of Teachers of English.

Young, E. (2010). Challenges to conceptualizing and actualizing culturally relevant pedagogy: How viable is the theory in classroom practice? *Journal of Teacher Education, 61*(3), 248–260.

CHAPTER 4

CRITICAL FAMILY HISTORY AS A STRATEGY FOR MULTICULTURAL HISTORY EDUCATION

LaGarrett J. King
University of Missouri–Columbia

As I am conceptualizing this chapter, I have just returned from my paternal side's family reunion in Texas. For three decades, my family reunion has grown from a meeting in a small church to a large annual picnic attended by hundreds of family members split between four Texas cities: Dallas, Longview, Houston, and Port Arthur. Each city has host families and they select the venue, develop family friendly activities, and cook food, which of course is delicious Bar-B-Que. The day (and sometimes night) is filled with fun, laughter, and history.

One constant activity is the retelling of our family's historical narrative. We begin with our patriarch, Tucker Davis, who was born in 1900 and lived to be 99 years old. He only had a third grade education, got married young, became a sharecropper, had seven children, became a widower, raised his children by himself, became a school bus driver and janitor in

Comprehensive Multicultural Education in the 21st Century:
Increasing Access in the Age of Retrenchment, pp. 59–79
Copyright © 2019 by Information Age Publishing
All rights of reproduction in any form reserved.

the school system, never remarried, and was able to obtain 100 acres of farmland while living during the nadir of African American life (Logan, 1954) in East Texas, one of the most violent and racist places in U.S. history (Fogg, 1999; Tuttle, 1972). As I have gotten older, we have begun remembering his children, my grandmother and great aunts and uncles who have passed; they serve as the seven branches to our family tree. Their history is filled with a legacy spanning the Harlem renaissance, the Great Depression, World War II, and legal Jim Crow.

Soon, narratives about their children will be told. These people include my father, his brothers and sisters as well as his cousins. This generation debated over the utility of Civil Rights ideology, attended both segregated and integrated schools, witnessed racial riots, were benefactors of some affirmative action programs, and became the generation that, in mass, moved from agricultural jobs to more industrial and White collar work. The last two generations include myself with all of my cousins and our children. Our generations can be defined through the emergence of hip-hop, technology, and now aspects of the Black lives matter movement. We are also more formally educated than previous generations and for most of our children, the only President they know is Barack Obama, the first Black man to serve that post. Through five generations, much has changed in our family history, yet for 116 years since my great grandfather was born, one constant remained, we all witness the struggle for racial equality and the fight for Black humanity. Nevertheless, to see, experience, and fellowship with five generations of the "Davis" clan, makes me proud but also provides a unique historicity into who I am, both as a member of a kinship group and as a Black male U.S. citizen who most likely has a slavery linage.

I argue that family histories are a type of curriculum and pedagogy that is normally ignored in schools. For Black people, family histories replace the erasure of Black culture, identity, and history brought upon from centuries of enslavement, oppression, and dislocation in the Americas. Unlike many history narratives presented in schools, my family history is interesting, culturally relevant, and provides me a macro understanding and perspective to complex U.S. historical dilemmas. Family histories also may be the only source of knowledge to understanding Black history as well as who individual Black people are within both a micro and macro context.

Therefore, when presented an opportunity to teach high students Black history during a summer enrichment program (King, Gardner-McCune, Vargas, & Jimenez, 2014), I immediately thought about students engaging in family history projects. Since I understood that many students found history boring and irrelevant (Howard, 2004; Loewen, 2007) or they have never had a formal family reunion such as mines, I thought the assignment had the potential to help students critically engage in historical inquiry as well as provide new and informative insight into who they are, through their families, within the grand U.S. historical narrative. This book chapter speaks to my beliefs by examining three years of classroom data of students engaging in a family history project.

CRITICAL FAMILY HISTORY

The family history project was developed based on Christine Sleeter's (2008) notion of critical family history (CFH, hereafter). Critical family history is a conceptual framework that helps investigate how power, particularly institutional and structural power, is historically embedded within the life histories of families (Sleeter, 2008). The overarching principles help students to understand that individual histories are influenced by the larger structures of society. Sleeter's original intent was to developed a concept to help White people, including her family, to understand how their Whiteness and/or immigrant status had been transformed and privileged throughout U.S. history. Since 2008, the concept has emerged with various insights into understanding how structural dynamics have influenced the family histories of indigenous populations, Asian Americans, Mexican Americans, and African Americans (Lee, 2013; Lee, Kumashiro, & Sleeter, 2015; Sleeter, 2014, 2016). In addition to examining larger societal structures, the concept is useful in teaching about historical methods of research including the examination of both primary and secondary sources.

Three principles are salient in exploring critical family history. The first is critical theory. Family history within a critical theory framework examines the notions of class and economics. Within U.S. structures, economics is defined through capitalism, which has a vested interest in a class hierarchy. Sleeter (2015) remarks that a class analysis through a capitalist lens helps understand family geography, how much they participated or was vested in the economic system, what class-based ideologies and decisions emerged as a result, and the possibility and limitation of family wealth.

The second principle is critical race theory. Critical race theory (CRT) examines the embedded nature of how race and racism has influenced the material realities of families. This principle highlights not *if* race plays a factor but *how* race has played a factor in life. CRT argues that race and racism is endemic and should be a major examination into its material influences on racialized persons. While racialization includes those considered to be Black, the concept also alludes to those who consider themselves White. For people of color, CRT provides space for counter stories through their voice and experiences that may oppose many dominant historical narratives. For Whites, CRT exposes Whiteness and helps expound on certain racial silences that do not fully ascertain a complete story of power and oppression.

The third principle is critical feminist theory. This concept details how gender is salient within life history. Through a feminist standpoint, family history attempts to uncover how patriarchal societies influenced gender oppression as well as the role women played as matriarchs. Sleeter (2015) notes that the concept "challenges us to consider how women were situated within the economy, embodied hierarchical structures based on gender, and how norms supporting equal relationships were taught and learned within the family" (p. 4). Additionally, gender agency is established as a way to ascertain the various actions taken by women to improve sexist conditions both on a macro- and microlevels.

When designing and implementing these principles, it is important to situate them as interlocking and not as separate entities. These power dynamics help guide the researcher into understanding the historical context of a given place in relation to the family. Sleeter (2015) explains that the principles, "identifies unjust social relationships, the roots of those relationships, and how they can be changed" (p. 3). These intersectional identities present a complex picture of various families, which makes learning history challenging and dynamic. To be clear, as critical feminist principle suggest, individuals and families are agentic but the three principles ensure that students understand the nexus of power relationships and the life histories of families.

BLACK HISTORY AND MULTICULTURAL EDUCATION

I developed this assignment because scholars have long lamented that K–12 history education, whether through curriculum or teacher instruction, is limited in the way Black history is constructed (Alridge, 2006; Brown & Brown, 2016; Epstein, 2010; King, 2014b; Woodson, 1933; Wynter, 1992). Black history is important to examine because researchers have detailed the subject's unique ability to help students (particularly Black students) disrupt and combat negative social and systemic notions of race and racialization, develop a positive self, cultural, and racial identity, increase academic achievement, help promote social justice and cultural diversity, assist critical thinking skills, and nurture mental health (Adams, 2005; Banks, 1971; Chapman-Hilliard & Adams-Bass, 2015; Grant, 2011; Merelman, 1993). Given the continued racism that exist within school structures (Brown & Brown, 2016; Ladson-Billings & Tate, 1995), which can hinder academic progress, Black history serves as one the remedies for Black student schooling success.

While there have been some major improvements in a quantifiable presence of Black history in the school curriculum (Wineburg & Monte-Sano, 2008), Black students have identified that history is one of their most disliked subjects (Loewen, 2007; Woodson, 2015). Scholars contend that Black students see Black history within traditional K–12 frameworks as deceptive because the stories continue to render the same Whitewashed historical characters, oppressive and victimized narratives, and racial liberal biases (Alridge, 2006; King, 2014a; Vasquez, Brown, & Brown, 2012; Woodson, 2016; Wynter, 1992). These limitations are further expounded when teachers lack knowledge or unwilling and not empathic enough to move past these simplistic renderings (Epstein, 2010; King, 2014b, 2016; Singer, 2008; Thornhill, 2014; Woodson, 2016). Therefore, Black students are left with what Ashley Woodson (2015) posited as a *contentious relationship* with the history curriculum because there is a level of distrust concerning the official history curriculum's epistemological approach in understanding the Black historical experience.

Educational researchers, therefore, have attempted to develop strategies such as multicultural education (Banks, 2004; Nieto & Bode, 2008; Sleeter & Grant, 1987) to help diversify history curriculum and make it more relevant for students of color (J. King, 1992; L. J. King, 2014a, 2016). While various definitions of multicultural education exist, I define it is an educational praxis that promotes equity through challenging oppression and bias in the school curriculum as well as through pedagogy and educational policies. Within the history curriculum, multicultural education, not only provides space for historical representation for Black people but multicultural narratives challenge, not reify, dominant narratives about race and racism that strive for ideological hegemony.

Sleeter (2015) notes that critical family histories are an extension of multicultural education because of its bottom-up approach to historical understanding. She explains:

> The bottom-up approach fits with my approach teaching multicultural education. It seems to me that inviting students to contribute their family stories-not the unexamined stories that repeat dominant narrative, but rather detailed and critical analyses of their ancestors' lives situated within a larger context- would provide a rich basis for considering what multicultural curriculum can be. (p. 8)

This description of how critical family history works, coincide with multiculturalist who believe that the curriculum should be conscious of power dynamics, which leads to challenging Whiteness and seeking and implementing strategies for societal transformation (May & Sleeter, 2010). K–12 Black history is considered the foundation of many multicultural approaches (Banks, 2004), therefore, the nexus between critical family history and multicultural education is appropriate. This chapter adds to notion that critical family histories can be used as a basis for multicultural education by centering history within the notions of the student's family can help history educators make the subject more engaging for students of color.

CRITICAL FAMILY HISTORY ASSIGNMENT

I used the concepts described above to develop a critical family history syllabus in a summer enrichment program titled *African American History: An Introduction*. The summer enrichment courses and residential program was held at a state university and was designed for high students from several rural counties in South Carolina (King, et al., 2014). The students, who were predominantly Black, began the program as rising sophomores and would return each summer until they were rising seniors. Throughout the three years, they took both life skills and college level academic courses in English, communications, computer science, and history, to name a few. At the conclusion of the program, if they attended all 3 years, the students received college credit to any college or university they decided to attend. I spent 3 years (2012–2015) with the program and taught this class to rising high school juniors ($N = 90$).

The rising juniors spent 2 weeks at the University. There were five class contact times, meeting every other day for 90 minutes. In addition to the allocated class time, students had opportunities to work on the class assignment outside of the regular meeting times. Since it was the summer and so abbreviated, I did not want students to learn passively through lectures or even group assignments. My goal was to help students understand that the nature of developing history is not static but is a fluid process based on how evidence is interpreted and manufactured to create narrative (Trouillot, 1995). I wanted to dispel the notion that what is learned as official history is not absolute truth but a collection of verifiable facts as well as silences and distortions based on individual bias. Since the students were rising juniors they have not had an opportunity to take a high school level U.S. history course, so I wanted to introduce them to historical inquiry through primary and secondary sourcing. My hope was to alter their understanding of history through their engagement of creating historical narratives about their families.

The critical family history assignment had three components. First, students would conduct a miniature oral history interview with a family member about a particular life moment tied to a larger historical event. The students had to find a relative (or suitable replacement) to interview and schedule a meeting time with them. Their responsibilities were to record the interview and because we had major time constraints, I did not require transcription but asked them to take detailed notes, which I collected later. Additionally, I informed the students that speaking with your oldest relative was great, but was not required as the purpose was to situate life histories with larger historical contexts. I also reminded that the histories did not have to be strictly tied to U.S. history; the event could encompass global or more localized historical events.

The second part of the assignment was for the students to contextualize the oral history. By contextualize, I wanted the students to juxtapose their family's narrative within the historic, social, political, and cultural context (Sleeter, 2015). To do this, the students completed two task. First, they had to gather a few primary sources from the historical time period that was under study. I recommended gathering newspapers, diaries, and old television news stories from YouTube or other media outlets. These sources served to accompany their family's stories about certain historical event.

Second, students had to use Sleeter's (2015) context questions framework (see Table 4.1) while completing their project. These questions served as a guide for the students in asking questions about the social and historical context of family, for each decade, in relationship to specific places where ancestors lived. It is important to note that the context question framework is the method for studying family histories through both primary and secondary sources. The framework is constructed as a chart where the vertical axis organizes the time period or decades. The horizontal axis is divided in three columns. The first column is dedicated to the family member(s) or event being studied. The second column or middle column is designated for the historical context. This column is reserved for the students to discover what happened historically in the town, county, and state where each family was, decade by decade. The last column is reserved for students to describe the social context. Social context asks about the relationships among various sociocultural groups in that location, decade by decade. In other words, students are engaged in a process that explores multiple historical narratives and not just one. Sleeter suggest the following questions as guide to help students understand the idea of social context:

- What other sociocultural groups were around (e.g., in the neighborhood, the town, the county)?
- Who wasn't around and why? Were there laws or policies that kept some groups away while others were favored? Specific ethnic groups may have been in the country or state but restricted to certain areas.
- What were relationships among sociocultural groups and gender groups in the time and place where your ancestors lived? Here, you can ask about power relationships and economic relationships (for instance, who worked for whom). How would those relationships have affected my ancestors' lives and viewpoints?
- What cultural communities and cultural norms existed? (Sleeter, 2015).

The context questions allow students to dig deeper into how historical eras may have influenced family members. These questions "explain how people lived, why they may have done things they did, how they were helped to hindered by unequal social relations, and values or experiences you may have inherited" (Sleeter, 2015). Additionally, these questions help students understand larger systemic questions related to racism, classism, and sexism.

Table 4.1.
Family History Chart

My family	Historical context	Social context
Factual data of family member	What historical event was happening during this decade? National and local events and laws that had relevance.	Who else was around? Who wasn't there, but could or should have been there? What values, norms were prevalent? What economic, political, cultural systems were there?

Third, students presented their family history narrative by creating a short presentation (PowerPoint, Prezi), complete with pictures (authentic or something representative) that described how their family history is located within the larger context of World, U.S., or any state's history. The presentation happened during the last class-meeting day.

CLASS SESSIONS

Since we only had four instructional opportunities with one day for presentations, I developed class sessions that helped students conceptualize historical context as well as help them with interviews and presentations. The first class period was titled, *what is history*, and included an introduction to Black history, the notion of historical narratives, and the critical family history project. This class period attempted to reorient students' notions of history as manufactured facts based on perspective. The notion of primary and secondary sources was introduced and the students began to think about family members they may want to interview.

The second class period was titled, *My Place in History*. This class was dedicated for setting up the family history project. In class we talked about the criteria for the assignment and began to see what they understood about their family history. I gave them a handout that asked them to trace their genealogy. They wrote how many family members they could remember, both on their mother and father side. I then asked them to write next to the names important historical events that happened during their relative's life span. A short clip from Henry Louis Gates, *Finding Your Roots* series from Public Broadcast System was played to give them an idea of the power of family historical narratives.

The third class was dedicated to learning how to conduct interviews. Students were taught to begin with easier or more biographical questions for their relatives. Questions were to move to more specific questions about themselves, the family, as well as larger historical moments during their life. During the second part of the class, the students created questions and interviewed their classmates and presented their findings at the end.

The fourth class was largely dedicated for the students to develop their presentations. The expectation was for students to interview family members a few days before. The computer lab was used for the students to gather all their data into presentation form. Students also used this time for additional research on larger historical contexts in order to synthesize that information into the presentation. The fifth day was dedicated towards presentations.

FINDINGS

Living Civil Rights: Stories From Grandparents

The students interviewed a variety of family members including their parents as well as uncles, aunts, and cousins. For the sake of brevity, I will focus on the critical family history projects centered on grandparents. Selecting the projects that featured grandparents are threefold. First, out of 90 critical family histories, 56 focused grandparents, for over 60% of all projects. Second, according to the students, their grandparents were born between the years of 1935–1960. Given that time period, all of the interviewees lived in southern states, which experienced major ideological and societal changes during formative times in their life. What is generally called the Civil Rights Movement, these life experiences are uniquely tied to South Carolina's well documented racist history (Bass & Nelson, 2002; Newby, 1973; Webster & Leib, 2001). Last, since the Civil Rights Movement and the racial upheaval that accompanied it are major topics taught in most states (Journell, 2008; Southern Poverty Law Center, 2011), examining the family narratives for this time period, therefore, is appropriate. This section will focus on the commonalities between the critical family history projects. Major themes were extracted highlighting how the students understood their grandparents' life experience as it relates to being racialized within the United States. The themes centered on racism in society, schools, and military.

Racism in Society

The majority of the interviews for the critical family history projects centered on how race and racism influenced the interviewees' upbringing. The majority of the interviewees were raised in small segregated rural towns in South Carolina and while the places they live may be classified as poor (according to census data), their families identified as working class. It was emphasized by the interviewees that Black and White people were treated differently by Jim Crow laws but interactions between the two races happened everyday through public settings such as the post office. Within public settings where Black and White people both congregated, there was a strict divide in where Black people could sit, enjoy a good meal, and be entertained. Through the narratives the students were told stories about Jim Crow, racial violence or the threat of, and unwritten racial rules that took the form of both internal and outward displays of subordination.

Racial violence or the threat of racial violence was a salient feature in many of the presentations. Students told stories about their grandparents witnessing or knowing someone who witnessed a lynching or some form of racial violence. One such example involved Jason's grandfather, who remembered as a child, a White man said that he would lynch him as response to him (Jason's grandfather) accidentally bumping the White man while playing. While Jason's grandfather (as well as others) emphasized that these occurrences of blunt threats of racial violence was not the norm and that he did not feel threatened in his everyday life by White people in their community, he did understand that there were unwritten racial rules. Lakeisha's grandmother noted this by saying, "there were some places you just did not go because it would be trouble." When asked why by Lakeisha, her grandmother words were similar to Loewen's (2005) explanation of sun down towns that forbid Black people in their town after night fall. She explained, "because we knew that Black people had their space and White people had their space and especially after certain times [of the day], we just did not cross." Kory, who was Lakeisha' cousin, said their grandfather noted that as a child, adults would tell him, "Don't make Mr. so and so mad because he was part of the Klu Klux Klan." Their grandfather was not certain if the rumors were true but it was implied that any "White person could be associated with the KKK" and if you did something that was against the racial norm, "something could happen to you physically."

Kenya's grandmother was the only participant to admit and have a personal connection with racist White people inflicting her family harm. Her grandmother told the story of her great grandmother's house being involved in a fire. She did not go into detail of what happened but mentioned that White people from the town did it. Kenya said that her grandmother did not know the entire story of why, but she said they were fairly certain that the culprits were White. It was later explained that her great grandfather was a local preacher and was involved with the NAACP in a larger city about one hour away. It was understood within the family story that his membership, he was not very active because of time and geography, was enough for the act of violence to occur.

About 20 presentations spoke about a well-known incident of racial violence that happened in Orangeburg, South Carolina. The racial massacre occurred at South Carolina State University, a local historically Black college or university in the late 1960s. The event which began as a protest to integrate a local bowling alley, involved student protesters at the University. On February 8th, two days after the bowling alley incident, the students built a bonfire in which a police officer attempted to extinguish the fire. The officer was hit by banister thrown from the crowd. Another patrolman fired his gun in the air to calm the crowd, other police officers claimed that they thought they were fired upon from one of the student protesters and shot into the crowd of students, killing three Black students and wounding 27 others (Bass & Nelson, 1984).

A few of the student's grandparents said that they knew some people who went to the school or was involved in the protest. Justin claimed that his grandfather was involved in the incident and was the only person to be convicted and sentence for the Orangeburg massacre. Justin told the story of how his grandfather was a Civil Rights activist and traveled around the country to help get Black people registered to vote. He did not provide great detail about the incident but noted that his grandfather was shot in the left shoulder and arrested for being an agitator. He was sentenced at trial and served 7 months of prison time. Justin asked his grandfather about his feelings about the incident:

> When you are targeted to be killed it creates some anger and bitterness. The three people who died in the Massacre were not friends but seeing them brutally murdered affected me so deeply. Even though I was shot, I knew I had to keep going on to get help. Many of the people I tried to help didn't make it. The law officials were just shooting randomly from a top of the hill."

The incident in Orangeburg had a great influence with the interviewees emotions and their racial consciousness. Taj's grandmother stated that while she was an hour away from Orangeburg, she was scared that the violence would invade her town. She explained, "a lot of Black folk was mad, a lot of White folk were mad and we did not want to see that anger come down here." John's grandfather mentioned, "I was mad a lot during that time." Not only did I hear about Orangeburg, but other things were happening around the country that I thought was not fair." Many of the grandparents noted that the Orangeburg incident influenced them to become more active in fighting against racial oppression leading to many of them joining various local and national Civil Rights groups.

Racism in Schooling

Another major theme presented throughout the critical family history projects were about the schooling experiences of family members. All of the students indicated that their grandparents attended segregated all Black schools at one point in their early educational experiences. Many of the grandparents were pioneers of integrated schools in South Carolina, which did not integrate until fall 1970, sixteen years after the ruling of *Brown v. Education*. The context of segregated and integrated schooling is important to consider for this population because almost all the families who were interviewed had a connection to the *Brown* case. Considered one the most influential Supreme court cases in the nation's history, Brown was a collection of five cases of school discrimination against Black student's education. One of the cases, *Briggs v. Elliot*, happened in the geographical region where most of these families lived at the time.

The *Brown* case within K–12 history classes elicit a narrative that implies a sort celebratory tone for integrating schools (Hess, 2005). Many Black people experienced *Brown*, differently. The unintended consequence of *Brown* closed many all Black schools, left Black educators unemployed, and forced Black school children to be taught by teachers who at worst was racist or at best culturally insensitive, which made Black children's schooling experience a site of violence (Bell, 2004; Ladson-Billings, 2004; Tillman, 2004). The families presented a very diverse narrative about their thoughts and experiences with integration with some juxtaposing their two experiences.

A few grandparents took the stance that *Brown* was a good thing for Black students. Alicia's grandfather mentioned that he was "upset with all Black schools because he wanted to get the same education as the Whites did." He remembered being happy that someone (the lawyers in *Brown v. Board*) was stepping in and that he got to go school with White people." Elisa grandmother noted that she attended all Black schools until she was 12 years old. She mentioned that going to an all-Black school made her feel "underneath the white students." She had a White friend and was sad that she did not go to school with her and it did have an effect of her as she felt that" she would never be equal with the Whites." When asked about her experience with integrated schools and segregated schools, Jill's grandmother stated, "it was different in terms of White teachers and classmates, but I guess it was a good thing, nothing happened to me that I can remember."

There were contrasting narratives, however. A few grandparents felt that their situation at all Black schools were fine and that integration was not needed and actually was more stressful. Jason's grandfather noted that because of segregated, "we did not know whether the white school had better education." In his words, "I had good [Black] teachers and Principals ... it was not as bad as it seems." Keisha's grandmother remembered that that the integrated schools were more of a problem than solution. She said, "It was a lot of racial tension back then and there were several riots and protest throughout the south ... my mother didn't want me to go to school because she feared I would not get along with White students." When asked about possible racism in schools, Janet's grandfather said, "I did not experience racism with my [White] classmates, it was the teachers who made it hard on me." Janet's grandfather words were true for many interviewees. For example, Calvin grandparents remembered that White kids would hit them with pebbles when they were walking to the all-Black school but when they attended the same school, they all played together. They noted, however, that they could tell that many of the teachers did not like them. Calvin grandmother said, "I don't remember them calling us [racist] names or anything but they [the White teachers] thought we did not belong, you could tell by their actions." For those interviewees who talked about integrated schools, their experiences of positivity and negativity was mixed. It must be noted, however, that even the positive stories did not indicate a sense of gaining a better education but a sense of having the opportunity to receive the same education.

Racism and Military

A third major theme that emerged from the critical family history projects were race and the military. Black people, mostly men, have participated in all U.S. conflicts but the history has been contentious because discrimination was as prominent in the military as it was in U.S. society (Webb & Herrman, 2002). The majority of family history centered on the student's grandfathers as Vietnam veterans. The Vietnam war was controversial and not well supported by U.S. citizens. Yet, the Vietnam war served as a turning point for Black involvement in the armed services as the conflicted represented [up to that point] the greatest percentage of

Black soldiers in history. The narratives told by the students indicated a diverse and complicated history concerning the Vietnam war including Post traumatic stress disorder and agent orange. Two major narratives are discussed, one narrative focused on the status of being a soldier especially a Black soldier in the U.S. and the second narrative told a stories of racism while protecting the country.

John's grandfather was proud to be a veteran. He served in the Vietnam war, working communications. John displayed pictures of the grandfather posing with his friend in Vietnam. When asked if he was scared, John's grandfather said, "being in that war had me scared at first, but I had to realize, I was doing it for the sake of my country." He said that everyone was proud that he was in the military. "As a Black man, the military was a good job with good benefits, better than most thing I could get while a civilian." The moniker that it was a good job was present in many of narratives presented by the students. Joey's grandfather explained that the military was the best decision he made from himself. He stated, "the military allowed me to provide for my family, it wasn't a lot of money, you know, but I felt I was doing better than some of my brothers at home." Natasha's grandfather proclaimed," The Vietnam war was a great experience. I got to fight for my country and gain leadership ranks while doing so; it was an awesome experience for a soldier who was just joining the military."

While certain projects detailed that the military was a good career opportunity for Black men and their families, a few project narratives stated the opposite. Ashley mentioned that her grandfather was a Vietnam veteran but hated the military and his experience as a soldier. She claims that he was drafted and only went to the military for fear of going to jail. Jerica mentioned that her grandfather thought the war was a "White man's war" but he served as a way to leave his small town and explore the world. Jackson told his grandfather's story of racial tension on military bases. "When you bring those country White boys with those city Black boys, it was a site to see. We all kinda kept to our own kind with nothing happening but I heard of some places where there were fights on the base between White and Black soldiers." Carey's grandfather's said, "well, we were fighting for democracy, to stop communism, but we [Black people] were still fighting in America for our rights."

Jeffrey's grandfather, who was drafted in the army in 1965 and relieved of duty in 1968, complained that civilians had no respect for Vietnam veterans. He said that people called him "a baby killer and that he felt disgusted and betrayed. In addition, he felt that as a Black man, the U.S. did not care about Black people. He cited the Orangeburg massacre (discussed in the previous paragraph) as an example. The incident happened while he was on military duty and he expressed distress over what had happened. "It was an outright crime how people, who were practically kids, were murdered the way they were." He mentioned that some of the White soldiers were happy when they heard about Orangeburg. He said, "I wanted to fight, I don't know why I didn't."

IMPLICATIONS

The critical family history projects represented the goals of multicultural history education by presenting the richness and complexity of historical narration that differed from most K–12 official history contexts. Critical family histories reorient U.S. history as not parts of a single narrative but helps represent the plurality of the nation's legacy. In other words, children do not learn *history* but they begin to learn about the *histories* of a given people. To promote U.S. history is always problematic not because it implies that only one narration will get privilege but that when multiple stories are attempted to be embedded, the new perspective will always be seen through the eyes of the dominant culture. Therefore, Whiteness, no matter how many racialized groups become stories within the meta-narrative, will become the default history, despite attempts at curriculum diversity.

With this in mind, critical family history projects, through the Black experience, alludes to reimagining what is considered Black history. While there exists a popular axiom that states that Black history is American history, the premise is a false one and does not delve into the complexity of historical narration. For Black history to be Black history, the narratives involve a distinct altering of the traditional narrative. Black people, in history, have a different historical trajectory than those who are considered White. This is not to say that White people, at various times, have not experienced hardship, discrimination, and lost; this is to say that Black people have unique histories that cannot be told through a single narration featuring a White epistemological framework. For example, as the critical family history narratives showed, Black Vietnam veterans experienced the added dimension of racism from U.S. society and from many times their fellow White enlistment. The interviewees noted that integrated schools may not have been the best strategy for Black school children at that moment. Black children left their schools and were forced to be taught by teachers who may have believed that they were inferior, therefore, creating a system that has propagated notions of achievement gaps and deficit thinking for the past four decades (Ladson-Billings, 2004). These narratives are typically left out of the history textbooks or teachers' instruction. It is important to note that the purpose of separating history through racialized lenses is not because of a need to segregate but out of a necessity to resist the default prism of Whiteness and gain as much historical insight from Black perspectives.

The critical family history assignment brought out the theme of race and racism and the major impact these constructs had with the student's grandparents. The students were able to understand how being racialized and acts of racism (both macro and micro) influenced their material reality. What is important to note is that these projects did not sensationalized racism. By this I mean, race and racism was clearly visible and tangible in the small rural towns where the interviewees lived but the narratives also highlighted racism's invisibility. For instance, the interviewees stated that they interacted with White people, had White friends but they just knew that at any given time violence could be inflicted upon them. Sometimes in the official history, racism is seen as something that is highly overt like calling a Black person a nigger or in the racial incident in Orangeburg, South Carolina. When viewing racism as overt, leaves out structural variables as well as the covert way the concept operates. Just knowing that "Mr. so and so" can harm you, without any physical contact or major announcement, exemplifies racism's hidden rules. In this context, racism does not need to be pronounced. It does not need to be overt, sensational actions but can be numerous subtle inactions that influences racial hegemony and the material realities of oppressed groups.

While there were some great insights brought about by the projects, they fell short on many aspects of critical family implementation. For instance, many of the projects missed some of the intersectional aspects of the grandparents lived experiences such as the influences of their class positions and gender constructs. Overwhelming the grandparents' stories all centered race and racism as salient life experiences, so naturally the students, who were inexperienced in historical narration and critical family history, narrated only aspects of race and racism. There were some chances to provide more nuance analysis based on class and gender. For example, when Joey's grandfather spoke about the military as way to provide financially for his family. Joey missed an opportunity to contextualize the economic conditions of many Black families during that period, the history that lead to those conditions, and examine the financial implications of military service.

Virtually no project attempted to fully examine Black women's lives juxtaposed with Black men. The narratives seemed to encompass a gender neutral framework, missing out on the unique historical experiences of Black women. By neglecting Black women's voices, therefore their history, reinscribes a traditional male centric K–12 history education. This critique within K–12 Black history is not new as sometimes in efforts to diversify the history curriculum, Black men (intersected with middle class, protestant, able bodied and heterosexuality) are privileged constructs (Hull, Scott, & Smith, 1982; Woyshner & Schocker, 2015). What the critical family history framework is missing is situating a theoretical positioning that seek to explore Black women's voices. While feminist theory is originally constructed to delve into the material realities of women and ensure that gender is a salient approach to family histories, this approach may not be enough. Proposing a Black feminist framework (Collins, 2000) assist with capturing the voices, the epistemological, and agency of a heteronormative patriarchal society. Adding to the critical family history contextual framework, it would have been interesting to learn how racism influenced gender, how Black girls and boys experienced integrated schools as well as the experiences of Black women in the Vietnam war or as civilians during war time.

CONCLUSION

Throughout this chapter, I explained that critical family histories can be used a way to expand the curricular and pedagogical thought surrounding history education. Using classroom presentation of rising high school juniors, who were mostly Black, I chronicled their family history narratives of the grandparents. The stories that were told gave voice to history and made this history tangible for many students who disliked the subject. When asked to rate the assignment and class from 1–5, the scores averaged to be 4. This was the first time many students even spoke to their families about family history. While I believe in critical family history as a learning tool because of its influence as a unique curricular and pedagogical tool, I leave us with a few ideas to consider about using critical family histories in the classroom.

Due to the newness of the instructional and pedagogical framework, there are a lot of questions surrounding the safeness of the approach. These concerns can have severe implications to students' learning and aspects of emotions when learning about themselves and their families. Strategies are needed for teachers to develop curriculum and pedagogical friendly strategies that approach "non-traditional families" such as transracial, LGBTQ, and students coming from the foster system.

We also need to gauge the level of violence critical family narratives may produce. By violence, I do not mean physical harm but a type of violence that is educative, symbolic, and psychological (Leonardo & Porter, 2010). Questions are needed concerning how racialized populations respond to possible historical connections to trauma from historic and systemic oppression. Additionally, how do White students reconcile their feelings if one or more of their relatives is a known bigot/racist/slave owner who enacted violence against another human. Last, how do we, as teachers, respond to family secrets of abuse, infidelity, or mental health. When looking for family stories, especially stories that elicit class, race, and gender analysis, the stories are not always positive and heartwarming. Teachers must have the tools to respond, support, and help students who may experience learning new and dangerous information about their families. Therefore, critical family histories can be a source for learning about histories but can also be a site of violence. Much work is needed in this area concerning critical family histories.

Nevertheless, as an instructor, I enjoyed helping students engage with family research and develop historical narratives. My goals for students was for them to understand the complexities of historical perspectives, create historical narratives, and the most importantly, to engage with their family's history through the connection with elders. Sara's words summed up what most students felt about the family history projects:

> At the end of this project, I learned history and stories that I will remembered. I really did learn. It wasn't boring ... I also found out so many interesting things about my family. Things I didn't know about my family. I really appreciate my family because they shape the world. If it weren't for them, we wouldn't be here. So we all should stop taking things for granted and appreciate what we have. Because we are truly blessed.

Sara's words are what the critical family history project is supposed to accomplish as multicultural education. It is the ability to personally connect with history and discover your identity.

REFERENCES

Adams, T. A. (2005). Establishing intellectual space for Black students in predominantly White universities through Black studies. *Negro Educational Review*, *56*, 285–299.

Alridge, D. (2006). The limits of master narratives in history textbooks: An analysis of representations of Martin Luther King, Jr. *The Teachers College Record*, *108*(4), 662–686.

Banks, J. A. (1971). Teaching Black history with a focus on decision making. *Social Education*, *35*, 740–745, 820–821.

Banks, J. A. (2004). Multicultural education: Historical development, dimensions, and practices. In J. A. Banks & C. A. McGee Banks (Eds.), *Handbook of research on multicultural education* (2nd ed., pp. 3–29). San Francisco, CA: Jossey-Bass.

Bass, J., & Nelson, J. (1984). *The Orangeburg Massacre*. Macon, GA: Mercer University Press.

Bell, D. (2004). *Silent covenants: Brown v. Board of Education and the unfulfilled hopes for racial reform*. Oxford, England: Oxford University Press.

Brown, A. L. & Brown, K. D. (2016). The more things change, the more they stay the same: Excavating race and the enduring racisms in U.S. curriculum. *National Society for the Study of Education*, *114*(2), 103–130.

Chapman-Hilliard, C., & Adams-Bass, V (2015). A conceptual framework for utilizing Black history knowledge as a path to psychological liberation for Black youth. *Journal of Black Psychology*, 1–29.

Collins, P. H. (2002). *Black feminist thought: Knowledge, consciousness, and the politics of empowerment*. London, England: Routledge.

Epstein, T. (2010). *Interpreting national history: Race, identity, and pedagogy in classrooms and communities*. London, England: Routledge.

Fogg, R. K. (1999, January). LONGVIEW'S RED HOT SUMMER. In *NAAAS Conference Proceedings* (p. 283). National Association of African American Studies.

Grant, C. A. (2011). Escaping Devil's Island: Confronting racism, learning history. *Race Ethnicity and Education*, *14*(1), 33–49.

Hess, D. (2005). Moving beyond celebration: Challenging curricular orthodoxy in the teaching of Brown and its legacies. *The Teachers College Record*, *107*(9), 2046–2067.

Howard, T. C. (2004). "Does race really matter?" Secondary students' constructions of racial dialogue in the social studies. *Theory & Research in Social Education*, *32*(4), 484–502.

Hull, G., Scott, P. B., & & Smith, B. (1982). *All the women are white, all the men are black, but some of us are brave*. New York, NY: Feminist.

Journell, W. (2008). When oppression and liberation are the only choices: The representation of African Americans within state social studies standards. *Journal of Social Studies Research*, *32*(1), 40.

King, J. E. (1992). Diaspora literacy and consciousness in the struggle against miseducation in the Black community. *The Journal of Negro Education*, *61*(3), 317–340.

King, L. J. (2014a). More than slaves: Black founders, Benjamin Banneker, and critical intellectual agency. *Social Studies Research and Practice*, *9*(3), 88–105.

King, L. J. (2014b). Learning other people's history: pre-service teachers' developing African American historical knowledge. *Teaching Education*, *25*(4), 427–456.

King, L. J. (2016). Teaching black history as a racial literacy project. *Race, Ethnicity, and Education*. doi:10.1080/13613324.2016.1150822

King, L. J., Gardner-McCune, C., Vargas, P., & Jimenez, Y. (2014). Re-discovering and re-creating African American historical accounts through mobile apps: The role of mobile technology in history education. *The Journal of Social Studies Research*, *38*(3), 173–188.

Ladson-Billings, G., & Tate, W. (1995). Toward a critical race theory of education. *Teachers College Record*, *97*, 47–68.

Ladson-Billings, G. (2004). Landing on the wrong note: The price we paid for Brown. *Educational Researcher*, *33*(7), 3–13.

Lee, J. (2013). The hidden four Ps and immigration. Retrieved from http://christinesleeter.org/hidden-four-ps/

Lee, J., Kumashiro, K., & Sleeter, C. (2015). Interrogating identity and social contexts through "critical family history." *Multicultural Perspectives*, *17*(1), 28–32.

Leonardo, Z., & Porter, R. K. (2010). Pedagogy of fear: Toward a Fanonian theory of 'safety' in race dialogue. *Race Ethnicity and Education*, *13*(2), 139–157.

Logan, R. W. (1954). *The Negro in American life and thought: The nadir, 1877–1901*. New York, NY: Dial Press.

Loewen, J. W. (2005). *Sundown towns: A hidden dimension of American racism*. New York, NY: The New Press.

Loewen, J. W. (2007). *Lies my teacher told me: Everything your American history textbook got wrong*. The New Press.

May, S., & Sleeter, C. E. (Eds.). (2010). *Critical multiculturalism: Theory and praxis*. New York, NY: Routledge.

Merelman, R. M. (1993). Black history and cultural empowerment: A case study. *American Journal of Education*, *101*, 331–357

Newby, I. A. (1973). *Black Carolinians: A history of blacks in South Carolina from 1895 to 1968* (No. 6). Columbia, SC: University of South Carolina Press.

Nieto, S., & Bode, P. (2008). *Affirming diversity: The sociopolitical context of multicultural education* (5th ed.). Boston, MA: Allyn & Bacon.

Tillman, L. C. (2004). (Un)intended consequences? The impact of *the Brown v. Board of Education* decision on the employment status of black educators. *Education and Urban Society*, *36*(3), 280–303.

Tuttle, W. M. (1972). Violence in a "Heathen" land: The longview race riot of 1919. *Phylon (1960–)*, *33*(4), 324–333.

Singer, J. A. (2008). *New York and slavery: Time to teach the truth*. New York, NY: State University of New York Press.

Sleeter, C. E., & Grant, C. (1987). An analysis of multicultural research in the United States. *Harvard Educational Review*, *57*(4), 421–445.

Sleeter, C. (2008). Critical family history, identity, and historical memory. *Educational Studies*, *43*(2), 114–124.

Sleeter, C. E. (2014) Multicultural curriculum and critical family history. *Multicultural Education Review*, *7*(1-2), 1–11.

Sleeter, C. E. (2015). Inheriting footholds and cushions: Family legacies and institutional racism. In J. Flores Carmona & K. V. Luschen (Eds.), *Crafting critical stories: Toward pedagogies and methodologies of collaboration, inclusion, and voice* (pp. 11–26). New York, NY: Peter Lang.

Sleeter, C. E. (2016, January). *Critical family history*. Retrieved from http://christinesleeter.org/critical-family-history/

Southern Poverty Law Center. (2011). *Teaching the movement: The state of civil rights education in the United States 2011*. Montgomery, AL: Kate Shuster.

Thornhill, T. E. (2014). Resistance and assent: How racial socialization shapes black students' experience learning African American history in high school. *Urban Education*. doi:10.1177/0042085914566094

Trouillot, M. R. (1995). *Silencing the past: Power and the production of history*. Boston, MA: Beacon Press.

Webb, S. C., William, J., & Herrmann, W. J. (2002). *Historical overview of racism in the military*. Patrick Air Force Base, FL: Defense Equal Opportunity Management Institute.

Webster, G. R., & Leib, J. I. (2001). Whose South is it anyway? Race and the Confederate battle flag in South Carolina. *Political Geography*, *20*(3), 271–299.

Wineburg, S., & Monte-Sano, C. (2008). "Famous Americans": The changing pantheon of American heroes. *The Journal of American History*, *94*(4), 1186–1202.

Woodson, A. N. (2015). "There Ain't No White People Here" Master narratives of the Civil Rights Movement in the stories of urban youth. *Urban Education*. https://doi.org/10.1177/0042085915602543

Woodson, A. N. (2016). We're just ordinary people: Messianic master narratives and black youths' civic agency. *Theory & Research in Social Education*, *44*(2), 184–211.

Woodson, C. G. (1993). *The miseducation of the Negro*. Washington DC: Associated Publishers.

Woyshner, C., & Schocker, J. B. (2015). Cultural parallax and content analysis: Images of Black women in high school history textbooks. *Theory & Research in Social Education*, *43*(4), 441–468.

Wynter, S. (1992). *Do not call us Negros: How" multicultural" textbooks perpetuate racism*. Peabody, MA: Aspire Press.

Vasquez Heilig, J., Brown, K., & Brown, A. (2012). The illusion of inclusion: A critical race theory textual analysis of race and standards. *Harvard Educational Review*, *82*(3), 403–424.

CHAPTER 5

FORTIFYING THE INTRAPERSONAL THROUGH ATTENDING TO THE INTERPERSONAL

Motivating Mathematics Self-Concept Through Fruitful Student-Teacher Relationships

C. Vandyke Goings
Westminster School in Atlanta, Georgia

Much of the discourse surrounding mathematics achievement in the Unites States focuses on gaps in scores disaggregated by categories, such as race. Gutierrez (2008) describes this narrow preoccupation as "gap-gazing." Giroux, Lankshear, McLaren, and Peters (Martin, 2007) attest that this kind of emphasis has been influential in establishing, maintaining, and disseminating a masternarrative used to position students of color, whom these data report as *underperforming*, as mathematically incompetent—

Comprehensive Multicultural Education in the 21st Century:
Increasing Access in the Age of Retrenchment, pp. 81–97
Copyright © 2019 by Information Age Publishing

or worse, incapable. Yet, the portrait communicated almost exclusively through a heightened attention to standardized test data is often incomplete. Raw achievement data may be a necessary component of the narrative—especially within the climate of No Child Left Behind—but they are not sufficient. Although these data are communicative, educators, researchers, and policymakers should be cautious in their interpretations and implications. *Curriculum and Evaluation Standards for School Mathematics* (National Council of Teachers of Mathematics, 1989) suggests that assessing students' beliefs about mathematics is an important component of the overall assessment of mathematical knowledge (Spangler, 1992). It recommends not only that educators are expected to be aware of students' mathematical beliefs, but also that considerable importance can be attributed to students' awareness of their own beliefs toward mathematics. These beliefs include the ways students conceive themselves in relation to and as doers of mathematics.

Although the refrain of the underachievement of African American students is frequently repeated, Cokley, Komarraju, King, Cuningham, and Muhammad (2003) suggest that "a thorough understanding of their academic self-concept may shed insight into this phenomenon" (p. 720). As Usher (2009, p. 278) maintains, qualitative inquiry can provide a nuanced understanding of how self beliefs are generated and developed by uncovering the "heuristic techniques" young students use to evaluate their academic competence. Attending to the voices of African American adolescent students who are able to reflect thoughtfully and communicate effectively about their learning has the potential to provide insights into the multiple mechanisms students employ to construct their conceptualizations mathematics self-concept. This chapter explores the ways that two African American students conceptualize and construct their mathematics self-perceptions.

Self-concept describes a collection of self-perceptions thought to be formed through experiences with the environment and the reflected appraisals of significant others (Pietsch, Walker, Chapman, 2003; Schunk & Pajares, 2005). Wigfield and Wagner (2005) indicate that self-concept is "made up of beliefs about many different aspects of self and evaluations of performance in different areas" (p. 228). Individuals perceive and evaluate themselves across a number of areas and specific dimensions. A distinction exists between individuals' perceptions involving the totality of self-knowledge and domain-specific perceptions of self. The general self-perceptions comprise the global self-concept. More domain specific self-concepts can comprise academic, social, emotional, and physical components. Academic self-concepts can encompass various subjects (for example, mathematics, science, language arts).

This analysis extends the work of the author's dissertation examining the mathematics competence and mathematics self-concept beliefs of six adolescent African American students. This chapter focuses on one particularly salient aspect of participants' comments about their mathematics experiences. That salient feature of students' educational experience is their interactions and relationships with teachers.

Evidence indicating the significance of positive relationships between students and teachers is increasing (Spilt & Hughes, 2015). Midgley, Feldlaufer, and Eccles (1989) assert that the effect of quality student-teacher relationships (STRs) is especially powerful during adolescence. High quality relationships that students have with teachers can foster student achievement (O'Connor & McCartney, 2007), along with emotional security and engagement. Furthermore, Bonner (2014) points out that in addition to fostering achievement, teachers often mediate student perceptions. Social support from teachers, and others, correlates with students' educational attitudes and behaviors (Somers, Owens, & Pilawsky, 2008), including aspirations and motivation. Martin and Dowson (2009) propose that STRs "affect achievement motivation by directly influencing motivation's constituent beliefs and emotions" (p. 328).

So, as it considers the salience of STRs in the educational experiences of students, this chapter emphasizes the contributions of these relationships to the construction of students' mathematics self-concept beliefs. This is achieved by examining qualitatively the cases of two adolescent African American students who, despite vastly different mathematics self-perceptions, reveal significant interactions with teachers and appreciate relationships with teachers as influential. This research uses qualitative semistructured interviews with students and their parents to construct rich cases. It highlights the effects of students' perceptions of these relationships in constructing robust mathematics self-concepts in ways that contribute to their academic success. Attending to the voices of African American adolescent students who are able to reflect thoughtfully and communicate effectively about their learning has the potential to illuminate some of the multiple mechanisms that students employ to resist and contest pejorative narratives of African American mathematical and intellectual ability that threaten their academic esteem and sense of self.

METHODOLOGY

Although the research from which this chapter is based was designed as a qualitative exploration, it used and referenced data from the administrations of a questionnaire, and subscales of an attitudinal scales instrument. The Self-Description Questionnaire II (SDQ-II; Marsh, 1992) measures academic self-concept in adolescents. This study used the 10 items focusing of mathematics self-concept as some of the prompts and probes in discussions with participants about their experiences with mathematics. Subscales from the Fennema-Sherman Mathematics Attitudes Scales (1976) were used to gauge students' feelings about (their) success in mathematics, their feeling about significant others' (parent, peers, teachers) thoughts about their ability, and the degree to which they perceive mathematics as a gendered [male] domain. Again, these instruments provided a springboard to explore student responses qualitatively by informing questions that guided interviews and other conversations with student (and parent) participants.

The two students highlighted in this chapter participated in a 2011 summer academic enrichment program at a university in the Southeast. They completed three interviews. In both instances, the pairs of students' parents were also interviewed. Each parent was interviewed once. Texts from focused interviews with students and parents formed the bulk of data for analysis as these data from instruments (SDQ-II, MIBI-t, Fennema-Sherman subscales) were clarified in the course of participant interviews. Students also composed mathematical autobiographies in which they gave details of significant periods in their development of their self-ideas involving their mathematical development.

Following this discussion of methodology is an introduction of two adolescent African American students. Gabourey struggles to establish a strong mathematics self-concept. Omari boasts a consistently robust mathematics self-concept. Gabourey and Omari describe themselves and their experiences with (classroom) mathematics. They includes in their descriptions discussions of interactions with teachers. The chapter considers how these students' interpretations of these interpersonal relationships with teachers can foster their intrapersonal development of mathematics self-concept beliefs.

Gabourey

Gabourey attends an independent coeducational elementary school. The school is grounded in frameworks of Christian faith and Jewish heritage. The school serves approximately 630 students during the 2011–2012 year with tuition for K–6 for the same year surpassing $19,000. The school provides more than 350 computers on campus with over 140 laptops and tablet personal computers.

Gabourey is 12 years old and entering the seventh grade. She is petite, but has considerable presence. Gabourey makes it clear that she does not like mathematics. She is affable and endearing. Her popularity helped her to garner a "Camper of the Week" award at the end of the first week of the program. She also secured an opportunity to offer student remarks at the program closing ceremony.

Mathematics Self-Concept Beliefs. When I first met Gabourey she was beginning her sixth grade year and disclosed that mathematics was "kind of like [a] 'downfall,' because I'm really not that good at math." Nearly a year and a half later, after completing the fall semester of her seventh grade year at an independent school, Gabourey is beginning to look at mathematics and her experiences with it more favorably. The shifts that occur in Gabourey's attitudes and feelings reveal a great deal about the development of her self-concept beliefs.

Gabourey's responses on the Self-Description Questionnaire (SDQ-II) (Marsh, 1992) document her transforming mathematics self-beliefs. The SDQ-II uses a 6-point Likert scale by which respondents describe how much a statement is very much unlike them (1) or very much like them (6). Gabourey's choice on four of the mathematics self-concept items remained the same between the year that separated SDQ-II administrations. These items were *I often need help in mathematics* (5), *I have trouble understanding anything with mathematics in it* (4), *I never want to take another mathematics course* (1), and *I enjoy studying mathematics* (3). Her response to two items increased by one unit: *Mathematics is one of my best subjects* (2 to 3), and *I get good marks [grades] in mathematics* (3 to 4). On the second administration of the SDQ-II, Gabourey indicated even more substantial changes in items that included *I look forward to mathematics classes* (1 to 3), *I do badly in tests of mathematics* (4 to 2), *I have always done well in mathematics* (1 to 3), and *I hate mathematics* (4 to 1). These changes in Gabourey's responses are encouraging and indicate a shift in her self-perceptions in the direction of a stronger mathematics self-concept.

Gabourey's history with mathematics illustrates the developmental nature of mathematics self-beliefs. Her experiences indicate that her mathematics self-concept has yet to stabilize. Mrs. Watkins, Gabourey's mother, recounts that when Gabourey was in kindergarten, "she felt like she could not perform math." In her mathematics journal, Gabourey recalls, "In the second grade all the way up to 3rd grade, I ... had a hard time in math. It was just always difficult for me." Her mother confirms, "By the time we got to the second grade with her, she was literally in tears. Mrs. Watkins explains that—perhaps as a result of certain mathematics deficiencies— Gabourey "came into the third grade thinking she wasn't good in math, and that she would fail, or not do well in math." After an encouraging fourth grade year that boosted Gabourey's confidence in her ability, she began to withdraw from mathematics recalling: "I was failing and there was just a point where I gave up and felt like I couldn't do it." But after fifth grade, Gabourey found that she became more attracted to mathematics in the sixth grade. In her mathematics autobiography, she writes, "At first I thought I was horrible at math. But then in the 6th grade, I realized I was able to do it, and do well at it."

Gabourey's verbal and written self-descriptions suggest that her mathematics self-concept is dynamic and in transition. She more generally describes herself as "funny, smart, small, flexible, [and] talented. Creative, and loving, caring." Gabourey further describes herself as

> A good math student, because I get it. And when I don't get it, I practice and then I still get it. So, I don't think I'm a great math student because, then, I would never get stuck. And I don't think I'm a bad math student, because I would never get the concepts. I'm a good math student because it's a little bit of both.

Even more specifically as a mathematics student, Gabourey characterizes herself as "intelligent, [and] patient." What remains consistent in her global and mathematics-specific descriptions is that they both include "smart" and "intelligent" respectively. Although she views herself as "smart" and "intelligent," she acknowledges difficulties with mathematical abstraction and recognizes her need, in some instances, to take more time to contemplate and figure more difficult possibilities.

In addition to aspects of her confidence, Gabourey also expresses other affective components of her mathematics self-concept. Primary among these affective components are her level(s) of enjoyment of mathematics and the degree she looks forward to mathematics (and, in some instances, her mathematics class). When asked how much she enjoys mathematics, Gabourey responds that on a scale from one to ten, from least to greatest, "It would probably be a seven and a half, or an eight. Yeah, it would be an eight." This certainly marks a shift from the days when she considered mathematics her "downfall." She notes, "It's easier for me in my math class right now [in 7th grade], 'cause I've already learned the stuff that we're redoing last year. So, it's the same right now." Her familiarity with the concepts facilitates her understanding. It is likely that she finds some fulfillment in a sense of accomplishment that might accompany her familiarity with mathematical content. This fulfillment from accomplishment possibly heightens her enjoyment of mathematics.

Gabourey also seems to find fulfillment in her capacity to understand mathematics and to perform well in it. She reports feeling better now about her experiences with mathematics than in previous years: "I just get it, I guess. 'Cause I just get it. It's not like the concept was any easier. But it clicked in my head." Perhaps the fact that she is now "getting it" and the mathematics is "clicking in her head" explains why Gabourey declares, "I like math now. And I'm doing well in it." She credits a great deal of her liking math *now* to her ability to figure out more problems. This marks a dramatic shift from 2 years ago, when Gabourey responded with a six

(Very much like me) to the SDQ-II prompt "I hate mathematics." During the following year—that is, upon the most recent SDQ-II administration—Gabourey's response to this item changes from a 6 ("Very much like me") to a 4 ("More true than false"). She is careful to clarify, "Now, it's not that I don't like math. I mean, I like multiplying and dividing and stuff. But it's not like I want to be like a mathematician, when I grow up." Gabourey's increasing fondness of mathematics has, for her, its perceptible limits.

She also explains that her enjoyment of mathematics "depends on what lesson we're learning.... It depends of what type of lesson we're learning." Gabourey enjoys multiplication, division, and the distributive property, but admits an aversion to fractions: "Fractions confuse me a lot. But as of today, I'm getting better.... Right now, I'm pretty good at it, I hope." Gabourey's statement is both hopeful and speculative. This dichotomy is also observed in Gabourey's response to the idea of taking more advanced mathematics courses. Gabourey definitively insists that she would not take more advanced courses "cause I don't think I'm there yet. I don't think I'm good enough yet." Memories of prior struggles with mathematics begin to assault Gabourey's self-concept beliefs and make her developing mathematical confidence more tentative. Through her comments, she reports a more optimistic, efficacious attitude, yet reveals a persistent struggle to overcome the doubtful apprehension that previously plagued her. Gabourey distinguishes that she tends to enjoy mathematics differently with different teachers "because they are more fun and can make learning math easy and fun." Gabourey implies that she does not particularly enjoy undergoing the rigors of difficult mathematical challenges.

Student-Teacher Interactions. The influence of teachers figures prominently in Gabourey's discussions of her mathematics self-beliefs. As she shares her experiences, Gabourey attributes some of the positive changes regarding her relationship to mathematics and her mathematics self-beliefs to relationships she had with some of her teachers. She credits these teachers with the power to affect affective shifts in student attitudes about mathematics and mathematics self-perceptions through clarifying concepts, often through differentiating instruction, and through demonstrating (other) acts of care. From Gabourey's discussions, demonstrations of care tend to suggest that particular (caring) dispositions are well suited for strengthening self-beliefs.

As Gabourey shared favorable interactions with teachers, she often began with the most fundamental notion that "good math teachers ... actually teach the students and ... they teach the students well." And part of good teaching, for Gabourey, is to explain concepts thoroughly to the point of student understanding, which may extend beyond teacher (or district) comfort. Gabourey maintains that the role of teachers is essential in how students view themselves as learners and doers of mathematics. She argues,

"[The teacher's role is] very important because the teacher is supposed to be the one who is teaching you the math concept. [It] … is very important because I have to get it the first time. But if I don't, the teacher has to be willing to help me through it." Gabourey expressed that effective teacher interactions "help me understand better."

Gabourey links her teachers' determination to teach, and the multiple approaches they use to reach students, to the notion that these teachers are demonstrating care for their students. Gabourey describes beneficial qualities in productive interactions with her teachers:

> She would go over it, if we had questions. And if you didn't have questions, to start working on problems … for homework. Or if we were going over a quiz, do some practice problems. And she would take as much time as we need to answer questions that we had.

Clearly, Gabourey prioritizes understanding and elevates teachers' efforts to facilitate student comprehension. It is also essential to Gabourey that her teachers are not only willing to answer questions, but that they also take "as much time as needed" to do so. In describing one of her favorite teachers, Gabourey points out that "she's fun, she's nice, and she's patient for some of us who don't get the concept as soon as others." She adds that this teacher and the seventh grade teacher she presently enjoys "both really care about teaching us something. So, they would both take time to answer questions." This capacity to teach with patience and sensitivity to students' needs is particularly significant for Gabourey in that she is cognizant of her history of having difficulty with mathematics and understands herself to be a student who may need more time to complete some mathematical tasks and exercises.

By extension, Gabourey includes in her distinction of effective and caring student-teacher relationships the initiative teachers demonstrate by differentiating their instruction to accommodate student needs. She appreciates teachers who "engage with the students." One of the ways that Gabourey prefers teachers achieve this with her is "if they just don't tell you like to do textbook pages all day. They actually try to make up review games for a big test or something."

In her description of her interactions with teachers, Gabourey highlights specific dispositions and emphasizes certain educator personality traits. The dispositions that teachers adopt and display, along with the characteristics they assume and demonstrate significantly determine the degree these educators are able to assist students' construction of robust mathematics self-concepts. The centrality of the teacher is apparent as Gabourey evaluates her affective shift. In addition, Gabourey's mother asserts that student interactions with teachers are instrumental in establishing and developing student confidence in mathematics. Mrs. Watkins attributes Gabourey's blossoming confidence during her early school years largely to the "great encouragement [she received] from her kindergarten teacher." Mrs. Watkins also maintains, "She's at least confident now that, depending on the teacher, … she can be successful in math."

The contrast depicted as Gabourey's recounted fifth- and sixth-grade experiences highlights interpersonal dynamics under which her mathematics self-concept languished and thrived. Gabourey states that her fifth grade teacher "was just tough. She was nice when it came to like just seeing her in the hallway or talking to her out of math class. But she was very hard and strict in math classes." Both her parents (in two separate individual interviews) used the word "rigid" to describe this teacher. Mrs. Watkins regrets this period when she witnessed Gabourey "starting to slide back into that 'Oh, I can't do math' [mindset]." Gabourey writes about this class and teacher in her mathematics autobiography, "I was failing and there was just a point where I gave up and felt like I couldn't do it. What caused that was my teacher." Gabourey attributes her withdrawal from mathematics, and from this mathematics class, exclusively to the teacher.

Conversely, Gabourey credits her recent sixth-grade and present seventh-grade interactions with teachers for shifting her mathematics self-concept more positively. She remembers her teacher in sixth grade "explaining," "helping," and offering "morning and recess help." Gabourey recollects in her journal, "At first I thought I was horrible at math. But then in sixth grade, I realized I was able to do it, and do it well. My mom and teachers helped me realize it too." Gabourey attributes the transformation of her mathematics self-concept to the realization fostered by her own collaborative efforts in concert with those of her mother and teachers.

The impact of these fifth- and sixth-grade interactions with teachers illustrates drastically different responses to relationships and experiences with teachers of different dispositions. Gabourey's accounts make clear that she responds more to interactions with teachers who she feels demonstrate compassionate and caring. These qualities sometimes broaden the student-teacher relationship beyond the walls of the classroom. She lauded the accessibility of a fourth-grade teacher:

> She's really nice to me, and everybody … just the way she talked, the way she explained stuff to us, and the way she supported us. She would help us with math problems. She would help us with any problems…. She could be your teacher and she can also be someone you could talk to.

Gabourey also finds motivation in her current seventh grade teacher's caring disposition:

She goes deeper [than] into just math. She's not just a math teacher. She loves us. And so, she wants us to do well in math, not because she wants … to brag about it to her other math teachers. She wants us to pass because she thinks that we can do well in math. And she knows we can do it.

Gabourey explains that she can tell that this teacher loves her and other students "by the way she teaches. And then it's like outside of class. She's my cheerleading coach also. So, she has a certain bond with all of her students." The bond of authenticity and compassion is one that motivates and encourages Gabourey to have a more positive experience. Gabourey also implies in her comments that she is further motivated by her teacher's confidence in her students' abilities.

Omari

Omari is a 13-year-old rising eighth-grader. He attends school in a city over 150 miles from the summer program. His public school serves almost 800 students. Approximately 86% of students are African American; 14% were Caucasian. Seventy three percent of the student population comes from economically disadvantaged families. The school had recently achieved Adequate Yearly Progress (AYP). Omari is easy to talk and listen to and made friends easily during the summer program.

Mathematics Self-Concept Beliefs. Omari has rather consistently maintained a strong mathematics self-concept. He has generally had favorable experiences with mathematics and mathematics teachers. Omari began attending a Montessori school in kindergarten. While he was in kindergarten, Omari "first realized that I was good at math." Omari recalls that when he was in kindergarten, second graders were taking a timed test, "I think on multiplication." Omari reports that his teacher did not see him when he grabbed a clipboard and "sat down with all the … second graders" and worked on the test." According to Omari, "I got about three-fourths done with it. I had done more than some of the second graders had done." The teacher was surprised when she discovered him taking the test and was, perhaps, more surprised by his performance. Omari remembers:

The teacher said, "What are you doing here?" And she asked, "Did you steal somebody else's paper?" I said, "No, this is my paper." She said, "Are you serious?" And so, she realized then that … I had a bigger aptitude than she thought I did.

Omari remained in the Montessori setting through the second grade. But this incident would come to typify experiences in which Omari would perform at levels beyond many of his peers.

Omari's mother, Mrs. Knight, recalls that Omari "learned his math facts quickly" and that "he was always a really good student." His father insists that mathematics "seems to just come to him naturally." He participated in a gifted program at a public school in the third grade. Both of Omari's parents came to advocate for work that was more consistent with Omari's ability during his third and fourth grade years. Despite doing "quite well" in a program for the gifted during both of these school years, the Knight family was disenchanted and disappointed at the disappointing lack of challenge the curriculum extended to Omari. Mr. Knight recalls a conversation with Omari's third grade teacher in which "we told her ... that he needs to be challenged because the stuff she was teaching in third grade, he'd already had."

Both Omari and his mother were frustrated with his fourth grade experience. The gifted component of his curriculum seemed to occur "just one day a week." Mrs. Knight remembers, "A lot of times he was bored and I would say, '[Omari], do you wanna go to some kind of math camp, or whatever?' And he would say, 'Oh, that'll just put me *another* year ahead of everybody else.' " Here Omari began to feel an uncomfortable burden associated with his intellectual acumen. Mrs. Knight feels that during this time instead of being stretched to accommodate additional intellectual stimulation, he often faced coursework and challenges with which he was already familiar.

What his mother views as institutional low expectations may have tempered Omari's academic motivation. During the fifth grade, he attended a Catholic school. As he began middle school in the sixth grade, he returned to a public school. She reports that in the sixth grade "they were okay not turning in their assignments.... I felt like the expectation [other people had] of him dropped—not just for him, but for the whole group." She is most disturbed by the prevalence of low expectations and its effects on her son: "he wasn't rising above that low expectation. And I knew he was capable of it.... I don't think he wanted to be the one to shine." Omari admits to this period of momentary surrender to the strong temptation to "be this stereotype that totally wasn't me."

Omari generally shares very positive feelings about mathematics. On the Self-Description Questionnaire II (SDQ-II), Omari's responses are remarkably consistent from 2011 to 2012 (Appendix O4). On a 6-point Likert scale ranging from 1: "Not like me at all" to 6: "Very much like me," Omari responds with a 6 on the item naming mathematics as "one of my best subjects," on the item reporting that "I have always done well in mathematics," and on the item claiming "I get good marks [grades] in mathematics." Omari also ranks highly the degree to which he "look[s] forward to mathematics classes." The only item, out of 10 specifically mathematics self-concept prompts, that changed at all reflected an increase in his enjoyment of studying mathematics (from 3 to 5).

Omari readily shares that many of his experiences in mathematics have been enjoyable ones. He writes in his mathematics autobiography that he was "so *happy*" in kindergarten when he took it upon himself to take a timed test for second graders, and upon being pleased (and surprised) by his competence, "the teacher called me out in front of the class and told everyone what I had done." He writes again about being "so *happy*" in the seventh grade after his teacher explained "how I was going to teach myself math." In a third instance, Omari recollects having identical emotions of happiness when, in the third or fourth grade, he began to comprehend factorization of numbers into primes using factor trees. Omari's enjoyment of mathematics is linked, then, to the *happiness* he experiences in pursuing and achieving mathematics competence and excellence.

Omari speaks about his mathematics competence with considerable confidence. He proudly affirms, "I love being good at math." In an early interview, he concedes, "I'm not the *best* math student in my class," but acknowledges that *the fact that some of his classmates come to him for help in mathematics "kinda boosts my self-confidence."* As a matter of fact, he describes a best friend and himself as "math geniuses."

Student-Teacher Interactions. Typically, Omari relates considerably positive affective relationships with mathematics. Much of his mathematics self-concept beliefs are expressed through motivational aspects, such as his interest and engagement in the domain. Omari affirms, "I have always been intrigued in math because of the teaching I got when I was young." He connects his interest in mathematics to his early pedagogical exposure. Many of Omari's comments about his relationships and interactions with teachers are couched in his embrace of the Montessori style of schooling to which he was exposed in kindergarten and continued at different subsequent levels. Most of these comments generally describe his teachers' interactions with students at large. In other words, his statements most often characterize the dynamics between teachers and groups of students, particularly an entire classroom.

Omari suggests that the Montessori setting freed teachers to demonstrate more flexible approaches to instruction. For example, in his experience teachers determined to a much greater extent the pace that the classroom moved as a whole. This was achieved through teachers distributing and sharing some authority to students in determining the pace and progress of exposure to the curriculum. Omari recounts the following middle school experience:

> For the first semester, she put a sign-up sheet and you had to sign up for your math
> time you wanted to meet with her. There was a book with lessons in it and you had to

do at least two lessons a week. And you had to meet with her. And so, basically, and you'd move at your own pace. If you needed to do a lesson again, then she'd let you do a lesson again. And it'd still count as a lesson. Everybody can move at their own pace.

Another vehicle through which teachers share authority with students is the Math Seminar. Math Seminar is a weekly recitation where students work, independently then collaboratively, to figure out problems assigned by the teacher days earlier. Omari explains:

They're word problem questions that have to do with what we're learning in math at that certain time or what we should have already learned. We have to find a way to work them out. You cannot talk to anybody. You cannot talk to your parents about it; you cannot talk to anybody. You have to work it out on your own.

Omari further explains that students argue the significance and validity of answers they propose: "We have to show our work, and then debate what our answer means. We never get the answer."

The fact that the teacher-as-facilitator of the Seminar does not give students the answer expands the focus from determining a mathematical solution to understanding and engaging in a process of mathematical discovery or implementation. Omari asserts, "They focus on the process—you knowing the process—not getting the right answer at the end." Omari explains that as classmates present and argue their respective solutions, "everyone looks at the process they did." Again, the students' focus not only on the final answer, but also, more importantly and specifically, on the comprehension and navigation of mathematically sound processes. The dynamics described also likely decenter the locus of authority from the teacher and relocates it more precisely among the students.

In his discussions about interactions with mathematics teachers, Omari generally speaks fondly of the accessibility and comfort he feels with them, particularly those in the Montessori setting. Omari reports that students "call them [teachers] by their first name." This suggests a deliberate effort on the part of the school to make relationships between teachers and students appear less formal and, perhaps, more proximal. Omari explained that he responded favorably to a number of teacher characteristics and qualities. One fundamental quality that Omari appreciated is his teachers' ability to clarify content, that is, to teach. For instance, he highly praised Ms. Star as a teacher who "explained it [mathematical content] well for a younger person to get it." In other words, she facilitated his understanding of mathematical concepts at an early age. Omari also explained that his teachers held high standards for achievement. They preserved academic rigor, but did so without insisting on rigidity. The accountability of students and the flexibility given to them as they complete curricular tasks evinces this. Omari respected his teachers' intolerance of mediocrity and apathy. He also respected how familiar his teachers were with his and his classmates' abilities. Omari appreciated the precision in his teachers' assessment of ability:

> They don't give us too much of a workload, but they don't give us too less.... And they know what is too much for the students. They know what the students need. And they know what is too much for them.

The teachers' familiarity with students' abilities provides a degree of comfort that helps make Omari and his classmates receptive to the teachers' expectations and challenges.

Omari especially enjoyed the academic attention and devotion he felt that some teachers lavished upon him. He described the personal attention that one of his teachers gives to evaluating his assignments. He commented that this teacher "will actually come and check over my work more that [he does] other people. Omari maintains, "He will check it as if I was at a different level—a higher level—because he knows that will help me for my benefit only. Because I have started working harder on the things that I do." In another instance, Omari expressed that he felt entrusted with responsibility for his own learning (and some of his own teaching):

> *One day she came up to three of us [students], 'cause she thought we were responsible enough to teach our own selves math. So, she gave us the book and she gave us the check-off list. So, we were able to teach ourselves the math. And then we'd do the work and the lesson and everything. And then, if we thought we were good.... If we thought we had it down pat, then we'd check the paper off and then have her look over our work. And then she'd sign it. And so, we could move on to the next lesson.*

Omari appreciates votes of confidence in his mathematical ability from his teachers as he undergoes the *challenges* of completing assignments at a *more competent* level.

IMPLICATIONS FOR FUTURE RESEARCH

The research summarized in this chapter has implications for educational researchers and for educators. It centers conversations with two adolescent African American students regarding experiences they have had with school mathematics. Not surprisingly, discussions about relationships and interactions with teachers featured prominently in their recollections. Gabourey and Omari credited mathematics teachers with fostering interest and intrigue in the discipline, encouraging confidence in their abilities, and demonstrating acts of caring inside and outside of teaching. The influence of these attributions on students' mathematics self-perceptions has implications for additional research on mathematics self-beliefs and how interactions with teachers can strengthen or weaken these beliefs.

This research explores mathematics self-concept beliefs of two adolescent African American students. As such, a natural extension of this research would be a more deliberate exploration of the intersection(s) of racial identity and mathematics self-concept beliefs. This kind of research would explore to what degree students subscribe to or, perhaps, reject narratives of (racial) ability in mathematics in constructing and developing their self-conceptualizations.

Additional areas of research into students' mathematics self-concept move toward examining school and classroom contexts. Omari shared that one aspect of his education that he enjoys is the Math Seminar in which he eagerly participates in his Montessori classroom. Omari responds positively to the classroom culture that the Seminar facilitates. This space of inquiry, argumentation, and defense inspires Omari's confidence to explore and take academic risks. More generally, Omari argues that in a number of his classroom experiences, his teachers allow student to demonstrate their initiative by freeing them to work—for the most part—at a pace that most suits them, provided they cover school curricular objectives. Omari finds liberation and encouragement in this kind of trust and distributed classroom authority. The trust embedded in this type of student-teacher interaction serves to fortify and reinforce Omari's mathematics self-concept. So, exploration of alternative school and classroom configurations and the cultures they create is a worthwhile direction to consider.

Omari's description of his favorable mathematics classroom environments, along with Gabourey's positive teacher discussions imply that further research is need to explore pedagogies and ideologies that scaffold robust mathematics self-concepts. For example, Ladson-Billings (1994) delineates social relations of successful educators of African American students who engage in culturally relevant teaching methods. She distinguishes that teachers adopting a culturally relevant perspective foster a "community of learners" and motivate "students to learn collaboratively" (p. 55). Omari witnesses this kind of community and motivation in his Math Seminar. Additionally, Ladson-Billings asserts that teachers practicing culturally relevant methods demonstrate "a connectedness with all students" and engage in relationships with students that extend "to interactions beyond the classroom and into the community" (p. 55). These were characteristics that Gabourey celebrated in her cheerleading coach and in her fourth- and seventh-grade teachers.

Since teachers comprise half of the student-teacher dyad, it is implicit that continued research on this group is necessary. Specifically, it makes sense to have qualitative investigations about student-teacher relationships that emphasize—or at least include—teacher perspectives. Also, as Gabourey and Omari highlight favorable characteristics of teachers that helped them nurture, restore, and/or fortify their mathematics confidence, further examination of teacher qualities is essential. This research should include attention to teacher propensities to interact differently with students of various abilities, races, genders, and other characteristics.

Finally, Gabourey and Omari responded largely to what they perceived as indications that theirs teachers cared about them. For Gabourey and Omari, teacher demonstrated care by committing to teach, by being accessible and responsive to their needs (extra time), by holding and maintaining high expectations for them and other students, and by challenging them to achieve while providing scaffolding when necessary. They implied that teachers' capacity to demonstrate care is instrumental in strengthening their self-beliefs regarding their mathematics ability. This particular quality of teacher care deserves special attention, as the investigation of the relationship of student-teacher interactions and relationships and student mathematics self-concept beliefs are explored, especially among students of color.

REFERENCES

Bonner, E. (2014). Investigating practices of highly successful mathematics teachers of traditionally underserved students. *Educational Studies in Mathematics*, 86, 377–399.

Cokley, K., Komarraju, M., King, A., Cunningham, D., & Muhammad, G. (2003). Ethnic Differences in the measurement of academic self-concept in a sample of African American and European American college students. *Educational and Psychological Measurement, 63*(4), 707–722.

Fennema, E., & Sherman, J. (1976). Fennema-Sherman mathematics attitudes Scales: Instruments designed to measure attitudes towards learning of mathematics by males and females. *Catalog of Selected Documents, 6*(1), 31.

Ladson-Billings, G. (1994). *The dreamkeepers: Successful teachers of African American children*. San Francisco, CA: Jossey-Bass.

Marsh, H. W. (1992). *Self Description Questionnaire (SDQ) II: A theoretical and empirical basis for the measurement of multiple dimensions of adolescent self-concept. A test manual and research monograph*. Macarthur, New South Wales, Australia: University of Western Sydney, Faculty of Education.

Martin, D. (2007). Mathematics learning and participation in the African American context: The co-construction of identity in two intersecting realms of experience. In N. Nasir & P. Cobb (Eds.), *Improving access to mathematics: Diversity and equity in the classroom* (pp. 146–158). New York, NY: Teachers College Press.

Martin, A. & Dowson, M. (2009). Interpersonal relationships, motivation, engagement, and achievement: Yields for theory, current issues, and educational practice. *Review of Educational Research, 79*(1), 327–365.

Midgley, C., Feldlaufer, H., & Eccles, J. (1989). Student/teacher relations and attitudes towards mathematics before and after the transition to junior high school. *Child Development, 60,* 981–992.

National Council of Teachers of Mathematics. (1989). *Curriculum and evaluation standards for school mathematics.* Reston, VA: Author.

O'Connor, E. & McCartney, K. (2007). Examining teacher-child relationships and achievement as part of an ecological model of development. *American Educational Research Journal, 44*(2), 340–369.

Pietsch, J., Walker, R., & Chapman, E. (2003). The relationship among self-concept, self-efficacy, and performance in mathematics during secondary school. *Journal of Educational Psychology, 95*(3), 589–603.

Schunk, D., & Pajares, F. (2005) Competence perceptions and academic functioning. In A Elliot & C. Dweck (Eds.), *Handbook of competence motivation* (pp. 85-104). New York, NY: The Guilford Press.

Somers, C., Owens, D., & Piliawsky, M. (2008). Individual and social factors related to urban African American adolescents' school performance. *The High School Journal, 19*(3), 1–11.

Spangler, D. (1992). Assessing students' beliefs about mathematics. *The Arithmetic Teacher, 40*(3), 148–152.

Spilt, J., & Hughes, J. (2015). African American children at risk of increasingly conflicted teacher-student relationships in elementary school. *School Psychology Review, 44*(3), 306–314.

Usher, E. (2009). Sources of middle school students' self efficacy in mathematics:A qualitative investigation. *American Educational Research Journal, 46*(1), 275–314.

Wigfield, A., & Wagner, A. (2005). Competence, motivation, and identity development during adolescence. In A. Elliot & C. Dweck (Eds.), *Handbook of Competence and Motivation* (pp. 222–239). New York, NY: The Guilford Press.

CHAPTER 6

AND HOW ARE THE BOYS?

Towards an "African American Male Pedagogy" to Promote Academic and Social Success Among Black Boys in Early Childhood Education

Nathaniel Bryan
Miami University (Ohio)

Brian L. Wright
University of Memphis

He who is well needs no physician.
—Mark 2:17

INTRODUCTION

In her most recent book titled *Educating African-American Children: And How are the Children?*, Boutte (2016) details the story of what is considered one of the fiercest and most intelligent East African tribes, the Maasai warriors, to draw attention to the dire need to prioritize the education of African

Comprehensive Multicultural Education in the 21st Century:
Increasing Access in the Age of Retrenchment, pp. 99–124

American children and to encourage culturally relevant teaching in public pre-K–12 schools. In so doing, Boutte emphasizes the way Maasai warriors exchange greetings with each other to make her points clear. She explains that when a Maasai greets another warrior, s/he asks the following question, "And how are the children?" The typical response to said question is, "All the children are well!" Therefore, the wellbeing of the children signifies not only the wellbeing of the individual but also the Maasai community (Boutte, 2016).

If we, as educators, ask each other this question with respect to Black boys, could we say with confidence that "all Black boys are well" in our nation's schools? Given our current schooling structure and the academic and social disparities of Black boys therein, it would nearly be impossible to answer this question with an affirmative response. From the time Black boys enter schools, they are not well (Wright & Ford, 2016). They become victims of institutional and structural inequities perpetuated by issues of race, racism, and classism, which position them as what Hill (2016) refers to as "nobodies" or what West (2001) considers "the least of them" in and beyond early childhood classrooms. These nobodies and the least of them are those who have been denied access to a high quality education as a result of social and institutional inequities (Hill, 2016; West & Buschendorf, 2015). In light of these troubling realities, we must say, "No, Black boys aren't well" in early childhood education; therefore, we must prioritize their educational experiences with uninterrupted urgency. We return to the opening passage of scripture to denote the importance of prioritizing the academic and social needs of Black boys in early childhood. In his attempt to share the importance of caring for people who were least cared for during his epoch, Jesus told his disciples, "He who is well needs no physician." To understand this biblical scripture from an educational perspective, it is essential to consider that children doing well in our nation's schools may not need as much or the type of culturally-specific interventions such as those appropriate for Black boys. In other words, schools are already culturally relevant and responsive to White children; whereas they are culturally irrelevant and unresponsive to Black children; thereby, impacting how they perform (Ladson-Billings, 2009; Wright, Counsell, & Tate, 2015).

Jesus was speaking about spiritual sickness and we invoke this same idea to suggest that institutional racism and classism have made Black boys spiritually "sick" in our nation's schools. The colorblind curricula and culturally unresponsive schooling practices are symptomatic of an inherent racist system that has adversely impacted the schooling outcomes for Black boys (Rashid, 2009). This sickness reflects what Kozol (1991) poignantly described as "death at an early age" and what Love (2013) and Williams (1991) call "spirit murder." Spirit murder is the "personal, psychological, and spiritual injuries to people of color through fixed, yet fluid and moldable, structures of racism, privilege, and power" (Love, 2013, p. 302). Like Fannie Lou Hamer we are 'sick and tired of being sick and tired' (Brooks & Houck, 2011) of early childhood and other programs failing to acknowledge and engage the brilliance that we know resides in Black boys.

We wonder what kind of impact it would have on the academic and social outcomes of Black boys in schools and society writ large if the question, "And how are the Black boys?," was asked each time we start national and state-level conferences and school board and faculty meetings. We also wonder whether such a question could possibly shift teachers' pedagogical and schooling practices and stereotypical beliefs and assumptions about Black boys. Finally, we wonder if such a deliberate question could potentially disrupt the persistent inequity in classrooms so that teachers may see the possibilities, promises, and potential Black boys bring to early childhood classrooms. In this conceptual chapter, we explore Bush and Bush's (2013) African American male theory (AAMT, henceforth) with implications for what we call African American male pedagogy (AAMP). The AAMP is a pedagogical framework constructed to promote the academic and social outcomes and experiences of Black boys in early childhood classrooms.

This academic work is important for several reasons. First, as previously stated, schools begin to fail Black boys in early childhood education. This systemic failure unfortunately persists throughout their school years (Rashid, 2009; Wright & Ford, 2016). As such, Black boys are placed at risk of not achieving future success in schools. We must be proactive instead of reactive in terms of finding solutions to better the schooling outcomes of Black boys in early childhood education and beyond.

Second, this line of inquiry is significant because the academic, social, and cultural needs of Black boys are often ignored and deemed insignificant in early childhood education. Given that schools are based on White middle-class norms (Milner, 2010), teachers cater to the academic and social needs from such backgrounds. Their ways of knowing and being are validated and reflected in curriculum and instruction and policy and procedures (Souto-Manning, 2013). Although unintentionally, even in strength-based scholarship on Black male students, the academic and social needs of young Black boys are undertheorized. For example, in a 2016 special issue of *Teachers College Record* titled, "Erasing the Deficits: What Works to Improve K–12 and Postsecondary Black Male Student Achievement" coedited by Warren, Douglas, and Howard (2016), few articles focus on the academic and social realities of Black boys in early childhood education.

Finally, few scholars (Bristol, 2015; Brown, 2009; ross et al., 2016) have used culturally relevant pedagogy and/or introduced pedagogical frameworks specific to improving the academic and social outcomes of African

American males. To improve the outcomes of boys of African descent globally and specifically within the United States, Bristol (2015) conceptualized the idea of "gender relevant pedagogy." Brown (2009) used culturally relevant pedagogy to support the academic and social needs of Black male students in a middle school setting. Similarly, ross et al. (2016) introduced "organic pedagogies" to build sociopolitical consciousness among Black males in a male development program. Although promising, these frameworks focus on the academic needs of adolescent Black male students in middle and secondary schools; which fails to account for the teaching and learning experiences of Black boys in early childhood education.

Recognizing the importance of locating ourselves in our research and scholarship, we share our positionalities. This is necessary in part to describe and explain to some extent our frames of reference that inform and shape our interpretations and analysis of the experiences of Black boys in early childhood education. In greater detail, we then provide an explanation regarding why we believe that Black boys are not well in early childhood education. In so doing, we offer an explanation regarding the need for culturally relevant pedagogical frameworks that are specific to African American boys prekindergarten through third grade. We follow the explanation with a brief overview of Bush and Bush's (2013) AAMT with implications for AAMP. We conclude with examples of a culturally relevant pedagogical framework educators can use to support the school readiness and success of Black boys in early childhood classrooms.

OUR POSITIONALITIES

We are both Black male professors at predominantly White institutions (PWIs) in the South. We were once Black boys in the public pre-K–12 schooling systems. Therefore, we bring our personal and professional perspectives and experiences to this work as advocates to improve the social-emotional and academic needs of Black boys in early childhood education. We see our work as a part of a larger quest to close opportunity gaps in an effort to create access and opportunities for Black boys to learn and thrive in early childhood. We want to see more Black boyss achieve at and/or above the level of academic success we have achieved. We both hold terminal degrees and are emerging experts in our professional field.

The first author is a clinical assistant professor at a PWI in the South. His research agenda focuses on the lived experiences, recruitment and retention, and constructed identities and pedagogical styles of Black male teachers in early childhood. His research agenda also focuses on the lived, schooling, and imaginative childhood play experiences of Black boys in early learning spaces. Therefore, he fully believes in the potential and possibilities of Black boys.

The second author is an assistant professor at a PWI in the South. His academic scholarship focuses on high-achieving African American boys, STEM education in the early grades, teacher identity development, and increasing Black and Latino men in early childhood. He is committed to the improvement of the academic and social outcomes of Black boys in early childhood education and beyond and as such, his commitment is reflected in more than a decade of his scholarship in the academy. His forthcoming book focuses on developing healthy self-identity and agency in African American boys; thereby, understanding why Black boys are not well in schools and providing solutions to make them well is a central part of his scholarly agenda. Our positionalities in mind, we turn to a more detailed discussion of why Black boys are not well in early childhood classrooms.

WHY BLACK BOYS AREN'T WELL IN EARLY CHILDHOOD CLASSROOMS

In order to ensure Black boys are well in public K–12 schools and subsequently society, educators need to have open and honest dialogue about why Black boys are not well. That is, despite the difficulty of such conversations, we must admit the ways institutional racism, and classism negatively impact their schooling experiences (Hopkins, 1997; Rashid, 2009; Wright & Ford, 2016). Most teacher education program fail to acknowledge the prevalence of racism; thereby, underpreparing its overwhelmingly White teaching force to acknowledge, discuss, and address issues of race and racism in pre-K–12 classrooms. We briefly focus on ways institutional racism and classism affect both the academic and social outcomes of Black boys in early childhood, which we argue, sets them up for failure in and beyond pre-K–12 schools. We also explore pedagogical frameworks which have been used to support Black boys but may not have been specifically constructed to do so in early childhood education.

The Academic Outcomes of Black Boys in Early Childhood Education

Early childhood education is foundational to the school readiness and success of Black boys and other children (Wright & Ford, 2016). However, like most children of color, the early years learning experiences of Black boys are not built on solid foundations due to issues of race, racism, and classism. Race(ism), and classism are threaded throughout the early years experiences of children of color. For example, most Black boys attend preschool and other early childhood programs where teachers are not and/or underprepared to support their social-emotional development and academic development. That is, some teachers are unable to teach in culturally responsive, relevant, and affirming ways instead they enact a color/culture-blind early childhood curriculum (Bryan, 2017; Rashid, 2009). On top of that, most early years programs are underfunded; thereby, lacking essential educational resources to support the learning outcomes of Black boys and other students of color (Rashid, 2009; Wright & Ford, 2016).

Consequently, the social-emotional and learning needs of Black boys are ignored and compromised. An empirical study conducted by Aratani, Wight, and Cooper (2011) suggest that Black boys leave kindergarten reading at lower levels. This means that they read two to three standard deviations lower than their White counterparts (Aratani, Wight. and Cooper, 2011). These scholars further contend that such low reading levels are consequences of inherent racist and classist early childhood educational practices. Considering that third and fourth grade reading scores are used to determine the need for future prisons, scholars have become concerned about the future trajectories of Black boys (Alexander, 2010; Allen & White-Smith, 2014; Bryan, 2017; Giroux, 2009). That is, if they are unable to read, they are more likely to become a part of the school-to-prison pipeline contributing to what Alexander (2010) described as "mass incarceration" of Black men in the criminal justice system.

In another early childhood study, titled "Different Tales: The Role of Gender in the Oral-Narrative-Reading Link Among African-American Children," conducted by Gardner-Neblett and Sideris (2018), they examined the oral narrative skills of 34 Black boys (and 38 girls). The study found that promoting oral narrative skills among African American children in preschool could have an impact on their reading skills in later schooling years. In terms of Black boys, the study demonstrated some promising findings in that while Black girls demonstrated success in reading in their first year of school, Black boys showed significant gains throughout their elementary school years. Therefore, oral narrative skills may have the potential to build strong reading skills among Black male students. The researchers argue that the results are not surprising because one of the dimensions of African American culture is a strong connection to oral storytelling. This study also supports Boykin's (1994) work where he acknowledges that one of the Black cultural dimensions is a strong connection to oral traditions. Given such promising findings, teachers should explore the effectiveness of oral storytelling to support the reading outcomes of Black boys in early childhood education. It is important that we note here, that while research has highlighted strong oration skills among Black children, we caution against essentializing cultural practices of any racial-ethnic group. By this we mean, attributing "natural" and/or "essential characteristics" that suggests that Black boys display and/or engage in particular practices because of their race, group affiliation, and gender (Wright, with Counsell, 2018).

Some Black boys who leave early childhood education also demonstrate low and/or below average performance in mathematics. According to Aratani et al. (2011), Black boys leave kindergarten scoring significantly lower than their White counterparts by performing three to five standard deviation lower in mathematics. Given the push for science, technology, engineering, and mathematics (STEM) education (Wright, Counsell, Goings, Freeman, & Peat, 2016), most Black boys will not only be excluded from and/or pushed out of these programs and into lower academic coursework, but this will limit their representation in future STEM careers. Although scholars have studied the effectiveness of culturally relevant mathematics practices among Black male students (Jett, 2013), to date, we do not have any studies on the effectiveness of culturally relevant mathematics teaching and practices among Black boys in early childhood education.

Ford (2013) suggests that Black boys and other students of color who perform low in both reading and mathematics will limit their chances for screened, referred, and assessed for gifted education and/or advanced placement (AP) coursework. Instead, they will be assigned to special education (Wright & Ford, 2016). Assignment to low ability classes and special education is damaging to not only their educational experiences of Black boys, but also their self-esteem. Suffice it to say that all of these consequences mean that Black boys will have limited opportunities for upward mobility in schools and society writ large (Edelman, 2006; Rashid, 2009).

The Social Outcomes of Black Boys in Early Childhood Education

On one hand, academic outcomes is one of the components where race, racism, and classism manifest themselves in the schooling experiences of Black boys. On the other hand, a hyperfocus on discipline as it relates to Black boys as early as preschool is another concern. As noted by the U.S. Department of Education Office of Civil Rights (2016) "2013–2014 Civil Rights Data Collection: A First Look," Black boys represent 19% of preschool enrollment; but 45% of preschool children receiving one or more out-of-school suspensions. These disturbing findings suggests that more is at play than the classic locating of problems with Black boys and their families. We know that when Black boys are ignored, not validated, viewed as "overly aggressive" and pushed out of school, they fall behind academically because they view school as not a place for them. This reality explains to some extent the academic gaps that remain between them and their White counterparts (Bryan, 2017; Wright & Ford, 2016). Wright and Ford (2016) argue that the disproportionate practice of disciplining Black boys is listed as the highest among all racial and ethnic groups in early childhood education.

Many scholars have theorized reasons Black boys as early as preschool become targets of disproportionate school discipline. Scholars including Dancy (2014), Ladson-Billings (2011), Goff, Jackson, Di Leone, Culotta, and DiTomasso (2014), and Rashid (2009) explain that instead of being viewed as children, Black boys are often viewed as less innocent and not worthy of protection. As a result of this dehumanizing view , they receive men-like punishment in early childhood education (and beyond). That is, they are either suspended or expelled or assigned to special education in the same manner they are assigned for low academic performance. Black boys are often assigned to what Wright and Ford (2016) call high incident areas of special education including emotional disability (ED). This area is subjective and based on culturally biased measures or assessments that do not reflect the cultural ways of knowing or being of Black boys. Bryan (2017) corroborates these scholars, when he offers that White teachers' biases and stereotypes, (which they are socialized into in society and teacher education programs), play a significant role in the way they target Black boys and when given the opportunity to serve as coaching teachers. He explains these teachers pass down what he coined as intergenerational legacies of negative views, biases, and stereotypes about Black boys to White preservice teachers. Bryan further adds that in order to shift teachers' mindset about Black boys, White preservice teacher must be prepared in teacher education programs to see the promise, potential, and possibilities of the Black male child. To that end, we explore pedagogical framework which will enable them to do so.

Pedagogical Frameworks to Support African American Males in Pre-K–12 Schools

Despite more than 40 years of academic scholarship on Black males students, there has only been one documented framework—African American male theory—geared specifically to support the academic and social outcomes of Black boys at the middle and high school levels (Bush & Bush, 2013). We introduce this theory in the next section of this book chapter as the impetus for our emerging pedagogical framework. In our overview of this theory we point out what is missing,is a pedagogical framework to support the academic and social outcomes of Black boys.

Although scholars have explored frameworks including culturally relevant pedagogy, culturally sustaining, and critical race pedagogy to improve the academic and social outcomes of Black boys in pre-K–12 school settings, to date, there is not a single culturally-specific framework to meet the school readiness and success of Black boys in early childhood education.

Building on Lynn's (2006) scholarship on culturally relevant Black male teachers teachers, Brown (2009) notes that in studying culturally relevant male pedagogues, scholars undertheorized how culturally relevant teachers influence the academic and social outcomes of Black boys in schools. Therefore, he constructed a study on Black male teachers and how they used culturally relevant pedagogy to support the academic success, cultural competence, and sociopolitical mindset of Black male students. In a 9-month qualitative study, Brown studied nine Black male teachers in an urban middle school setting finding that culturally relevant Black male teachers were successful in using different pedagogical styles to support learning among their students inside and outside of the classroom. Brown described these pedagogues as "enforcers," "negotiators," and "playful." According to Brown, each of these performance styles consisted of distinct roles. The enforcer style of performance "seeks abrupt and immediate enforcement of defined expectations" (p. 424). The negotiator style of performance asks questions and seek students' input. The playful style of performance is used both inside and outside of the class and allows the performer to use jokes, debates, and other engaging activities to "break the monotony of the schoolwork and motivate students" (p. 424). Considering that Brown explored culturally relevant Black male teachers in middle school settings and the ways they influenced the outcomes of adolescent Black male students through culturally relevant teaching, we still need to know how culturally relevant pedagogies impact the academic and social outcomes in early childhood classrooms.

Filling that gap, Bryan (2016) conducted a 9-month qualitative study to investigate the constructed identities and pedagogical styles of three culturally relevant Black male kindergarten teachers in early childhood classrooms. He found that these teachers self-identified as culturally relevant teachers and demonstrated fictive kinship in the lives of their Black males students. By culturally relevant and fictive kin, we mean that Bryan discovered that these teachers supported their students in academic and nonacademic ways by fostering collaboration and building solidarity with the Black community to do so. Similarly, they used culturally relevant pedagogic performance styles including hip-hop and mathematics literacies to engage and improve the learning outcomes of their Black male students.

In a 3-year qualitative research study conducted in an urban school district, ross et al. (2016) examined the organic pedagogies of five Black male teachers in a specialized program within an urban school district. The purpose of this district-wide program was to provide academic and social support to adolescent Black male students in urban high school settings. The researchers found that these male pedagogues applied pedagogies grounded in "racialization and re-humanization." That is to say, addressing issues of race and racism were central to the teaching and learning process; thereby emphasizing the importance of shared humanity and collective goals between teacher and students. Focusing on the teaching and learning process of Black boys in early childhood education, we see our pedagogical framework as building on the concept of "racialization and re-humanization." Therefore, in the same manner scholars (Lynn & Jennings, 2009) have transformed critical race theory into a pedagogical framework (i.e., critical race pedagogy), we desire to do likewise by examining AAMT with implications for what we call AAMP.

Understanding AAMT With Implications for AAMP

In the 2013 special issue of the *Journal of African-American Males in Education* (JAAME), Bush and Bush (2013) introduced the AAMT. The AAMT is drawn from an amalgamation of theories including Afrocentricity, Bronfenbrenner's bioecological systems theory, culturally relevant pedagogy, and critical race pedagogy. Bush and Bush (2013) theorize that to improve the academic and social outcomes of Black boys in schools, educators should consider six important tenets, which we will introduce and explain in turn. First, educators must understand that "the individual and collective experiences, behaviors, outcomes, events, phenomena, and trajectory of African American boys and men's lives are best analyzed using an ecological systems approach" (Bush & Bush, p. 10). In other words, Black boys live in diverse contexts that shape and impact in a bidirectional manner how they live. Based upon Brofenbrenner's bioecological theory, these contexts include the microsystem, mesosystem, exosystem, macrosystem, and chronosystem. Taking each of these systems into account in relation to the process of development in relation to Black boys certainly indicates the complex nature of the effects of contexts on children's development

The microsystem focuses on an individual's immediate environment/ world (home/school) in terms of cultural attitudes, beliefs, and practices that include, but are not limited to , ideologies, personality and the influence of other important human and societal connections including family, peers, friends, schools, neighborhoods within the individual's world (Brofenbrenner, 2005; Bush & Bush, 2013). Bush and Bush's (2013) construction of the microsystem within the AAMT however, differs from Brofenbrenner's (2005) in that they divide the microsystem into two parts. These parts include the inner and outer microsystems (Bush & Bush, 2013).

The inner microsystem "captures components such as a person's biology, personality, perceptions, and beliefs" (Bush & Bush, 2013, p. 8). The outer microsystem encompasses "the intellectual gifts and the interactions familial, home, peer groups, neighbors, and school environments" (Bush & Bush, 2013, p. 8).

The mesosystem is also a component of both the Bush and Bush's (2013) AAMT and Brofenbrenner's (2005) bioecological theory. It is where the microsystems interact with other. In other words, as Bush and Bush explained, "it is the connection between the home and the school, family and peer groups and the like (p. 8). These scholars also extend the mesosystem by linking the inner and outer microsystems to what they call the "subsystem." The subsystem "provides the space to consider the influence and involvement of such matters as the supernatural and spirit, the collective will and archetypes" (p. 8). Furthermore, the exosystem includes external environments, which influence how an individual lives, namely community factors and settings and places of employment or lack thereof.

According to Bush and Bush (2013), the macrosystems includes "larger cultures or systems, which can be physical, emotional, ideological that may affect an individual's development" (p. 8). For example, Johnson and Bryan (2017) note how racial violence not only impacts the physical and emotional development of Black male professors in the academy but also how it adversely impacts Black boys in communities. The chronosystem also plays a vital role in the AAMT and the bioecological theory. It focuses on sociohistorical and sociopolitical transitions and changes within the environment (Bush & Bush, 2013).

Second, educators should know that there is something unique about "being male and of African descent." In other words, Black boys and men possess unique gifts and talents that must be acknowledged and valued. These gifts and talents as a collective group and individuals must be recognized, understood, and engaged. Such an intentional focus on these said gifts and talents must be reflected and interwoven throughout every aspect of microlevel and macrolevels of schooling process including curricula, pedagogies (Bush & Bush, 2013).

Third, educators need to acknowledge that "there is a continuity and continuation of African culture, consciousness, and biology that influence the experiences of African American boys and men" (Bush & Bush, 2013, p. 10). Therefore, AAMT centers the importance of African ways of knowing and being in the experiences of Black men and boys. Said more pointedly, although Black boys and men are not spatially situated in Africa, Africa is biologically situated in them and that the schooling experiences of Black boys and men must be "anchored in Africa" (p. 8). Bush and Bush (2013) warns that "research [and other schooling practices] on African American boys that [do] not take into account for the impact of Africa in America runs a significant risk of producing incomplete and faulty results" (p. 8). For this reason and more, Black boys "underperform in and beyond early childhood classrooms" (Rashid, 2009).

Fourth, educators must believe that "African American boys and men are resilient and resistant" (Bush & Bush, 2013, p. 10). That is to say, they must acknowledge that Black boys come from a legacy of African descendants who knew how to survive in the midst of racial and economic hardships; therefore, like their ancestors, African American boys have a unique desire to overcome challenges they face in school and society (Boutte, Johnson, Wynter-Hoyte, & Uyoata, 2017; King, 2005). AAMT acknowledges and values this self-determination among Black men and boys in such a way that it argues against deficit ideologies and beliefs that may describe them as having biological and cultural deficiencies, which prevent them from overcoming and succeeding. Rather, AAMT problematizes socially-constructed systems of inequity that become barriers for Black boys and men. These barriers include but are not limited to White-dominated school curricula, limited access to gifted education and other advanced course including AP, and limited access to postsecondary education (Wright & Ford, 2016).

Another component of the AAMT is that Black boys' and men's resilience and resistance is the the rejection and resistance of White cultural ways and knowing and being (Bush & Bush, 2013). Bush and Bush (2013) are clear that AAMT does not align with cultural resistance and oppositional theories including those constructed by John Ogbu and Signithia Fordham. Conflating education with schooling, Ogbu (1991) and Fordham and Ogbu (1986) argue that Black male (and female) students resist and reject education because valuing it is seen as "acting White" (Bush & Bush, 2013). AAMT sees Black male resistance as a strength instead of a weakness, particularly as it has been reflected in many social movements. Alongside Black women, Black men and boys have demonstrated social resistance in movements including #BlackLivesMatter (Hill, 2016).

Fifth, educators should acknowledge that "race and racism coupled with classism and sexism have a profound impact on every aspect of African American boys and men" (p. 8). Drawing from critical race theory (CRT), Bush and Bush (2013) emphasizes in the AAMT that race is an ever-present reality in the schooling and societal experiences of Black male students. The AAMT also accounts for what CRT scholars (Cook & Williams, 2015; Crenshaw, 1991) call the intersectionality of race and racism, which is the idea that race collides with other forms of oppressions. This idea builds on the notion that the schooling and societal experiences of Black boys should be viewed from a bioecological theory perspective as race and racism are entrenched within these systems (Bush & Bush, 2013).

Finally, educators must understand that the focus and purpose of study and programs concerning African American boys and men should be the pursuit of social justice. The AAMT is grounded in the idea that as the African and racial consciousness of Black boys and men is emphasized, they must also be encouraged regarding that consciousness (Bush & Bush, 2013). In other words, similar to culturally relevant and critical race theory, sociopolitical consciousness, which is embedded in the AAMT, requires specific social justice actions (Bush & Bush, 2013). Given these components of the AAMT, as previously mentioned, what is missing from this work is a pedagogical framework to support the school readiness and success of Black boys in early childhood education.

To that end, the remaining components of this book chapter focuses on making connections between AAMT and AAMP and providing a pedagogical framework that early childhood educators can use to support both academically and socially Black boys in early childhood classrooms. Although our pedagogical model focuses on Black boys in early childhood education, this model can be expanded meaning that it is not limited or limiting and may be beneficial to Black boys at varying educational levels and boys from other Indigenous and historically marginalized groups including Latino-American and Native-American boys.

TOWARDS AN
AFRICAN AMERICAN MALE PEDAGOGY (AAMP)

Given the need to explore curricula, pedagogies and programs to better support Black boys and men (Bush & Bush, 2013), we propose our pedagogical framework—African American Male Pedagogy (AAMP). It includes five pedagogical dimensions we extrapolate from the six tenets of AAMT. In order to engage in AAMP, we recommend teachers apply simultaneously all five dimensions of AAMP.

We also provide a few pedagogical examples from the classrooms of Black male teachers in early childhood education to make our points clear. Mr. Javien, Mr. Henry, and Mr. Tal are kindergarten teachers and participated in a larger 9-month qualitative study, which investigated their constructed identities and pedagogical styles (see Bryan, 2016). The first author also shares pedagogical examples from his coteaching in a second grade classroom. Though we draw from the pedagogical examples of Black male teachers in early childhood education, our focus on them is not to suggest that Black females and other teachers cannot use the AAMP to support Black boys in early childhood classrooms. We know that Black females have always contributed to the academic and social success of Black boys and other males of color (Siddle-Walker, 2000; Ladson-Billings,

2009). Similarly, we have witnessed the potential and possibilities of White teachers who have also contributed positively to the academic and social outcomes of Black boys (and girls) in pre-K–12 schools (Boutte, 2016; Ladson-Billings, 2009). To that end, it is our desire to provide snapshots of Black male teachers because we want to demonstrate that they are more than "role models," "father-figures, " and "disciplinarians, " as they are often socially constructed in both theory and practice. Rather, we want to provide counterstories, which portray them as effective pedagogues who can influence the academic and social outcomes of Black boys with whom they work in early childhood classrooms.

Below we explain each dimensions of AAMP. Like Bush and Bush (2013), we admit that similar to AAMT, AAMP is not a new pedagogical construction. It draws from and builds on several existing culturally specific frameworks including Afrocentricity, culturally relevant, culturally sustaining, and critical race pedagogies, and bioecological theory. However, what is new about this pedagogical framework is that it not only provides some pedagogical perspectives to improve the school readiness and success of Black boys, but it also challenges the field of early childhood to move beyond color- and cultural blindness in curricula and schooling practices. Similar to most young children of color, Black boys "underperform" because of the overemphasis on curricular content and practices including "developmentally appropriate practices" (DAP) in early childhood classrooms. DAP is a color and culture-blind curricular approach, which not only does harm to Black boys but also advantages/privileges White children at their expense (Boutte, 2016; Cannella, 1997). Boutte (2016) contends that while early childhood educators are sworn to "first do no harm to children," which is myopically interpreted as enacting physical and not pedagogical harm to young children, most teachers do not consider the damaging effects of the DAP and other color- and cultural-blind curricular renderings. With such considerations in mind and our desire to see schools as sites of healing for Black boys, we propose the AAMP. AAMP include the following tenets.

1. Teaching and Learning Should be Based on the Multidimensional Realities Black Boys Bring to Early Childhood Classrooms

Because Bush and Bush (2013) propose that the experiences of African American boys and men should be analyzed through a bioecological theory lens, we contend that effective teaching and learning should be grounded in a bioecological theory approach to promote academic and social success among Black boys. In other words, early childhood teachers should consider how the microsystem (inner, outer, and subsystems), macrosystem, exosystem, and chronosystem inform the everyday lived realities of Black boys to engage them in the teaching and learning process that is culturally responsive and responsible to their strengths and needs. Drawing from these systems will enable educators to place many factors regarding Black boys at the center of teaching and learning and not ignore that context matters. These factors may include, but are not limited to, Black boys' personality, sexuality, family and extended family, spirituality, and cultural ways of knowing and being, and socioeconomic status. Considering that teachers should build positive relationships with all students (Ladson-Billings, 2009), acknowledging the cultural and personal identities (multidimensional realities) Black boys bring to classrooms is a sure-fire way to get to know them.

Understanding how the macrosystem levels (e.g., hip-hop culture) inform the lives of his Black boys, Mr. Javien, a 35-year old male, uses hip-hop pedagogy to teach them. Mr. Javien finds hip-hop useful in assisting his students to expand their vocabularies. Mr. Javien uses Jay-Z and Beyonce, hip-hop musical icons, as examples to help his students understand the term "headliner." After Mr. Javien used the word in a sentence, many of his students still did not understand its meaning. Immediately one of his Black boys, Keith, who was sitting at the front of the class asked, "What is that?" Mr. Javien then explained to his students:

> Let me help you understand what a headliner is. You know when you go to [a] Jay-Z or Beyonce concert, they are the headliners because they are in-charge on the stage. There ain't no headliners in this class. You understand that Keith?

The integration of sight words and other vocabulary terminology seem to be an essential component of Mr. Javien's kindergarten classroom, which many of his Black boys take advantage of to build their own vocabulary. Mr. Javien draws from hip-hop artists to make those connections to help his students better understand vocabulary words. Similarly, although he helps his students build their vocabularies in Standard American English (SAE), Mr. Javien also demonstrates his understanding of how the macrosystems inform the home language his students speak. He does not devalue the African American Language (AAL)[1] they bring to the classroom, but he incorporates their linguistic diversity or English variety into the learning process to make cultural connections between him and his students as he uses double negation such as "aint no" to make his points clear. Double negations are acceptable constructions of AAL (Boutte, 2016; Smitherman, 1999). This is his ways of code-switching, code-mixing or translating orally between SAE and AAL and allowing his students to implicitly and explicitly know that he values both SAE and AAL as acceptable languages in his early childhood classroom.

Similarly, knowing how the inner microsystem level (e.g., biological makeup) shapes the lives of his Black boysand drawing from his own personal experiences as a young Black boy in public pre-K–12 schooling system, Mr. Henry, a 25-year old Black male, takes an extremely flexible approach to managing the classroom climate. He contends that traditional "classroom management" approaches are not flexible and problematic for Black boys who are full of energy and verve. Instead of forcing his Black boys s to sit during the duration of his classroom lessons, he allows them to freely move throughout the classroom to relieve themselves of the monotony of the early childhood classrooms. He also plans engaging on-hands lessons, which require them to be actively involved in the learning process. One of those engaging activities includes mathematics basketball where he enables his male students to shoot hops as they solve mathematics problems (see Bryan, 2016). It is important to note here, that we reject the tendency to view activities for boys such as sports as appealing to all boys, Black boys especially with respect to basketball and football. The aforementioned example is just but one way to connect with some Black boys. We understand there are Boys who may not play within the traditional constructions of Black masculine childhood play expectations (Bryan, 2018).

2. Teaching and Learning Should be Grounded in the Uniqueness Black Boys Bring to Early Childhood Classrooms and Should Encourage Their Resilience and Resistance in Schools and Society Writ Large

Due to the struggles African American people, especially men, have faced and continue to face in American society, Bush and Bush (2013) assert that being male and of African descent are unique identities and as such, this uniqueness is often expressed through their abilities to remain resilient and resist in the face of injustices. Mr. Tal, a 24-year Black male, believes his Black boys to be unique in that considering the challenges they face in their urban school, they are self-determined and knew how to fight. By fight mean, their use of agency to act upon their environment or a change the outcome of a situation or one's circumstances. He continues to affirm their uniqueness by teaching them to be resilient. Drawing from his own personal struggles to pass the PRAXIS II, the teacher certification exam, he is adamant about sharing his story with his students to encourage them to not give up when they find the rigor of the kindergarten class too difficult to master. He sees himself in his students and he knows if he could have passed the PRAXIS exam after four attempts that his male students could likewise overcome the difficulty of the classroom. Stories of Black boys' uniqueness, resilience, and resistance are employed throughout his early childhood curriculum as he provides his Black male students images of "mentors on paper" (Thompson, 1996) through authentic African American children's literature that ensures that Black boys see themselves in books.

3. Teaching and Learning Should be Afrocentric in Nature and Should Help Black Boys Build African Consciousness

Afrocentricity is central to the AAMT (Bush & Bush, 2013). Therefore, we propose that it should guide the teaching and learning process for Black boys. This is an important concept because Asa Hilliard (1995) argued that African American children were ethnic before they were raced, and that they must understand their ethnic connection to Africa. In other words, Black children must know that the history of the descendants of enslaved Africans does not start with the enslavement of African people (Boutte et al., 2017; King, 2005). Instead, it should start with more empowering stories which portray African people as kings and queens who have made and continue to make extremely notable contributions to the world.

In the Afrocentric tradition, African-centered people often refer to other Black people as "brother" and "sister" (Brown, 2009; X & Haley, 1965). Mr. Javien uses this approach to culturally affirm and to build a sense of pride among his Black boys. Throughout any given day in his kindergarten classroom, he could be heard praising his Black boyss by using terms such as, "Very good my brother" and nice job my brother," which demonstrates his intimate, cultural connections to them. He believes that this way of affirming them lets them know he is in struggle with them. Similarly, he pushes the African concept of "ubuntu" or the idea of "what is mine is yours" in the teaching and learning process. Therefore, what Boykin and Cunningham (2001) consider African communalism or a strong sense of collaboration is felt throughout his classroom, which he sees as a way to build fictive kin relationships among his students. In such a way, he encourages his students to teach and to be responsible for the wellbeing of each other in both academic and social ways. This idea challenges the traditional Eurocratic structure of the early childhood classroom where young children are often dependent on the knowledge and guidance of the teacher and are encouraged to compete with each other espousing the nature of American schooling (i.e., individualism, independence, and competitiveness). A departure from this way of schooling, he encourages his students to see themselves as working towards common academic goals and as being knowledgeable experts in their own learning process.

Teaching a 9-week unit on African contributions to the Lowcountry of South Carolina, Dr. B. explained to a group of Black boys in second grade how many of the Lowcountry traditions are grounded in African cultural ways of knowing and being. He uses examples of the sweetgrass baskets and the Gullah language to make connections to authentic African made baskets and spoken languages in West Africa. The students were able to develop an understanding that Africa is considered the cradle of civilization and that all knowledges began in Africa. He also informed the students that they can connect all content areas including mathematics, science, and geography to Africa; thus, they should develop an interest in those areas because their ancestors invented these fields of study. Dr. B also read several books including *We Be Gullah* to help students develop African consciousness. Including such books is his way of integrating Diaspora literacy into the curriculum. Boutte et al. (2017) define Diaspora literacy as books which reflect " Black people's knowledge of their collective story and cultural dispossession" (p. 68).

Although Bush and Bush (2013) do not place specific emphasis on where teachers should engage Afrocentricity in the AAMT, we believe that educators should first address African contributions in the AAMP before they discuss issues of race and racism with Black boys. As previously mentioned, this idea follows Hilliard's (1995) point that Black people were ethnic before they were raced. Furthermore, we find centering Afrocentricity more humanizing and a way to build African pride among Black boys, which can counter the dehumanizing effects of having to grapple with issues of rac(ism) and gender that tend to circumscribe their experiences in and outside of school.

4. Teaching and Learning Should Place Specific Emphasis on Understanding Issues of Race and Racism, Anti-Blackness, and the Intersections of These and Other Forms of Oppression

Because AAMT acknowledges that issues of race and racism influence the everyday lived realities of Black boys (and men) (Bush & Bush, 2013), the AAMP also emphasizes the centrality of race and racism. Therefore, we contend that after engaging the Afrocentric dimension of AAMP, educators should center race and racism in the teaching and learning process. Some early childhood scholars may argue that addressing issues of race and racism may be inappropriate at such early stages and that young children do not understand issues of race and racism (Boutte et al., 2017). However, like other scholars (Boutte 2016; Boutte et al., 2017; Boutte, Lopez-Robertson, & Powers-Costello, 2011), we argue that young children do understand the impact of these social constructions. In a study designed to demonstrate the ways young Black and Brown children understood issues of race and racism, Boutte et al. (2011) shared narratives regarding how young children were able to connect institutional racial discrimination to their personal and familial lives (see also Derman-Sparks & Edwards, 2010).

Therefore, Black children, boys in this case, need to come to understand both individual and systemic racism at the early stages in their educational careers so that they can develop a deeper sense of how individual and institutional racism works. In order to deepen students' knowledge bases regarding individual and institutional racism, we recommend that early childhood teachers engage in explicit conversations with young Black boys about individual and institutional racism and how it affect their lives, which can only be achieved if teachers possess cultural competence regarding matters of race, class, and gender. Mr. Henry, who we mentioned earlier, engaged a Black boy, a White girl, and a White boy in a literacy circle where he used the book titled *The Story of Martin Luther King, Jr. by Johnny Ray Moore* to scaffold and talk explicitly about issues of individual and institutional racism through the live of Dr. Martin Luther King, Jr. Drawing from the information in the book, Mr. Henry explained what segregation was and how it was enacted during Dr. King's time. Using each child as an example, he informed Roland, the only Black boy in the group, that he would not be able to attend school with Kate (White girl) and John (White boy). Roland began to ask why such was the case. Mr. Henry explained that laws prohibited Black and White interaction and supported the separation of White and Black people in public spaces. Mr. Henry continued to share that as a Black male teacher, he could not teach Kate and John during segregation. Roland briskly asked questions one after the other "So you mean you couldn't be their teacher?" and "I couldn't play with Kate?" Though Mr. Henry's lesson was within the initial stages of developing the racial awareness of his students, it was extremely courageous as most early childhood teachers do not engage these conversations, despite the fact the the lives of Black boys are negatively influenced by these social constructions (Bryan, 2017). Roland's participation in the literacy circle demonstrated his interest in the topic of race and racism.

Mr. Javien, who was also introduced earlier, often had informal conversations with his Black male students about the importance of making right decisions. These conversations were designed to help them understand how bad choices negatively impact Black boys. Mr. Javien engaged such conversations because he wanted his Black boys to understand how they are targeted in schools and society and are often treated more harshly in comparison to their White male counterparts. We caution, such conversations must be done with knowledge, skill and care to ensure that Black boys and other children do not come away feeling disempowered based on their race, but rather empower to know they can make a difference in their school and community.

Although Bush and Bush (2013) acknowledge the importance of African American boys and men understanding race and racism, we want to go further by suggesting that African American boys and men need to understand the workings of anti-Blackness. As a result of the varying histories people of color have with racism in America, we understand that marginalized groups presently experience issues of race and racism differently and AAMP desires to acknowledge these said differences. For example, African Americans have had to endure Jim and Jane Crow segregation and policies and laws of the land still reflected in efforts to differentiate between Black and White citizens. As mentioned earlier, mass incarceration is one of those examples. Though Black and White men engage in similar crimes, Black men are often faced with longer convictions and harsher punishment for crimes (Alexander, 2010).

Therefore we draw from the works of Dumas and ross (2016) on Black critical theory, which underscores the importance of exploring anti-Blackness. Anti-Blackness addresses the specific ways Black bodies endure and experience racism (Dumas & ross, 2016). We argue that as a part of AAMP, it is essential to engage what we call a "Black critical pedagogy," which explicitly addresses anti-Blackness. Because of the recent introduction of Black critical theory to the field of education (Dumas & ross, 2016), we do not have a pedagogical example from an early childhood classrooms. However, we want to return to an example we provided earlier in this section to demonstrate ways educators can address anti-Blackness in early childhood classrooms.

Revisiting Mr. Javien's classroom example, we want to argue that he could have not only spoken about how Black boys are systematically targeted, but he could have also placed a particular emphasis on anti-Blackness to illustrate the differences in racialized histories and between the experiences of Black people, males in this case, from other racialized groups. Given that understanding of numbers is a basic skill that most young children are required to learn in early childhood education, data which reflects the differences in the number of shootings of Black males including Trayvon Martin, Mike Brown, and Jordan Edwards who are killed by White cops and vigilantes in comparison to White and other males of colors could possibly make clear the idea of anti-Blackness.

AAMT explains the importance of considering the multiple experiences of African American boys and men. Therefore, we suggest that early childhood educators who take up the AAMP must help Black boys understand how race, racism, and anti-Blackness intersects with other forms of oppression. Grounded in CRT scholarship, intersectionality locates other forms of oppression including gender (gender expression), class, and sexuality and how they intersect with race and racism. In other words, Black boys are not only targeted because they are Black but also because they are male (Bryan, 2017; Howard, 2014; Wright, Counsell et al., 2016). AAMP emphasizes the importance of understanding that the intersections of Blackness and maleness constitute misfortunes in every aspect of society and schooling for Black boys and men.

Drawing from his own personal and professional experiences with race and racism as a Black man, Mr. Henry expressed the importance of having high expectations for his Black boys in kindergarten and having high expectation of themselves as a way to confront racist, stereotypical assumptions about Black boys and men. Because of the particular ways in which society discriminates against Black males, he understands the difficulties associated with being Black and male and demands that his Black boys perform their best in every situation. He also knows the difficulties Black females face but sees his Black males as those who are often given permission to fail. He explained that one of his high-achieving Black boys in his kindergarten classroom attempted to submit an assignment that did not represent his best work. Mr. Henry explained to Joshua, a Black boy, that the assignment was not acceptable and required the student to redo it. He saw reinforcing high expectations as a way for his student to reinforce high expectations for himself in a school system and society designed for him to fail.

5. Teaching and Learning and Black Male Support Programs (i.e., Mentoring Programs) Should be Grounded in Social Justice Activism

Because knowing about issues of race, racism, and anti-Blackness is only one component of eradicating issues of inequities, like AAMT, we propose a social justice activism component to our pedagogical framework. Similarly, in the same manner, critical race praxis adds an action-oriented component to critical race theory (Stovall, 2013), we do likewise to help educators and Black boys to see how social justice activism can affect their experiences in and outside of school. The idea of social justice activism also builds on Bush and Bush's (2013) idea concerning the need to enhance Black boys' natural abilities to reject and resist. That is, Black boys and men must learn to push back against Eurocentric ways of knowing and being, which may be emotionally and spiritually damaging to them.

In his classroom, Mr. Henry taught his Black boys (and other students) the importance of engaging in social justice activism. For example, teaching a lesson on standing up for what is right, Mr. Henry shared a scenario with his students during which he explained that the school principal had decided to discontinue recess and that students were no longer able to use the playground during school hours. Many of the students became upset about the principal's decision and decided to write letters to dissent and protest. To explain other ways to engage in social justice activism, Mr. Henry drew from contemporary examples including #BlackLivesMatter to help his students understand the importance of their voice and the different ways social justice activism can be enacted to affect change in society.

While these are a few pedagogical examples of how these teachers used the AAMT, they are not exhaustive. We encourage teachers to use these examples to find ways to employ AAMT with their Black boys in their own way and in ways that understand, recognize, and are sensitive to the range of diversity within, between and across Black boys.

CONCLUSION

Although the schooling experiences of Black boys have been under investigation and scrutiny for more than 40 years, there has been extremely few studies which problematized issues of race, racism, and classism and how they negatively inform Black boys' experiences in school. Similarly, few scholars have explored theoretical and pedagogical frameworks to support the academic and social success of Black boys in schools. Instead, until recently, scholars have focused primarily on the cold sterility of negative school statistics surrounding Black boys, most of which have blamed Black boys for the problems they inherit in schools (Warren, Douglas, & Howard, 2016). Toldson and Johns (2016) contend that many scholars and researchers have been awarded many grants and financial aid to conduct research on what they call "the Black male in crisis" narrative. However, our work is constructed to work against such deficit laden narratives to provide early childhood teachers' solutions to better support Black boys early on in their schooling careers; thereby, drawing from Bush and Bush's (2013) African American male theory, we propose what we call the African American male pedagogy (AAMP), which is grounded in the multidimensional realities of Black boys, caters to the uniqueness Black boys brings to classrooms and encourages their resistance and resilience in schools and society writ large, places Afrocentricity at the heart of their educational experiences, and encourages social activism in an unjust society. This framework is important and scholars and early childhood practitioners are encouraged to use it to improve the schooling and educational experiences of Black boys. Because until our schools do a better job of educating Black boys beginning in early childhood to the highest level of achievement, our society will forego untapped potential that includes a vast and diverse reservoir of human talent. It should be our goal to recognize all human talent, as educators. In so doing, when we are asked the question, "And how are the Black boys?," we want to respond with confidence, honesty, and integrity, "All the Black boys are well!"

NOTE

1. AAL is a systematic, rules-governed language, which is spoken by more than 95% of African American speakers (Boutte, 2015; Smitherman, 1999).

REFERENCES

Allen, Q., & White-Smith, K. (2015). "Just as bad as prison": The challenge of dismantling the school-to-prison pipeline through teacher and community education. Equity and Excellence, 47(4), 445–460.

Aratani, Y., Wight, V. R., & Cooper, J. L. (2011). Racial gaps in early childhood: Socio-emotional health, developmental, and educational outcomes among African-American boys. Retrieved from http://www.nccp.org/publications/../text_1014

Alexander, M. (2010). The new jim crow: Mass incarceration in the age of colorblindness. New York, NY: The New Press.

Boutte, G. (2016). Educating African American children: And how are the children? New York, NY: Routledge Press.

Boutte, G., Johnson, G., Wynter-Hoyte, K., & Uyoata, U.E. (2017). Using African diaspora literacy to heal and restore the souls of young Black children. International Critical Childhood Policy Studies, 6(1), 66–79.

Boutte, G., López-Robertson, J., & Powers-Costello, B. (2011). Moving beyond colorblindness in early childhood classrooms. Early Childhood Education Journal, 39(5), 335–342.

Boykin, A. W. (1994). Afrocultural expression and its implications for schooling. In E.R. Hollins, J. E. King, & W. C. Hayman (Eds.), Teaching diverse populations: Formulating a knowledge base (pp. 243–273). Albany, NY: State University of New York Press.

Boykin, A. W., & Cunningham, R. T. (2001). The effects of movement expressiveness in story content and learning context on the cognitive performance of African American children. Journal of Negro Education, 32, 256–263.

Bristol, T. (2015). Teaching boys: Towards a theory of gender-relevant pedagogy. Gender and Education, 27(1), 53–68.

Brofenbrenner, U. (2005). Making human beings human. Biological perspectives on human development. Thousand Oaks, CA. SAGE.

Brown, A. (2009). Brotha gonna work it out: Understanding the pedagogic performance of African American male teachers working with African American male students. Urban Review, 41, 416–435.

Brooks, M. P., & Houck, D. W.(2011). The speeches of Fannie Lou Hamer: To tell it like it is. Jackson, MS: University Press of Mississippi.

Bryan, N. (2018). Playing with or like the girls: Advancing the performance of multiple masculinities in Black boys' childhood play in U.S. early childhood classrooms. *Gender Education, 2*(3), 1–18.

Bryan, N. (2017). White teachers' role in sustaining the school-to-prison pipeline: Recommendations for teacher education. *Urban Review, 49*(2), 326–345.

Bryan, N. (2016). *Towards a multidimensional framework: Exploring the constructed identities and pedagogical styles of Black male kindergarten teachers in the South* (Unpublished dissertation). University of South Carolina, Columbia, South Carolina.

Bush, L., & Bush, E. (2013). Introducing African-American male theory. *Journal of African American Males in Education, 4*(1), 6–17.

Cannella, G. S. (1997). *Deconstructing early childhood education. Social justice and revolution*. New York, NY: Peter Lang.

Crenshaw, K. (1991). Mapping the margins: Intersectionality, identity politics, and violence against women of color. *Stanford Law Review, 43*(6), 1241–1299.

Cook, D. A., & Williams, T. (2015). Expanding intersectionality: Fictive kinship networks as supports for the educational aspirations of Black women. *Western Journal of Black Studies, 39*(2), 157–166.

Dancy, T. E. (2015). (Un)Doing hegemony in education: Disrupting school-to-prison pipelines for Black males. *Equity & Excellence, 47*(4), 476–493.

Derman-Sparks, L., & Edwards, J. O. (2010). *Anti-bias education for young children and ourselves*. Washington, DC: NAEYC.

Dumas, M. & ross, k. (2016). "Be real Black for me": Imagining BlackCrit in education. *Urban Education, 51*(4), 415–442.

Edelman, M. (2006). Losing the children, early and often. *The Crisis Magazine*. Retrieved from https://www.childrensdefense.org/wp-content/uploads/2018/08/crisis-mag-losing-the-children-2007.pdf

Ford, D. (2013). *Recruiting and retaining culturally different students in gifted education*. Waco, TX. Prufrock Press.

Fordham, S., & Ogbu, J. (1986). Black students' school success: Coping with the burden of 'acting white.' *Urban Review, 18*, 176–206.

Garner-Neblett, N., & Sideris, J. (2018). Different tales: The role of gender in the oral-narrative-reading link among African-American children. *Child Development, 4*(1), 1328–1342.

Giroux, H. A. (2009). *Youth in a suspect society: Democracy or disposability?* New York, NY: Palgrave McMillan.

Goff, P., & Jackson, M., & Di Leone, B. (2014). The essence of innocence: Consequences of dehumanizing Black Children. *Journal of Personality and Social Psychology, 106*(4), 526–545.

Hill, M. L. (2016). *Nobody: Casualties of America's war on the vulnerable, from Ferguson to Flint and beyond*. New York, NY: Atria Books

Hilliard, A. G. (1995). *The maroon within us: Selected essays on African American community socialization*. Baltimore, MD: Black Classic Press.

Hopkins, R. (1997). *Educating Black males: Critical lessons in schooling, community, and power*. New York, NY: SUNY Press.

Howard, T. (2014). *Black maled: Perils and promises in the education of African American males*. New York, NY: Teacher College Press.

Jett, C. (2013). Culturally responsive collegiate mathematics education: Implications for African American students. *Interdisciplinary Journal of Teaching and Learning, 3*(2),102–116.

Johnson, L., & Bryan, N. (2017). Using our voices, losing our bodies: Michael Brown, Trayvon Martin and the Spirit Murder of Black Male Professors in the Academy. *Race Ethnicity, and Education, 20*(2), 163–177.

King, J. (2005). *Black education: A transformative research and action agenda for the new century.* New York, NY: Routledge.

Kozol, J. (1991). *Savage inequalities.* New York, NY: Broadway Paperback.

Ladson-Billings, G. (2011). Boyz to men? Teaching to restore Black boys' childhood. *Race, Ethnicity and Education, 14*(1), 7–15.

Ladson-Billings, G. (2009). *The dreamkeepers: Successful teachers of African American children* (2nd ed.). San Francisco, CA: Jossey-Bass.

Love, B. (2013). "I see Trayvon Martin": What teachers can learn from the tragic death of a young Black male. *Urban Review: Issues and ideas in Public Education, 46*(2), 292–306.

Lynn, M. (2006). Education for the community: Exploring the culturally relevant practice of Black male teachers. *Teachers College Record, 108*(12), 2497–2522.

Lynn, M., & Jennings, M. (2009). Power, politics and critical race pedagogy: A critical race analysis of Black male teacher pedagogy. *Race, Ethnicity and Education, 12*(2), 173–196.

Milner, H. R. (2010). *Start where you are but don't stay there: Understanding diversity, opportunity gaps, and teaching in today's classroom.* Cambridge, MA. Harvard Education Press.

Ogbu, J. (1991). Cultural diversity and school experience. In. C. E. Walsh (Ed.), Literacy as praxis: *Culture,language, and pedagogy* (pp. 25–50). Norwood, NJ: Ablex.

Rashid, H. (2009). From brilliant baby to child placed at risk. The perilous path of African American boys in early childhood education. *Journal of Negro Education, 78*(3), 347–358.

Ross, K., Nasir, N., Given, J., McKinney de Royston, M., Vakil, S., Madkins, T., & Philoxene, D. (2016). "I do this for all the reasons America doesn't want me to: The organic pedagogies of Black male instructors. *Equity and Excellence, 49*(1), 85–99.

Siddle-Walker, V. (2000). Valued segregated schools for African American children in the South, 1935–1969: A review of common themes and characteristics. *Review of Educational Research, 70*(3), 253–285.

Smitherman, G. (1999). *Talkin that talk: Language, culture, and education in African America.* New York, NY: Routledge.

Souto-Manning, M. (2013). *Multicultural teaching in the early childhood classroom: approaches, strategies, and tools Pre-school-2nd grade.* New York, NY. Teachers College Press.

Stovall, D. (2013). Fightin' the devil 24/7: Context, community, and critical race praxis in education. In M. Lynn & A. Dixson (Eds.), *Handbook of critical race theory in education.* New York, NY: Routledge Press.

Thompson, M. C. (1996). Mentors on paper: How classics develop verbal ability. In J. VanTassel-Baska, D. T. Johnson, & L. N. Boyce (Eds.), *Developing verbal talent: Ideas and strategies for teachers of elementary and middle school students* (pp. 56–74). Boston, MA: Allyn and Bacon.

Toldson, I., & Johns, D. (2016) Erasing deficits. *Teachers College Record, 118*(6), 1–7.

U.S. Department of Education Office of Civil Rights. (2014). *Civil Rights Data Collection. Snapshot: School Discipline.* Retrieved from http://ocrdata.ed.gov/Downloads/CRDC-School-Discipline- Snapshot.pdf

Warren, C., Douglas, T., & Howard, T. (2016). In their own words: Erasing deficits and exploring what works to improve K–12 and postsecondary Black male school achievement. *Teachers College Record, 118*(6), 1–4.

West, C. (2001). *Race matters.* Boston, MA: Beacon Press.

West, C., & Buschendorf, C. (2014). *Black prophetic fire.* Boston, MA. Beacon Press.

Williams, P. J. (1991). *The alchemy of race and rights.* Cambridge, MA: Harvard University Press.

Wright, B., with Counsell, S. (2018). *The brilliance of Black boys: Cultivating school success in the early grades.* New York, NY. Teachers College Press.

Wright, B. L., Counsell, S. L., & Tate, S. L. (2015). We're many members, but one body: Teachers and African American males co-constructing the culture of the classroom community to increase access and empowerment. *Young Children, 70*(3), 24–31.

Wright, B. L., Counsell, S. L., Goings, R. B., Freeman, H., & Peat, F. (2016). Creating access and Opportunity: Preparing African-American male students for STEM trajectories prek-12. *Journal for Multicultural Education, 10*(3), 384–404.

Wright, B., & Ford, D. (2016). "This little light of mine": Creating early childhood classroom experiences for African-American boys PreK-3. *Journal of African American Males in Education, 7*(1), 5–19.

X., M., & Haley, A. (1965). *The autobiography of Malcolm X.* New York, NY: Grove Press.

CHAPTER 7

RESPONDING TO TEACHERS' PERCEPTIONS OF AFRICAN AMERICAN MALES

Addressing Bias in the Special Education Referral Process

Charmion Briana Rush
Western Carolina University

Gretchen G. Robinson
University of North Carolina at Pembroke

RESPONDING TO TEACHERS' PERCEPTIONS: ADDRESSING BIAS IN THE SPECIAL EDUCATION REFERRAL PROCESS

Significant disproportionality based on race and ethnicity in the identification and placement of African American students in special education programs has been a significant issue for over 40 years (McKenna, 2013; Hosp & Reschly, 2004). In spite of mandates to eliminate disproportionality, this challenge has been extraordinarily resistant to change. According to the

Comprehensive Multicultural Education in the 21st Century:
Increasing Access in the Age of Retrenchment, pp. 125–142
Copyright © 2019 by Information Age Publishing

U.S. Department of Education (2007), the disproportionate representation of African American students exists nationwide. For instance, African Americans make up 17% of public school students, and 27.3% receive educational services for emotional and behavior disorders (EBD) (U.S. Department of Education, 2005). Compared with students with a European American background, African American students are 2.88 times more likely than European American students to be labeled as intellectual disabled (ID) and are 1.92 times more likely to be identified with emotional disturbance (ED) (McKenna, 2013; Skiba, Poloni-Staudinger, Gallini, Simmons, & Feggins-Azziz, 2006). Researchers point to numerous possible contributors to the influences, past experiences with racism, issues with the definition of ED, school demographic factors, educator perceptions, the delivery of inappropriate instruction, and inadequate research (McKenna, 2013; Kearns, Ford, & Linney, 2005).

A more recent theme in the literature addressing disproportionate representation lies with the group of professionals who have the most direct influence over the entrance of students into special education programs, that is, the general education teachers who typically initiate the referral process. Despite mandates for fairness and appropriate evaluations, researchers have found that the referral process may not be as objective as presented. Given the overrepresentation of African American students who receive special education services, questions of bias and misidentification have been raised. According to Mamlin and Harris (2000), once a referral has been made, the referred child will be less likely returned to the general education classroom because a need for special education has been identified. Furthermore, teachers' perspectives, classroom practices, curriculum expectations, and students' characteristics either minimize or maximize a student's possible referral for special education (Dunn, Cole, & Estrada, 2009).

To extend this point, research has indicated that referral practices of general education teachers have gone beyond identifying the level of learning difficulties but also depend on student behaviors and gender. In a study conducted by Wehmeyer and Scwartz (2001), it appeared that certain student behaviors, particularly the behaviors of boys, led to special education referrals more often than other observed behaviors. In particular, the identified behaviors were significantly greater for male students when compared to their female counterparts. Unlike girls with learning difficulties who are more likely to internalize behavioral problems, boys with learning difficulties generally displayed more task-commitment problems and disruptive behaviors than boys without learning difficulties (Wehmeyer & Scwartz, 2001). More recently, Dunn's (2006) qualitative study revealed that general education teachers used five main referral criteria relating to behavior: (a) inattentiveness, (b) need for assistance, (c) inability to apply the presented information, (d) inability to complete tasks, and (e) students' "look" (i.e., the student's demeanor/comportment projecting a disposition or attitude of not wanting to learn).

THEORETICAL FRAMEWORK: CRITICAL RACE THEORY (CRT)

To understand teachers' perceptions of African American students and the reasons why they refer them for underachievement and behavior issues, it seems reasonable to analyze this phenomenon using critical race theory (CRT). Initially begun in the discipline of legal studies by Derrick Bell and other minority scholars as a response to racial oppression in law and society (Delgado & Stefancic, 2001), CRT has been used by many educational scholars as a theoretical and/or interpretive framework to analyze the realities of racial politics in education (Closson, 2010). In particular, this theory is used to analyze the way current inequalities are connected to earlier, more overt, practices of racial exclusion (Closson, 2010; Dixson & Rousseau 2005). CRT has been extended and applied to many educational disciplines such as academic motivation, performance, intercultural interactions, and teacher perceptions (Ladson-Billings, 1998; Solorzano & Villalpando, 1998). According to Solorzano and Yosso (2002), critical race theorist who have focused on schooling, CRT in education is defined as "a framework or set of basic perspectives, methods, and pedagogies that seek to identify, analyze, and transform those structural and cultural aspects of education" (p. 25). CRT provides a historical overview on how society constructs schools and categories to maintain subordinate and dominant racial positions in and out of the classroom. Critical race theorists asks such questions such as this one: What roles do schools, school processes, and school structures play in the maintenance of racial, ethnic, and gender subordination in American society?

Arguably, one of the most important contributions of CRT to the field of education in general is its robust theorization of race (Ross, 2009; Jennings & Lynn 2005; Ladson-Billings & Tate 1995). As an aspect of educational research, CRT confronts and challenges traditional views of education in regard to issues of meritocracy, claims of color-blind objectivity, and equal opportunity. CRT posits that racism is endemic in society and that racism has become so deeply engrained in society's and schooling's consciousness that it is often invisible (Delgado Bernal, 2002; Delgado & Stefancic, 2001; Solorzano & Yosso, 2002; Villalpando, 2003). As opposed to fixed conceptualizations of racial identity, CRT scholars conceptualize race (and all other racial identities) as being socially constructed (Chang, 2002; Matsuda, Lawrence, Delgado, & Crenshaw 1993).

The theory has been further developed in an effort to show how inequities are reproduced over time through institutional practices, decisions groups, and individual actions (Skiba, Knesting, & Bush, 2002). One important implication of CRT is that such actions or processes may be implemented by individual or institutional habit patterns without ever reaching a conscious level of awareness on the part of those who participate in those institutional actions. For example, the interactional and evaluative techniques routinely used by teachers may not be adequate to fully identify the intellectual resources and talents of low-status children, who are subsequently assessed as poor performers (Stanton-Salazar, 1997). Unchallenged, such patterns can unintentionally recreate and reinforce existing inequities in school processes.

CRT is offered as a lens and as a theoretical tool for engaging understandings of issues of whiteness and how ideologies of whiteness influences attitudes to fixed conceptualizations of racial identity. To be specific, CRT is particularly important regarding the role of teacher attitudes toward, expectations of, and beliefs about African Americans prior to pre-referral as it provided the theoretical framework for the development of my research questions and data collection.

In a mixed methods study, Rush (2012) examined the extent to which classroom teachers' perceptions affect the referral and disproportionate representation of African Americans in special education programs. The goals of the study were to (a) provide in-depth descriptions of general educators' perceptions regarding factors affecting overrepresentation of African Americans in special education, (b) identify the relationship between teacher demographics and teacher perceptions of what prompts referrals for special education services, and (c) explore African American student characteristics (i.e., ethnic background, gender, and SES) considered significant by general education teachers prior to special education referrals. In particular, the study intended to identify specific student characteristics and other variables that influence educators' decision making. The following questions guided this research:

1.   What are general educators' perceptions regarding factors influencing the overrepresentation of African American males for special education?,

2.   What student characteristics (i.e., ethnic background, gender, and socioeconomic status) are considered significant by general education teachers prior to the referral of African American males' assessment for special education?, and

3.   Do the teacher's demographic characteristics influence reasons for referrals?

The study took place in a midsized school district in North Carolina where 45% of the students are White, 31% are Black, 18% are Hispanic, 2% are Asian, 4% are multiracial, and less than 1% are Native American, this district has addressed the overrepresentation of minority youth in special education for more than 10 years (Child Count Reports, 2010). As related to the total student population, both African American males and females had been over identified for special education services. The most prominent area of concern was the eligibility for the category serious emotional disability (SED). As reported in 2010 federal child count data, North Carolina's counts of children ages 3 through 21 receiving special education and related services under IDEA (Part B), a total of 206 students in the district were reported receiving services in the SED category (Child Count Reports, 2010). Of that total, 140 students were reported as African American; 30 students were African American females and 110 students were African American males. This disproportionate rate averages 70% of African Americans placed in special education. In contrast, student counts by race and disability reported 51 students as White (25%), 13 students as multiracial (0.063%), 1 student as Hispanic (0.004 %), 1 student as Native American (0.004 %), and 0 Asian students were identified as SED.

A total of 256 teachers from 42 elementary schools participated in the study. Two hundred and five participants (85%) were females; 28 (13%) were male, with two participants not responding. A majority of the survey respondents, 140 (65%) indicated their ethnicity as Caucasian. A total of 58 (27%) were African American, 7 (3%) were Hispanic/Latino, two (1%) were Asian, and none were Native Americans. Seven respondents (3%) indicated "other" as their ethnicity. Age of respondents ranged from 21 to 70 years. Regarding number of years teaching, the largest group, with 56 respondents (25.6%) indicated they had taught 10 to 14 years. The next largest group of 41 (19%) respondents taught 5 to 9 years. The third largest group had 35 (16%) had been teaching 15 to 19 years, followed by 28 (13%) respondents who only had zero to 4 years of experience. Forty-one (41) respondents taught more than 20 years and approximately 24 respondents taught more than 30 years. The smallest group, more than 40 years, had two respondents. Regarding highest degree earned, of the 216 participants, 108 (50%) earned bachelor's degrees. Surprisingly, just as many educators earned master's degrees, 104 (48%) total. And, 2 (1%) respondents earned terminal degrees. The majority respondents held current license in the state of North Carolina and every elementary grade level was represented (kindergarten-fifth grades). A large number of survey respondents indicated they received multicultural training and/or cultural sensitive training during their preservice training and though the current system which they are employed. A total of 181 (84%) indicated "yes" and 35 (16%) indicated "no" on this item.

In contrast, 82 (38%) reported receiving disability training and 132 (61%), results that are nearly the opposite to those related to cultural sensitivity training. However, those who did receive disability training reported information related to nearly all areas of eligibility (specific learning disability, other health impaired, SED, intellectual disability; as well as speech and language impaired, autism, visual impaired, and orthopedically impaired.

A 47-item survey, *Gresham-Revised* (GR), was adapted from Dr. Doran Gresham's original instrument (Gresham, 2005), and developed with questions specifically addressing factors for referral and teacher demographics. The survey included five sections. Section I of polled participants' level of agreement to 29 statements regarding bias, ethnicity, socioeconomic status, parental involvement, and medical and environmental factors related to factors that may contribute to the referral of African American students prior to special education. A 5-point Likert-type scale measured teacher perceptions of these variables as linked to pre-referrals (Likert, 1932; Suter, 2006). Ratings included "strongly disagree," "somewhat disagree," "neither agree/disagree, "somewhat agree," and "strongly agree." Section II was an open-ended question that required a narrative response in regard to any additional factors that they perceived to be critical in the overrepresentation of African American males as pre-referral candidates. Section III consisted of 15 demographic questions concerning the characteristics of the respondent. Section IV was an open response question that asked for further elaboration or comments from the preceding section. Section V asked participants to volunteer for an interview conducted by the researcher at a later time in a location to their choice. If "no" was selected, the survey ended and the respondent was thanked for his or her time and participation. If "yes" was selected, a separate link allowed volunteers to submit their name, phone number, and e-mail address.

To potentially identify indicators of systematic bias without directly questioning participants if, in their perception, systematic bias exists within the system, an interview protocol was also developed. Based on their willingness, 12 participants were contacted by the researcher to further inform emerging findings reflective of teachers' perceptions.

RESULTS

Survey data were analyzed using means and standard deviations, as well as multivariate analysis of variance (MANOVA) and interview data were coded to verify common themes and/or emergent issues that recurred in the data (Powell-Taylor & Renner, 2003).

Quantitative Results

Based on response rates, the levels of "agreement" and levels of "disagreement" were used to identify reasons significant for African American male referrals for special education. In ranking order, prominent factors included (a) environmental factors (e.g., exposure to drugs and violence); (b) hereditary factors (e.g., prenatal exposure to drugs; biological transmission of mental illness, etc.); (c) certain biases (e.g., racial prejudice) on the part of the student's families; (d) low socioeconomic status (e.g., being raised by economically poor parents or guardians); (e) biases (e.g., racial prejudice) on the part of the student; (f) students' use of culturally different speech patterns or slang; (g) lack of clarity in school guidelines for special education referrals; (h) being raised by a single mother; (i) subjectivity in the county referral process; and (j) African American males being raised by extended family (e.g., aunt, uncle, or grandmother).

To examine what factors/student characteristics are considered significant by general education teachers prior to referral of African American students for special education, a factor analysis was performed to determine the strength of the relationships among specific survey items, completed using the principal component method. Initial analysis confirmed four factors for the data. Factors loadings indicated "raised by an extended family," "cultural biases," "ineffective training," and environment.

The communality was used to describe the relative importance of the reasons for referral. The student walking styles, the student hair styles, the students' style of dressing, being raised by adopted parents and being raised by two biological parents were among the top 10 reasons for referral of African American students. From the factors perspective, the cultural biases (e.g. racial prejudice) on the part of the educators and raised by extended family.

To analyze whether or not teachers' demographic characteristics influence reasons for referral, multivariate analysis of variance (MANOVA) was performed to determine the main effects of gender, ethnicity, age, highest degree obtained, years of experience, multicultural training and disability training on the reasons for referrals of the African American students.

Overall, the MANOVA criteria showing a significant effect identified ethnicity, highest degree earned, years of experience, and a lack of disability training. MANOVA test criteria for the hypothesis of no overall ethnicity effect showed a significant ethnicity main effect with Wilkes $\Lambda = 0.131$, $F_{(145,504)} = 1.77$, and $p < 0.001$.

Tukey's Studentized Range Test also showed that there was significant difference in the means of all the dependent variables except there are more in the elementary school population, heredity factors, and environmental factors. There was significant difference in the means of ethnicity between the teacher and the student, cultural beliefs and or differences between the teacher and the student, students' hair style, hereditary factor, environmental factors, being raised by single mother, being raised by single father, being raised by extended family, being raised by legally separated or divorced parents, and being raised by economically poor parents or guardians.

MANOVA test criteria for the hypothesis of no overall Years of Experience effect showed a significant Years of Experience main effect with Wilkes $\Lambda = 0.0903$, $F_{(232, 798)} = 1.25$, and $p < 0.05$. Tukey's Studentized Range Test also showed that there was significant difference in the means of inappropriate teacher training, lack 'of clarity in school guidelines for special education referrals, negative preconceptions about the behavior of African American males, students' walking styles, being raised by adopted parents, raised by foster patens, being raised by extended family, and being raised by legally separated or divorced parents

MANOVA test criteria for the hypothesis of no overall disability training effect showed a significant disability training main effect with Wilkes $\Lambda = 0.5660$, $F_{(29,101)} = 2.67$, and $p < 0.001 < \alpha = 0.05$. Tukey's Studentized Range Test also showed that there was significant difference in the means of Q5 Lack of clarity in school guidelines for special education referrals, and Q23 being raised by two biological parents.

MANOVA was also performed to determine interaction effects between gender and ethnicity, gender, ethnicity and highest degree obtained, gender and years of experience, multicultural training and ethnicity and disability training and Ethnicity on the referrals of African American students. All analysis used questions 1 to 29 as dependent measures. Overall, there was only one interaction effect identified. MANOVA test criteria for the hypothesis of no overall ethnicity and disability training interaction effect showed a significant ethnicity and disability training interaction effect with Wilkes $\Lambda = 0.4135$, $F_{(58,202)} = 0.193$, and $p < 0.001$ ($\alpha = 0.05$).

Qualitative Results

The qualitative portion of the survey included two open-ended items. Section II of the survey instrument asked the follow-up question, "*Are there any other reasons that you believe to be critical about the overrepresentation of African American males as pre-referral candidates that has not been addressed?*" The other response question, in Section IV of the survey, asked the participant to provide "additional comments" pertaining to any portion of the survey. In all, a total of fifty-five ($n = 55$) individuals responded to the first question and thirty ($n = 30$) responded to the second question.

Finally, to complement the survey data with richer information about referral-related topics, semistructured interviews were utilized. In Section V of the survey instrument, participants were given the opportunity to volunteer to be interviewed by the researcher at a later time. In all, a total of 23 participants ($n = 23$) volunteered to Section V of the survey instrument. However, only 12 ($n = 12$) interviewees were chosen for this study. Interviewees were chosen based on their availability and willingness to meet with the researcher. An interview protocol was used to facilitate and guide the discussion for a twelve ($n = 12$) interviewees.

All qualitative responses were used to enrich the research questions: (a) *What are general educators' perceptions regarding factors influencing the overrepresentation of African American males for special education?*, and (b) *What factors/ student characteristics (i.e. ethnic background, gender, and SES) are considered significant by general education teachers prior to referral of African American students for special education?* Ideally, the opened-item responses addressed research question one and the interviews provided insight to research question two.

Pen Response Survey Items

Are There Any Other Reasons That You Believe to be Critical About the Overrepresentation of African American Males as Pre-referral Candidates That Has Not Been Addressed?

The most common reason among responded comments to this open-response item suggested that African American males are overrepresented as pre-referral candidates because there is a lack of parental involvement. Other common reasons dealt with issues related to poverty, student behaviors, ineffective behavior management strategies, failure to use differentiated instruction, lack of early intervention strategies, high stakes testing, accountability, subjectivity in the referral process, educators' perceptions of African American males as low achievers, a lack of parental knowledge in the referral process, a lack of teacher and parent communication, media influence, an influx of African Americans in the population, a lack of multi-cultural training, and African American males raised in a single family home.

Collaboration with families. Respondents viewed the lack of parental involvement and support, lack of parents' understanding of the referral process, and lack of communication in the African American home as reasons for pre-referral. Repeatedly, respondents suggested that more home-school partnerships would reduce the need for referrals and thus, the problem of overrepresentation. Proactive and collaborative partnerships included parental involvement with homework, more interaction within the schools, reinforcement with literary skills, and stronger parental skills/parental training in the home environment.

Similarly, responses report that in the referral process, teachers may not provide open dialogue with the parent. In large, the lack of communication leads to high referrals based on the sole opinions and beliefs of teacher. Data suggested that, more often than not, the lack of communication between teacher, parent, and school ultimately lead to identification and a label.

Responses also noted that teachers fail to communicate with African American parents about student performance. And, in turn, African American parents fail to become active partners in the referral process. As a result, teachers and other professionals make important decisions for African American males with limited parental input. Data suggest that the lack of parental involvement is due to parents effectively knowing "how" to advocate for their child(ren). According to responses, this "lack of knowledge" is predominant in the low socioeconomic levels of the African American community.

Effects of poverty. According to responses, there is a common concern by teachers about the impact of poverty in relation to a child's development and learning potential. The negative effects of poverty such as high crime, drug abuse, lack of prenatal care, and the stability of the family contributes to poor developmental outcomes and low educational achievements. Simply put, based on "certain regional locations," African American males will be "inevitably be referred and thus disproportionality represented."

Similarly, general educators report that African American male referrals stem from those students who are raised by a single parent and/or extended family. Data suggest that educators believe that African American male candidates are often the same individuals who may have young parents with little to no parental skills; this includes a lack of early intervention skills and follow-up support. It is also suggested that students raised in such an environment lack the necessary male role model necessary for personal growth and advancement.

Behaviors. Responses indicate inappropriate behaviors by African American males and ineffective behavior management strategies within the classroom setting contribute to an increase of special education referrals. Data suggest that behavior issues stem from a variety of sources including the student, parental involvement, educators, and school/administration. Likewise, teachers reported that administration fails to support the staff. When it comes to administrators supporting teachers from inappropriate behaviors displayed from students and parental action, there is little to none.

Data-based decision making. Responses for this theme indicate that the pressure from high stakes test-based performance influxes African American referrals. Data suggest that administrators and teachers feel pressure to increase accountability ratings. As such, both teachers and administrators tend to recommend African American males as special education candidates to reduce low performing scores. Also, it is implied that this population is overrepresented because, often than not, those students who need instructional support are not able to obtain the services due to the demands of "teaching to the test," an educational practice where curriculum is heavily focused on preparing for a standardized test. As such, other instructional implementations (e.g., remediation) are lacking.

Cultural understanding. Responses indicate that referrals occur because teachers lack multicultural experiences and training. Data suggest the lack of training occurs at both levels; with preservice and veteran teacher.

Subjectivity in the referral process. According to participant respondents, subjectivity in the referral process contributes to higher referrals of African American males. Data suggest that educators tend to make predetermined decisions to identify and qualify a student for special education services, prior to any formal testing. In contrast, data suggest that educators believe that African American males are overrepresented in special education because they tend to be misdiagnosed.

Differentiated instruction. Differentiated instruction, the ability to design and deliver effective learning experiences, was identified as another reason for referral. In sum, educators reported an inability to address the learning needs and preferences of African American male students due to biased judgments, a lack of training and choices made by district/administrative authorities concerning delivering the curriculum.

Early intervention strategies. The lack of early intervention strategies ultimately leads to an increase of special education referrals for African American male students. Data suggest the importance of early childhood prevention and early intervention programs prior to formal school training are crucial in setting the foundation for lifelong learning. In particular, general educators believe that early intervention strategies are particularly important for African Americans coming from poverty-related backgrounds.

Educators' perceptions of African American males as low achievers. Media come to represent our social realities (Brooks & Herbert, 2006). As this theme indicate, much of what educators know and understand about African American males is based on the perceptions, images, and symbols portrayed by television, film, music, and other media. Likewise, data suggest that many adverse depictions of the male tend to make them candidates for referrals. For example, one educator response indicated that African American males were identified as individuals that are feared.

Finally, respondents indicated that a "cultural disconnect and stereotypical view of African American males as a low achievers" contribute to high referrals.

Sectional IV (of the Survey Instrument): Additional Comments

Of the 30 responses, most of the comments given for this section of the survey paralleled themes identified in Section III of the survey instrument. This included responses related to early intervention strategies, lack of parental involvement, ineffective behavior management, African Americans raised in single parent families, subjectivity in the referral process, poverty, lack of parental multicultural education training, poverty, and cultural differences.

Interviews

Section five of the survey instrument asked participants to volunteer for semi-structured, informal interviews conducted by the researcher during a time and location of their choice. From the 22 respondents, the researcher chose a total of 12 ($n = 12$) classroom teachers from kindergarten to fifth grade. The twelve ($n = 12$) interviewees were chosen based on their willingness and availability. Each participant agreed to participate in a single, digitally-recorded interview lasting approximately 30 minutes. The main purpose of the interview was to generate data relative to referral reasons that would supplement and deepen those obtained through the survey. Each interview began with this question: Think about an African American male student you have referred. What were you reason(s) for referral? A series of follow-up followed: *If academic, what area(s) (reading, writing, and math)? [Subquestions: What is the student's current functioning level? Describe the student's level of difficulty; What informal assessments were used prior to referral; What formal assessments were used prior to referral?], If the student was referred for behaviors, describe the occurring behaviors? [Subquestions: Were the behaviors significant to impede the student's learning and that of others? (If yes,) describe the student's behavior?]; What other factors were considered critical to referral?* Additional questions included these: *How does socioeconomic status and family conditions affect your decision to refer an African American male; How does parental involvement affect your decision to refer an African American male?; How does culture affect your decision to refer African American males? How do environmental factors affect your decision to refer an African male?* The closing question was as follows: *Do you wish to add anything else we may have missed?* This allowed each participant the opportunity to end each interview with closing comments.

Educators' Views Regarding Referrals

The most frequent reasons given for special education referrals were for academics, with the most prominent area identified in reading. However, teachers admitted the underlying reason for referral was viewing a student as needing assistance:

> *I knew he was having difficulty. To be honest, my "gut" feeling felt like that there was something. I thought that he was missing something. To tell you the truth, that's where it originally started I had to go with my "gut" feeling.* (Fourth-grade teacher, 1)

As required for the identification process, all teachers reported using both informal and formal assessments to determine student's functional levels. A majority of the teachers identified students' functioning levels at least two grade levels behind. The most frequently mentioned assessment involved teachers' observations of students' inability to apply presented information in their work.

Those students referred for behavior problems were described "*acting out*" as result of struggling. Significant behaviors often included misbehavior perceived as a means to avoid work. "Other" factors related to referral identified the importance of parental involvement. This included inconsistency of home/parental support with academics and the overall lack of authentic parental involvement in the child's education.

Whether the following questions were too sensitive in nature or, whether true accounts were given, interviewees reluctantly admitted that socioeconomic status, parental involvement, culture and environmental factors can be reasons for initial referrals of African American males. As reported, regardless of race, "these factors have to be taken in consideration at some point because *they are all tied in together*." Identified were the results of poverty (e.g., limited resources), parental involvement (e.g., students raised in single parent homes), culture (e.g., White versus African American culture; *two ways to act*), and environmental factors (e.g., exposure to drugs and violence).

CONCLUSIONS

Rush's (2012) study was founded on the assumption that the broader historical and cultural contexts encompass differences of cultural incongruity in terms of teacher attitudes, expectations, beliefs, and understanding of African American culture and learning styles (Delgado & Stefancic, 2002). With the best intentions, teachers who are unfamiliar with African American cultures may inadvertently make invalid special education referrals based on unconscious bias and stereotypes (Losen & Orfield, 2002). A clear need exists to understand the complexities of teaching students from culturally diverse backgrounds. As educators address the demographic divide (Gay & Howard, 2000), teachers must face the reality that they will continue to come into contact with students whose cultural, ethnic, linguistic, racial, and social class backgrounds may differ from their own. Teachers need to recognize the ways in which race constructs their identities and their perceptions of their students.

The responses provided in the quantitative sections of the survey seem to suggest that there are several factors influencing the referral of African American males for possible special education services. The most prominent reasons were being raised by extended family, cultural biases among teachers, ineffective trainings for teachers, and student environmental factors.

In contrast, the qualitative data from interviews were not as clear. For example, interviewees denied that race affects referrals but, then again, factors related to race (such as poverty, parental involvement, culture, and environmental factors) had to be taken into consideration because these issues are not separate issues.

IMPLICATIONS AND FUTURE RESEARCH

The goal of this chapter was to draw attention on the impact of teachers' perceptions of African American males during the pre-referral process. Based on overall findings, what can be concluded is that reasons for referral vary. These include the effects of poverty, disruptive behavior, unstable homes, lack of parental involvement, and teacher trainings. Students were also referred for less obvious reasons such as cultural bias (in the student's walk, talk, and dress). However, the overarching reason for referrals implied that race and culture matters in every aspect. As Banks (2006) noted, this complex relationship (that between race and culture) varies with respect to the extent to which individuals adopt characteristics associated with a particular group or internalize values and standards associated with that group.

The results of the study are significant in that they address real and very pressing factors related to the disproportionate placement of African American male students in special education. The results are also important in that the findings can help general educators and others in the field to examine their inner perceptions, and in turn change their thinking and their behavior. In addition, this research helps professionals to embrace the possibility that individuals in responsible positions should seek and eliminate the unconscious or conscious acts that may limit African American students from reaching their potential.

The study revealed several areas that need further study. One area of particular importance is clarity in the procedure of referral implementation. Future research in this area should focus on how to structure professional development to maintain a quality pre-referral structure. This includes redesigning guidelines of the pre-referral and intervention process. For example, in the traditional pre-referral process or response to intervention (RTI) procedures, a systematic examination of classroom and teachers variables should be included.

In addition, variables relating to teacher effectiveness with multicultural populations, student cultures, curriculum aspects, cognitive styles and overall quality to learning should be carefully taken in consideration as part of pre-referral process (Atwater, 2007; Rudea, Klinger, Sager, & Velasco, 2008). Likewise, research also should investigate the impact of professional development opportunities and trainings such as multicultural education and cultural awareness to determine if components of these trainings (such as diversity strategies, culturally relevant methods, and the implementation of research-based interventions) would better prepare teachers to work with a broader spectrum of children and thus become more effective at ameliorating this unyielding problem.

Research could consider the impact that standardized testing itself is having on the referral process. That is, another means to extend this research would be to compare a typical standardized curriculum classroom setting with an educational environment focusing on learning styles to determine how this alternative method might affect the number of students referred for special education services. To expand on the findings of this study, future research also should include a more nationally representative sample of teachers. A replication of this study in a different demographic is recommended to address similar findings with different dynamics. For example, certain aspects are unique to urban areas, whereas other rural and suburban factors may be generalizable to rural and suburban areas.

Additionally, a replication of the study would be beneficial if special education teacher's perceptions were included in the data. This study only included the perceptions of the general education teachers, because they are usually the first involved with the pre-referral process. However, since special educators are also knowledgeable about students who struggle academically and need intervention in regular instruction, they should also be included in the sample. These teachers also would have valuable perceptions to share.

REFERENCES

Atwater, A. S. (2007). An investigation of teacher's 'color-blind' racial attitudes and diversity training experiences: Implication for teacher education. *Journal of Education & Human Development, 1*(2), 1–15.

Banks, J. A. (2006). *Race, culture, and education: The selected works of James A. Banks.* New York, NY: Routledge.

Brooks, D. E., & Hébert, L. P. (2006). Gender, race, and media representations. In B. Dow & J. T. Wood (Eds.), *Handbook of gender and communication* (pp. 297–317). Thousand Oaks, CA: SAGE.

Chang, R. S. (2002). Critiquing "race" and its uses: Critical race theory's uncompleted argument. In F. Valdes, J. M. Culp, & A. P. Harris (Eds.), *Crossroads, directions, and a new critical race theory* (pp. 87–96). Philadelphia, PA: Temple University Press.

Closson, R. (2010). Critical race theory and adult education. *Adult Education Quarterly, 60*(3), 261–283.

Delgado Bernal, D. (2002). Critical race theory, LatCrit theory, and critical raced-gendered epistemologies: Recognizing students of color as holders and creators of knowledge. *Qualitative Inquiry, 8*(1), 105–126.

Delgado, R., & Stefancic, J. (2001). *Critical race theory: An introduction.* New York, NY: New York University Press.

Delgado, R., & Stefancic, J. (2002). *Critical race theory: The cutting edge* (2nd ed.). Philadelphia, PA: Temple University Press.

Dunn, M. W. (2006). It was written all over him: Classroom teachers' referral criteria for special education services. International Journal of Special Education, 21(2), 124–139.

Dunn, M. W., Cole, C., & Estrada, A. (2009). Referral criteria for special education: General education teachers' perspectives in Canada and the United States of America. *Rural Special Education Quarterly, 28*(1), 28–37.

Dixson, A., & Rousseau, C. (2005). And we are still not saved: Critical race theory in education ten years later. *Race, Ethnicity and Education, 8*(1), 7–27.

Gay, G., & Howard, T. (2000). Multicultural teacher education for the 21st century. *The Teacher Educator, 36*(1), 1–16.

Gresham, D. (2005a). *General educators' perceptions about the overrepresentation of elementary aged black males identified as students with emotional disturbance* (Doctoral dissertation). George Washington University, Graduate School of Education and Human Development, Washington, DC.

Hosp, J. L., & Reschly, D. J. (2004). Disproportionate representation of minority students in special education: Academic, demographic, and economic predictors. *Exceptional Children, 70*, 185–199.

Jennings, M. E., & Lynn, M. (2005). The house that race built: Critical pedagogy, African-American education, and the re-conceptualization of a critical race pedagogy. *Educational Foundations, 19*, 15–32.

Kearns, T., Ford, L., & Linney, J. A. (2005). African American student representation in special education programs. *The Journal of Negro Education, 74*, 297–310.

Ladson-Billings, G. (1998). Just what is critical race theory and what's it doing in a nice field like education? *International Journal of Qualitative Studies in Education, 11*(1), 7–24.

Ladson-Billings, G., & Tate, W. (1995). Toward a critical race theory of education. *The Teachers College Record, 97*(1), 47–68.

Likert, R. (1932). *A technique for the measurement of attitudes.* New York, NY: Archives of Psychology.

Losen, D., & Orfield, G. (2002). *Racial inequity in special education.* Cambridge, MA: Harvard Education Press.

Mamlin, N., & Harris, K. R. (2000). Elementary teachers' referral to special education in light of inclusion and pre-referral: Every child is here to learn . . . but some of these children are in real trouble. *Journal of Education Psychology, 90,* 385–396.

Matsuda, M., Lawrence, C., Delgado, R., & Crenshaw, K. (1993). *Words that wound: Critical race theory, assaultive speech, and the First Amendment.* Boulder, CO: Westview Press.

McKenna, (2013). The disproportionate representation of African Americans in programs for students with emotional and behavioral disorders. *Preventing School Failure, 57*(4), 206–211.

North Carolina Child Count Report. (2010). Retrieved from http://www.ncpublicschools.org/ec/data/childcount/reports/December

Powell-Taylor, E., & Renner, M. 2003. *Programme development and evaluation: analysing qualitative data.* Madison, WI: University of Wisconsin-Extension.

Ross, S. N. (2009). Ross critical race theory, democratization, and the public good: Deploying postmodern understandings of racial identity in the social justice classroom to contest academic capitalism. *Teaching in Higher Education, 14*(5), 517–528.

Rueda, R., Klinger, J., Sager, N., & Velasco, A. (2008). Reducing disproportionate representation in special education: Overview, explanations, and solutions. In T. C. Jimenez & V. L Graf (Eds.), *Education for all: Critical issues in the education of children and youth with disabilities* (pp. 131–166). San Francisco: Jossey Bass.

Rush, C. B. (2012). *General educators' perceptions of African American males prior to pre-referral.* The University of North Carolina at Greensboro). *ProQuest Dissertations and Theses,* 169. Retrieved from http://search.proquest.com/docview/1022503531?accountid=131239. (1022503531).

Skiba, R. J., Knesting, K., & Bush, L. D. (2002). Culturally competent assessment: More than nonbiased tests. *Journal of Child and Family Studies, 11*(1), 61–78.

Skiba, R. J., Poloni-Staudinger, L., Gallini, S., & Feggins-Azziz, R. (2006). Disparate access: The disproportionality of African-American students with disabilities across education environments. *Council for Exceptional Children, 72*(4), 411–424.

Solórzano, D. G., & Villalpando, O. (1998). Critical race theory, marginality, and the experience of minority students in higher education. In C. Torres & T. Mitchell (Eds.), *Emerging issues in the sociology of education: Comparative perspectives* (pp. 211–224). Albany, NY: State University of New York Press.

Solorzano, D. G., & Yosso, T. (2002). Critical race methodology: Counter-story-telling as an analytical framework for education research. *Qualitative Inquiry, 8*(1), 23–44.

Stanton-Salazar, R. D. (1997). A social capital framework for understanding the socialization of racial minority children and youths. *Harvard Education Review, 67*(1), 1–41.

Suter, W. N. (2006). *Interactions to research: A critical thinking approach.* Thousand Oaks, CA: SAGE.

U.S. Department of Education, Office of Special Education and Rehabilitative Services, Office of Special Education Programs. (2005). *27th Annual Report of Congress on the implementation of the Individuals with Disabilities Education Act, 2005, Vol.1.* Retrieved August 5, 2008, from http://www/ed/gov/about/reports/annual/osep/2005/partsv-c/27th-vol.pdf

U.S. Department of Education, Office of Special Education and Rehabilitative Services, Office of Special Education Programs. (2007). *29th annual report of Congress on the implementation of the Individuals with Disabilities Education Act, 2007, Vol.1.* Retrieved August 31, 2010, from http://www2.ed.gov/about/reports/annual/osep/2007/parts-b-c/29th-vol-1.pdf

Villalpando, O. (2003). Self-segregation or self-preservation? A critical race theory and Latina/o critical theory analysis of findings from a longitudinal study of Chicana/o college students. *International Journal of Qualitative Studies in Education, 16*(5), 619–646.

Wehmeyer, M., & Schwartz, M. (2001). Disproportionate representation of males in special education services: Biology, behavior, or bias? *Education and Treatment of Children, 24*(1), 28–45.

CHAPTER 8

STUDENTS WITH DISABILITIES

Making Idea Transition Services Work

Rhonda L. Sutton-Palmer
Independent Researcher

James Coaxum, III
Rowan University

Ted N. Ingram
Bronx Community College, CUNY

BACKGROUND OF THE PROBLEM

Transitions from high school to postsecondary education and employment can be particularly challenging for students with disabilities (Bangser, 2008). According to Burgstahler and Kim-Rupnow (2001), students with disabilities are less prepared to meet the challenges of adulthood, more likely to continue to live with their parents after high school, and engage in fewer social activities. Nationally, less than eight percent of students with disabilities graduate high school with a job, are enrolled in post-

Comprehensive Multicultural Education in the 21st Century:
Increasing Access in the Age of Retrenchment, pp. 143–172
Copyright © 2019 by Information Age Publishing
All rights of reproduction in any form reserved.

secondary education, are involved in community recreation and leisure activities (Condon & Callahan, 2008). School completion is one of the most significant issues facing special education programs nationally (Gaylord, Johnson, Lehr, Bremer, & Hasazi, 2004). According to Wagner et al. (1991), as cited in National Center on Secondary Education and Transition (NCSET, 2004):

> The National Longitudinal Transition Study (NLTS) found that approximately 36% of students with disabilities exited school by dropping out. The NLTS data also revealed that risk factors such as ethnicity and family income are related to dropout rates, and that some groups of special education students are more apt to drop out than others. Of youth with disabilities who do not complete school, the highest proportions are students with learning disabilities (32%), and students with emotional and behavioral disabilities (50%). (p. 8)

Transition planning is a formal process of long-range cooperative planning that will assist students with disabilities to successfully move from school into the adult world (New Jersey Department of Education [NJOE], 2010) while transition services are a coordinated set of activities for a student with a disability that is designed within a results-oriented process (NJDOE, 2006).

> Students with disabilities often have trouble meeting graduation requirements, and concern is mounting about the relationship between students' academic experiences and the formulation of post-school transition plans that address how students will access postsecondary education, employment, and community living opportunities. (Guy, Shin, Lee, & Thurlow, 1999; Johnson, Sharpe, & Stodden, 2000a; Johnson & Thurlow, 2003; Policy Information Clearinghouse, 1997; Stodden & Dowrick, 2000a, 2000b, as cited in NCSET, 2004, p. 3)

Poor post-school outcomes have been linked to the lack of vocational preparation, transition planning, and linkage to existing adult services and supports prior to graduation (Condon & Callahan, 2008). Most young people are receiving little to no career guidance outside the home, and not enough from their parents (Hurley & Thorp, 2002). Lack of career guidance leads to high school graduates who are undecided about their career goals or who will make poor decisions that they will regret later in life (Hurley & Thorp, 2002). A lack of special educators prepared with specific abilities in secondary transition to facilitate students' successful movement from high school to adult life is a significant variable in poor adult outcomes for students with disabilities (Benitez, Morningstar, & Frey, 2009; Blalock et al., 2003; Morningstar, Kim, & Clark, 2008).

In general, past research has shown that students with disabilities achieve postschool outcomes at a much lower rate than do their non-disabled peers (Mithaug, Horiuchi, & Fanning, 1985; Sittlington & Frank, 1990). Another study found fewer than half of students with disabilities were employed full time two years following their high school graduation (Wagner et al., 1991). However, more recent research shows improvements in that 31% of students with disabilities access post-secondary education within two years of leaving high school (Newman, 2005, as cited in Williams-Diehm & Lynch, 2007, p. 14).

As the end of high school approaches, so does the termination of a structured environment and pre-college support systems (Burgstahler & Kim-Rupnow, 2001). Having a particular disability can affect transition planning, and students with disabilities experienced higher stress, lower peer social support, and poorer adjustment than do other students without disabilities (Hoppe, 2003). Students who drop out of school tend to have backgrounds that include poverty, parents who are less well educated, homes in which academic skills such as reading are neither valued nor modeled, and the presence of multiple family stressors (e.g., drugs and alcohol, divorce, abuse) (Leone et al., 2003).

PROBLEM STATEMENT

Research involving individual education plan (IEP) document reviews has characterized transition goals as vague, overly broad, or template, suggesting that limited attention may be given to aligning transition plans with youths' unique characteristics and individual goals for life after high school (Carter, Trainor, Sun, & Owens, 2009; deFur, 2003). Transition plans are often in name only, many are ineffective, and some may thwart the goals of young adults (Cooney, 2002). Consequently, transition planning too often becomes an afterthought rather than the primary focus that guides secondary special education service decisions (deFur, 2003).

According to the Federation of Families SC (n.d.), "Because students with disabilities often experience limited success after leaving high school, many new IDEA 2004 provisions seek to improve transition planning so that students with disabilities can be more successful in their adult lives" (p. 1). The National Center for Educational Statistics (2006) revealed that while attendance by students with disabilities in postsecondary institutions has increased in past decades, only 12% of individuals with disabilities graduated college (Dowrick, Anderson, Heyer, & Acoster, 2005, as cited in Garrison-Wade, 2012, p. 1). Young adults with disabilities continue to face significant difficulties in securing jobs, accessing postsecondary education, living independently, fully participating in their communities, and accessing necessary community services such as healthcare and transportation (Gaylord et al., 2004). The National Association of Special Education Teachers (NASET, 2007) argues that,

> Teachers and parents of disabled students face a very difficult task when it comes to trying to maneuver through all the red tape, options, forms, etc. that are involved in the special education process. Nowhere is that procedure more intense and important than in the transition of disabled children to adulthood. (p. 1)

Many secondary education school students with disabilities are in dire need of results-oriented transition services. Additionally, the federal government holds state education agencies responsible for the implementation of transition services to students with disabilities (Katsiyannis, deFur, & Conderman, 1998). Even though transition services are firmly mandated by the federal government, it is evident that many schools still have difficulties implementing this critical component. Additionally, the standards-based reform movement has shifted the attention of educators from preparation for work and career toward academic performance outcomes for all students (Bassett & Kochhar-Bryant, 2006). Despite all that has been learned and accomplished regarding research-based secondary transition practices, they are rarely implemented and sustained at local schools (Benz, Lindstrom, Unruh, & Waintrup, 2004).

PURPOSE OF THE STUDY

The purpose of this qualitative study was to examine the perception of the special education teachers, administrators, and guidance counselors at Michael J. Hawkins High School regarding the present transition planning process. Teachers who do not understand transition planning are less effective in ensuring that the students receive the maximum benefits resulting from the transition plan (Williams-Diehm & Lynch, 2007). Given these needs, it is crucial for educators and other professionals to better understand the individual and program level components that may support effective transition outcomes (Lindstrom et al., 2007).

Additionally, we examined how confident the special education teachers, students with disabilities, administrators, and guidance counselors felt that students with disabilities were prepared to transition from high school to adulthood. "The role of secondary education administrators, including but not limited to principals, guidance directors, curriculum supervisors, department chairs, and special education directors, is important to the success of students with disabilities" (Boscardin, 2005, p. 21). The need for all-inclusive transition programming and establishment of personal goals is a critical issue for educators and professionals dealing with students with special needs (Dowdy, Carter, & Smith, 1990). Successful transition from secondary education is becoming recognized as a chief indicator of the effectiveness of our educational system for preparing youths and young adults for employment, postsecondary education, military service, and adult independence (Bassett & Kochhar-Bryant, 2006). The central research question that frames the study was: What were the perceptions of the high school special education teachers, school administrators, and guidance counselors regarding the present process for implementing transition services to students with disabilities?

TRANSITION PLANNING AND TRANSITION SERVICES

The Office of Special Education and Rehabilitative Services (OSERS) established transition as a policy and funding priority in the early 1980s. In 1984, U.S. Assistant Secretary of Education for Special Education and Rehabilitation, Madeleine Will, proposed Bridges from School to Work as a conceptual model of transition. In 1985, educational researcher, Andrew Halpern, proposed a revised and expanded conceptual model of transition that included residential, employment and social interpersonal networks under the rubric of community adjustment. In 1989, OSERS funded the implementation of the National Longitudinal Transition Study from 1987–1993 that included over 8,000 youth ages 13–21. Students were interviewed over 2 intervals: 2 years or less post-school and 3–5 years post-school. In 1991, OSERS established and funded the Systems Change in Transition priority. In 1996, The National Transition Alliance was funded to provide technical assistance to states receiving STW development and implementation grants. In 1990, IDEA passed and included provisions for transition services. In 1992, the Rehabilitation Act was amended to include the same definition of transition as IDEA. In 1994, the School-to-Work Opportunities Act was passed that required the inclusion of all students. In 1998, the Workforce Investment Act linked amendments of the Rehabilitation Act to generic employment services. In 1999, the Ticket to Work and Work Incentives Improvement Act included incentives to return to work and to seek employment related to health care and cash benefits.

Transition services, as mandated by IDEA, are intended to assist students with disabilities during their school years with "an array of activities aimed at increasing employability" (Test, Aspel, & Everson, 2006, p. 223). The National Joint Committee on Learning Disabilities' (NJCLD) position makes it clear that providing transition plans and services is crucial in assisting youth with disabilities to prepare for adult life (Clark, 1996).

Good transition plans reflect the student's personal choices, preferences, and needs across a variety of domains including education, employment, community living, and recreational experiences (Bakken & Obiakor, 2008; Brooke & McDonough, 2008; Brooke, Revell, & Wehman, 2009). A number of studies have indicated that an atmosphere of a shared and open dialogue among all parties is an essential component for transition planning activities to be effective (Cooney, 2002).

The transition planning process is critical to assuring the success of students served through special education services (Williams-Diehm & Lynch, 2007). Sitlington and colleagues (2007) argue that transition planning is an integral part of the educational process for students with disabilities during the secondary school years and serves as the foundation for planning for adult roles. "A final critical aspect of transition planning for students with disabilities is self-determination, which has been defined as 'one's ability to define and achieve goals based on a foundation of knowing and valuing oneself' "(Field & Hoffman, 2002, p. 164). Despite the significant attention and resources devoted to developing and implementing transition services for youth with disabilities, we continue to see a disturbing picture for youth with disabilities in transition (Cushing & Parker-Katz, 2012). According to Gaylord et al. (2004):

> Effective transition planning and service depend upon functional linkages among schools, rehabilitation services, and other human service and community agencies. However, a number of factors have stood as barriers to effective collaboration, including (a) lack of shared knowledge and vision by students, parents, and school and agency staff around students' post-school goals and the transition resources necessary to support students' needs and interests; (b) lack of shared information across school and community agencies, and coordinated assessment and planning processes, to support integrated transition planning; (c) lack of meaningful roles for students and parents in the transition decision-making process; and (d) lack of meaningful information on anticipated post-school services needed by students and follow-up data on the actual post-school outcomes and continuing support needs of students that can be used to guide improvement in systems collaboration and linkages. (p. 2)

Helping students with disabilities to secure post-high employment is the main priority of special education teachers responsible for transitioning these students to adulthood (Eisenman, 2003).

The Role of Special Education Teachers and Transition Planning

Depending on the nature and severity of the disability, special education teachers and parents may play more of an ongoing role in the child's life even after he or she leaves secondary education (NASET, 2007). Notwithstanding, helping students with disabilities to secure post-high employment is the main priority of special education teachers responsible for transitioning these students to adulthood (Eisenman, 2003). Many educators in secondary education settings understand the need to help students engage in meaningful career exploration and to foster positive beliefs and behaviors in students that will lead to success in future workplace and/or college settings (Deemer & Ostrowski, 2010). According to Smith, Gartin, Murdick, and Hilton (2010), "Special Educators are responsible for facilitating the transition process by encouraging parent and student participation and facilitating their participation in transition planning" (p. 2).

Although families piece together support networks, invest personal resources, and juggle multiple roles and responsibilities to help their children achieve fulfilling futures, teachers must ensure that they equip parents with needed information and resources (Ankeny, Wilkins, & Spain, 2009). Transition related best practices, namely self-determination practices, may not be widely applied in the public schools in which future educators are obtaining experience (Young, 2007). Furthermore, several first-year teachers felt that because these practices were not employed in their schools, it would be difficult to implement these best practices since there appeared to be little support and knowledge about this approach (Young, 2007).

Because schools rely heavily on special education teachers to implement and manage transition planning and services, it is disconcerting that teachers feel unprepared in those areas (U.S. General Accounting Office, 2003). Addressing federal mandates regarding both the delivery of transition services and access to the general education curriculum has been a challenge for secondary education special educators (Lee, Wehmeyer, Palmer, Soukup, & Little, 2008). Conderman and Katsiyannis (2002) conducted a survey of 132 secondary special education teachers in Wisconsin and their results coincided with similar teacher surveys done by Asselin, Todd-Allen, and deFur (1998). Results of their findings indicated that special education teachers carry an ever increasing work load through the addition of multiple roles and responsibilities. In addition to providing direct classroom instruction, teachers listed other time consuming tasks such as writing IEPs and lesson plans, and conducting assessments. According to Benitez et al. (2009) and Knott and Asselin (1999), teachers' level of confidence in providing transition services were found to vary significantly. These surveys of teachers also revealed that those who rated themselves high in their transition knowledge and competencies were found to be most likely to be documenting and implementing transition practices when compared to those who rated themselves lower. Nonetheless, more experience in the teaching field did not result in higher ratings, perhaps because transition mandates, agencies, and paperwork have changed over time. Furthermore, many teachers felt that they lacked the training necessary to be successful in transition plan development and rated their incidences of transition practice implementation as low (Knott & Asselin, 1999). Knott and Asselin (1999) surveyed 217 teachers in Virginia and found that those who gained transition information through attending conferences were most likely to rate themselves as confident in their background knowledge above those who participated in transition related college courses.

Ten years later Benitez et al. (2009) surveyed 557 teachers across 31 states looking for their perceptions of transition knowledge and levels of implementation. Despite a decade to become familiar with transition practices, Benitez et al. showed results similar to Knott and Asselin (1999). Both studies found that teachers of students with mental retardation or multiple disabilities were most likely to feel confident in implementing transition practices compared to teachers of students with learning disabilities. Each study also pointed to teacher apprehension when collaborating with outside service agencies. Despite interagency collaboration being listed as the fourth most important factor in creating successful transitions by teachers, Knott and Asselin found it ranked 25th out of 31 total competencies implemented by those same teachers. Ten years later, out of six domains of transition competency, teachers report collaboration as fifth with regards to levels of preparation and frequency of implementation (Benitez et al., 2009). These two studies, done 10 years apart, present similar findings that suggest improvements in transition may need more than just time.

Based on their research study, Williams-Diehm and Lynch (2007) insist:

> The primary step in creating effective transition planning is to fully educate teachers on the transition process. Teachers must not only hear the legal requirements but also be convinced of its importance in predicting and guiding post-secondary success of the students. Teachers who do not understand transition planning are less effective in ensuring that the students receive the maximum benefits resulting from the transition plan. (p. 8)

Given these needs, it is crucial for educators and other professionals to better understand the individual and program level components that may support effective transition outcomes (Lindstrom et al., 2007). In addition to impacting educational opportunities for students, legislation has increased the involvement of school counselors with students with disabilities (Milsom, 2002).

THEORETICAL FRAMEWORK

The theoretical framework for this study is grounded in the transition planning framework. "Transition planning framework blends multiple standards in a process of continuous, systematic planning and decision making to define and achieve postsecondary goals" (Bassett & Kochhar-Bryant, 2006, p. 9). Transition planning is a student-centered activity that requires a collaborative effort. At Michael J. Hawkins High School, the responsibilities for transition planning needs to be shared by the students, parents, and secondary education personnel, and postsecondary personnel, all of whom are members of the transition team (NJCLD, 1994). "Effective transition planning programs are characterized by the consistent involvement and participation of appropriate individuals" (National Council on Disability, 2000, as cited in Levine, Marder, & Wagner, 2004, p. 2). Creating a transition planning process at Michael J. Hawkins High School is essential in that it allows case managers to follow a systematic and thoughtful process of planning a post-school environment for our students with disabilities. For students with disabilities to grow into adults who can function successfully in society, secondary education educators must provide school services that prepare them for the transition to adulthood (Dowdy et al., 1990; Zigmond, 2006).

Hulett (2007) "described transition planning as the eighth component to the individual education plan (IEP) process and is a requirement for every student's annual IEP" (as cited in Tucker, 2012, p. 25). The transition planning process should be results driven to produce high-quality outcomes for postsecondary living (Miller, Lombard, & Corbey. 2007). "The transition plan must be reviewed annually and a statement of the needs or services must be included in the IEP" (Tucker, 2012, p. 25). During an IEP meeting the team must review the student's courses of study, training, supported employment, integrated employment, adult services, community participation, and independent living skills (Tucker, 2012). In addition, they must look at community agencies that assist with the child and these services are at no cost to the student (Miller et al., 2007). As stated previously, transition planning includes a coordinated set of goals and objectives to meet the transition needs of students with disabilities as they transition into postsecondary life (NJDOE, 2006). The IEP should include vocational education, community living, home and family issues, financial planning, recreation and leisure, mobility, and health issues. The student should be the focus of transition planning by taking into account the desires, talents, interests, and preferences of the child (NJDOE, 2006; Wehman, 2011). Vocational training, postsecondary options, and continuing education opportunities should be included in the transition process (Snell & Brown, 2006).

Transition planning requires that service providers develop and implement plans that describe the services provided, assessment and evaluation measures, obligations of team members, person who are part of the plan, and plausible service agencies (Overton, 2009). Team members include the special educators, general educators, community agencies, student, family members, possible psychologists and counselors, rehabilitation specialists, and other designated individuals who could provide support in the transition planning (Overton, 2009; Wehman, 2011). Additionally, the student and parent should be included in the transition planning process at all stages to secure greater positive outcomes at the postsecondary level (Etscheidt, 2006). Unfortunately, at Michael J. Hawkins High School, parental participation is very poor during IEP meetings and other necessary meetings. According to Tucker (2012):

> The National transition goals, which are outlined in IDEA 2004, include promoting self-determination and self-advocacy, ensuring that students have access to the standards-based curriculum, increasing graduation rates, providing access to full participation in postsecondary education and employment, increasing parent participation, improving collaboration for optimum school, and post-school outcomes, increasing the availability of qualified workforce, and encourages full participation in community life, including social, recreation, and leisure opportunities.
> (p. 29)

METHODOLOGY

Qualitative research is best suited for research problems in which you do not know the variables and need to explore a particular phenomenon (Cresswell, 2009). Data were obtained through interview protocol as we sought to learn from the participants. The participants for this study consisted of eight special education teachers, one school administrator, and three guidance counselors. Interview with participants from a database composed of words. Additional data were gathered through observational protocol, in which the researchers records notes about the behavior of participants. These notes derived from participants at work will become of the qualitative database.

SETTING AND CONTEXT

Michael J. Hawkins High School (MJHHS) is a large urban high school in New Jersey. The city population in the 2010 census was 77, 344. In 2010–2011, over 14,000 students were enrolled in the school district. Based on this school's low socioeconomic status, it receives Federal Title 1 funding and is also an Abbott District school. In 2009, MJHHS had 62% of students eligible for free or reduced price lunch programs while New Jersey overall had 30% of eligible students for free or reduced price lunch programs. Eligibility for the National School Lunch Program is based on family income levels.

Student Ethnicity in 2009 was Black 74%, Hispanic 24%, and White 1%. In 2009, MJHHS had 10 students for every full-time equivalent teacher. The New Jersey average is 12 students per full-time equivalent teacher. The student population is approximately 1,016 with 39% of students classified with a disability. The teaching staff consists of approximately 61 teachers with 14 being special education teachers.

MJHHS is one of New Jersey's "persistently lowest achieving" schools in terms of academic achievement and is a recipient of the NJ School Improvement Grants (SIG). Schools are identified either because of consistently low test scores or graduation rates below 60 percent. As part of the SIG we were required to adopt and implement the Turnaround model. The Turnaround model requires that the district replace the school's principal, unless that principal has been hired in the last two years as part of a reform effort (New Jersey Department of Education, 2011). The Turnaround model also requires schools to extend learning time for students, use student data to inform instruction, and implement strategies such as financial incentives, increased opportunities for promotion and career growth, and more flexible work conditions to recruit and retain high-quality staff. Lastly, the Turnaround model contains an additional requirement to replace no less than 50% of the staff.

FINDINGS

According to Bolman and Deal (2008), understanding the perceptions of an organization's members is critical to implementing change. The methods used to collect faculty and staff perceptions were one-on-one interviews. The researcher received valuable information from the special education teachers, guidance counselors, and school administrators' questionnaires. The responses gave the special education teachers, guidance counselors, and school administrators an opportunity to express their perception regarding the present process for implementing transition services to students with disabilities; how well they believed that their students were prepared for life after high school; and how MJHHS could effectively assist students with disabilities in transitioning from high school to adulthood. We used priori themes and one "justification for using priori themes is that the importance of certain issues in relation to the topic being researched is so well-established that one can safely expect them to arise in the data" (School of Human & Health Sciences, 2007, p. 1). The priori themes identified were: (1) Understanding IDEA and transition services; (2) Curriculum and resources; (3) Students' preparedness for life after high school; and, (4) Effective transition services program at MJHHS.

Understanding IDEA and transition services. Teachers who do not understand transition planning are less effective in ensuring that the students receive the maximum benefits resulting from the transition plan (Williams-Diehm & Lynch, 2007). In regards to the participants' understanding of IDEA as it pertains to transition services, several responses seem to reflect that some special education teachers were aware that transition services were required and were supposed to prepare students for work, college, community, adult life and include the students' interests, goals, strengths, abilities, and skills:

"IDEA is geared towards helping this population as they begin to prepare to leave the world of special education in order to make a successful transition from the context of secondary school to the next phase; either further schooling or work."

"Transition services were to reduce the dropout rate of students with disabilities and plan their desired post school vision. Students express their preferences, interests and vision for their adult life."

"Transitional plan should be implemented at 16 years old. The family, teachers, and other stakeholders (schools, businesses, etc.,) should develop/ implement a plan for student's transition from high school and info the community. The plan should focus on goals and strengths."

"High school students should have a plan for what they will pursue after high school. It is on the IEP and involves career opportunities and skills to earn a living."

"My understanding is that students are to be assisted by school staff to transition into work, or higher education after high school."

One guidance counselor commented:

> The services are to begin at the age of 14, I believe. They are to be exposed to various agencies within the community as well as develop a plan to implement upon graduation. They are to be registered with DVR/DDD.

The Michael J. Hawkins High School child study team (CST) coordinates with the Division of Vocational Rehabilitation Services (DVRS) to ensure that our seniors are in contact with DVRS to make a seamless transition from the CST transition services to DVRS. According to the New Jersey Department of Labor and Workforce Development (2010):

> the goal of the Division of Vocational Rehabilitation Services (DVRS) is to connect with the student while in high school - working with the family, child study team, and guidance counselors to develop a plan for transitioning the student from high school to work. A broad array of individualized services is available to help students achieve their employment goals.

After the student finishes school, DVR services focus on gaining work skills needed to achieve an employment goal and job match, job placement, and follow-up. (p. 1)

Unfortunately, some of the participants were not aware of who was responsible for implementing and monitoring transition services. Subsequently, the teachers that are most effective in helping students with special needs prepare for college are usually the teachers of honors and college prep courses (Conley & Venezia, 2003). The following participants indicated on their questionnaires that they were either unaware of or not familiar with the transition services, IDEA, and transition planning process for special education students:

"I was not aware that special education students were supposed to receive services for transition before leaving high school."

"I am not familiar with the transition process for my students, as the process is handled by the CST/counselor? Not sure."

I am not familiar with our students' IEP and how transition services are documented. I do however have access to student's IEPs, and can therefore read the plans, and educate myself. Though I have been invited to some IEP meetings, I have not been able to attend.

The sole administrator participant commented: "Students with disabilities are eligible for services until age 21. They will be placed in least restrictive environment. Numerous categories of disabilities (i.e., SLD, LD, MCI, MD, ED, ODD)."

According to Katsiyannis et al. (1998, p. 57), the federal government holds state education agencies responsible for the implementation of IDEA, making state educational agencies the catalyst for providing transition services to students with disabilities. If students with learning disabilities are to maximize their chances for postsecondary vocational and educational success, schools and Vocational Rehabilitation agencies must do a better job in transition programming (Dowdy et al., 1990). For students with disabilities to grow into adults who can function successfully in society, secondary educators must provide school services that prepare them for the transition to adulthood (Zigmond, 2006).

Curriculum and resources. It has been argued that one of the reasons for the lack of postsecondary success for students with disabilities is that many high school programs fail to provide adequate services needed to ensure success for these students (Johnson, Stodden, Emanuel, Luecking, & Mack, 2002, as cited in Gillis, 2006, p. 12). Although some teachers provide transition services, it is not universal. The need for all-inclusive transition programming and establishment of personal goals is a critical issue for educators and professionals dealing with students with special needs (Dowdy et al., 1990). Helping students with disabilities to secure post-high employment is the main priority of special education teachers responsible for transitioning these students to adulthood (Eisenman, 2003). The results revealed that the participants did not share or use the same criteria to incorporate transition services into their curriculum. Consequently, according to the following special education teachers' comments, it was quite obvious that there was no transition services curriculum available or authorized by the school district:

"I am an in-class support teacher in various subjects but whenever the opportunity arises I encourage student to take advantage of career day, and also discuss career opportunities and higher education."

> I am a history teacher so it is easy to incorporate I have resume homework, I use currents to explore jobs that can come out of the current news. I discuss dreams and back up plans. I utilize technology in my lessons and researches. I allow outside agencies to present in my class.

> Special education teachers assist their students' not only academically but career awareness. Teachers strive to help their students in academic and career awareness so they can be prepared for everyday life after they complete school. Teaching routine skills such as writing a check or making a grocery list are ways special education teachers are assisting their students succeed after graduation.

> I teach careers in my classroom. This is allowing students to get an idea of what jobs are awaiting them in the world. I teach writing checks, how to dress for success, paying bills, manners, and anything else needed for my students to be successful.

"I use AGS Math program that covers community activities. Also, I often infuse real life stories about my experiences or others. I know that I also give the actual employment test that Forman Mills uses."

Addressing federal mandates regarding both the delivery of transition services and access to the general education curriculum has been a challenge for secondary special educators (Lee et al., 2008). The following responses seem to reflect that either the participants did not incorporate transition services in the classroom, they incorporated them whenever opportunities arose to discuss career opportunities, there were limited resources, or that they do teach life skills and career:

"I teach life skills and careers but limited with the lack of resources provided by the school (learning material, books, etc.)."

"I do not incorporate a lot of transition services after reading this questionnaire but would try to put these ideas in my future lesson plans."

"I do not formally incorporate career awareness and planning, employ-ability skills or foundational knowledge to the students that I come into contact with. I offer suggestions as to career and training opportunities usually through oral discussions."

Two special education teachers shared that the high school impedes their progress to provide transition services by the lack of resources, no curriculum for life skills and careers:

"The lack of resources (technology, learning material, etc.,) as well as partnership with the learning and business community has impeded ideal transitional services."

"No curriculum for life skills or careers."

This is consistent with the findings of Conley and Venezia (2003) and Neumark (2004) who reveal that some special education teachers have noted that a lack of resources inhibited their ability to fully implement career development activities or programs. Dowdy et al. (1990) insist that many students with disabilities desperately need a high school curriculum with a greater emphasis on their transitional needs. According to Bassett and Smith (1996), without special educators' participation, new initiatives, such as transition for students with disabilities, will not move forward successfully, and students will not be afforded opportunities that should be available.

These comments are also supported with the findings by Wasburn-Moses (2006) who argued that too often special education teachers are expected to teach academic skills as well as provide students with the life and vocational skills necessary for selfsufficiency. In reality, it is difficult for special education teachers to coordinate the IEP goals with specific transition classroom activities and address the New Jersey Core Curriculum Content Standards (NJCCCS) at the same. As revealed by Neumark (2004), some schools' staff members have noted that a lack of resources inhibited their ability to fully implement career development activities or programs. Teachers play a major role in helping students prepare for college, yet they do not have the resources they need to give students accurate information (Conley & Venezia, 2003).

A special education teacher commented:

> The classroom/special education teacher does not formally prepare the students with disabilities for life as adult citizens and workers in the 21th century. Our daily schedule does not include any of this preparation. Except, maybe the self-contained classes. Vocational training/skill development may be electives offered as part of the students' class schedule.

Mastropieri (as cited in Wasburn-Moses, 2006) states "that special education teachers are required to work in different settings (e.g., resource room, general education classroom) and tailor instruction to students with a variety of special needs" (p. 21). Until recently, the concept of transition has implied a separate post-school planning process in which students with disabilities worked with special educators to develop transition plans while students without disabilities worked with guidance counselors to develop graduation plans (Bassett & Kochhar-Bryant, 2006). Several guidance counselors shared:

"I am in the process of working with staff, colleagues and child study teams regarding this process: students are provided fair and equal opportunities, but receive accommodations and modifications identified in the Individualized Education Plan/Program."

"Guidance counselors cannot ensure that teachers satisfy this goal. Guidance counselor can, however, meet on a regular basis with each class to assist in developing these skills via classroom guidance lessons."

"I am a first year guidance counselor and have been lead to believe that such evaluation and monitoring is reserved for the special education teachers' supervisors, department chairpersons, and administration."

Williams and Katsiyannis (1998) stated, "A primary implication of the 1997 Amendments to the Individuals with Disabilities Education Act is the need for all educators to share in the responsibility for services provided for all students including those with disabilities" (p. 17). Although legislation encourages greater school counselor involvement with students with disabilities, little research has been conducted to examine the actual roles that school counselors perform for those students (Milsom, 2002).

"The role of the school counselor in the lives of students with disabilities is often not clearly understood, and this ambiguity can lead to role confusion for practicing school counselors" (Marshak, Dandeneau, Prezant, & L'Amorneaux, 2009, p. 6).

"The first problematic view is that the responsibility for addressing the needs of students with disabilities is a matter for the special education department, not the school counselor or school counseling program" (Marshak et al., 2009, p. 6).

"The widespread belief that students with disabilities belong to the special education department further marginalizes them and does not allow them to benefit from the school counselor's expertise or the school counseling programs" (Marshak et al., 2009, p. 6).

The counselor's training and expertise in career development and academic planning will definitely come into play during this time of need. Challenges that school counselors confront range from basic disability awareness to ability to participate in interagency collaboration (Gillis, 2006). Another significant implication for school counselors is administrative support and improved understanding of the professional role of the school counselor in serving students with disabilities (Gillis, 2006). In order to enhance the transition process for students with disabilities, school counselors must familiarize themselves with the following legislative acts: Individuals with Disabilities Act (IDEA); No Child Left Behind (NCLB); Americans with Disabilities Act of 1990 (ADA); and The Rehabilitation Act of 1973 (ASCA, 2010; Naugle, Campbell, & Gray, 2010).

Principals can assume a leadership role by encouraging and establishing links with community agencies, promoting a transdisciplinary approach to the assessment and planning process, assisting in the development of specific policies and procedures relevant to the process, and ensuring that adequate resources are devoted to assessment and planning (Levinson & Palmer, 2005, p. 13). Disappointingly, out of six administrators contacted, only one administrator completed the administrator questionnaire. This administrator appeared fairly knowledgeable of the transition services requirement for students with disabilities (Field Notes, April 12, 2012). She stated that the students were fairly to moderately-prepared to transition from high school to adulthood based on career inventory assessments and IEP exit interviews. She also indicated that the high school implements and monitors transition services through guidance, CST, special services personnel, and teachers. Lastly, she stated that she evaluates and monitors how special education teachers incorporate transition services into the curriculum through monitoring lesson plans, walk-throughs, classroom observations, and conferences with staff.

Administrators must provide staff members with adequate training, access to support personnel, and opportunities for professional development regarding best practices in teaching students with disabilities (Martínez & Humphreys, 2006; Thurlow, 2005). According to Gillis (2006), "Few school districts are preparing their administrators and professional staff to combat the obstacles for students with disabilities and their families" (p. 8). Training for building administrators is often sporadic and lacking in continuity that often results in one or two day workshops on a special education topic. Many principals report that they receive little or no training for supervising special educators (NJCLD, 1994). McLaughlin and Nolet (2004) offered additional implications for school principals who want to foster a collaborative culture in order for students with disabilities to receive appropriate transition services. They suggested the following five things a principal needs to know about special education:

(a) Understand the legal entitlements of special education; (b) understand how to match effective instruction with the learning characteristics of students; (c) understand that special education is a program, not a place; (d) know how to meaningfully include students with disabilities in assessment; and (e) know how to create an inclusive environment in school settings. Even with all of these components in place, principals may continue to face challenges in providing effective transition services for students with disabilities. (as cited in Gillis, 2006, p. 9)

Throughout the transition planning process the building administrator and school counselor play an important role in working with special educators to monitor the implementation of each student's transition plan. According to Levinson and Palmer (2005), principals can promote the importance of staff member attendance and provide input at transition planning meetings.

One special education teacher commented: "Administration should implement an accountability system. Once a proper process is put in place to ensure that students with disabilities are fully prepared to transition at the end of their high school year."

"Additional challenges are presented for school administrators who either do not know or do not have the resources to provide adequate transition services" (Gillis, 2006, p. 8). Stephens and Nieberding (2003, as cited in Gillis, 2006) affirmed the major lack of opportunity for building principals to secure the knowledge and understanding for implementing and sustaining special education programs in their schools. Stephens and Nieberding (2003, as cited in Gillis, 2006),

> suggested the need to accommodate principals by providing them with stipends or scholarships, materials, child care, distance learning, and video conferencing as methods of professional development to compensate for their lack of knowledge and understanding of special education law, implementation of the law, and supervision of special education programs in their buildings. (p. 10)

School administrators are vital members in assuring that students with disabilities are included in as many postsecondary opportunities as their nondisabled peers (Gillis, 2006). School administrators must set a positive and effective climate in the school that is conducive for school faculty and staff to buy into supporting the needs of students with special needs. Based on the lack of administrative support of this study, it substantiates why the students with special needs are not receiving the transition services that they so greatly need.

Students' preparedness for life after high school. After more than two decades of federal transition legislation, students with disabilities continue to have significantly poorer post-school outcomes as compared to their peers without disabilities. One reason for these outcomes is that educators are inadequately prepared to provide the services required under the Individuals with Disabilities Act (IDEA) (Anderson et al., 2003). The questionnaire results revealed that a majority of participants indicated that the students were not prepared for life after high school, but each of the participants had various comments to reflect this finding:

"It is difficult to observe the students with disabilities and monitor their progress to adulthood. The student's IEPs would be the indicator which would reveal that they have any career pans for life after high school."

"Generally, most of the students have to further develop life skills (communication skills, time management, etc.) to be an effective employee. The students also have to be exposed to different careers to develop their goals and career aspirations."

"I think it is difficult based on the weakness of our economy and the lack of hard work ethic."

Most of our students don't have an idea of what they would like to do after high school. Based on my observation many of students are not prepared to enter adulthood. They think that adulthood is having any kind of job so they can buy the latest fashion, car rims, electronic devices and to start a family. They have no idea what all of this entails. Asked about role models, answered NFL players, entertainers and basketball players.

"They do not seem to be knowledgeable about what is need for post-secondary or vocational/career success."

My observations suggest that my students are ill-prepared for adulthood. However, because I live in this city I often see former students. For some of them, the "light" goes on and they are able to find employment and sustain themselves.

A few participants felt that the students were prepared and/or have had the opportunity to be prepared for life after high school. Students with disabilities are given the opportunity as the general population to meet with grade level guidance counselors to plan and discuss career goals. They also have a very supportive Child Study Team that helps prepare them for the next step after high school. Some of my students are focus and are well prepared to transition in to adulthood. The students who are not are the students who have been allowed to cut class run the halls for years. They disturb other classes and become problem in halls and attendance and community. They can be 18 and still not have enough credits to be in the sophomore year. These students are nonproductive due to the lack of administration from being support by the BOE guidelines.

"In the past, students with disabilities were given various opportunities to have outreach services, assistance with assessment with assessment's and services for preparation beyond high school; such as Division of Vocational Services, Counseling Programs, etc."

By conducting classroom guidance sessions I can say which students are ready and which students need more directions. Those students that follow through with our appointments, DVR appointments, job applications, testing appointments, college visits ... are ready. Others are still awaiting someone else to complete and follow through on the task or having really big dreams that at this time are unattainable and need smaller steps to achieve. Without the willingness to take the small steps the ultimate goal will not be achieved.

I have observed that most of the students with disabilities are as prepared and sometimes even more prepared to transition from high school to adulthood than some regular education students. Many of these students appear to take special interest in vocational classes and do well in them.

The administrator participant revealed: "Students were fair to moderately-prepared for life after high school and this is indicated through career inventory assessment and IEP exit interviews."

In contrast, another participant felt:

"It was difficult to observe and monitor students' progress to adulthood." The data analysis also revealed that the study participants (guidance counselors and administrator) who spent the least amount of time with the students in the classroom felt that the students were more prepared for life after high school. Consequently, the majority of the special education teachers spent the most time with the students and felt that the students were not prepared for life after high school.

Effective transition services program at Michael J. Hawkins High School. Many students with disabilities desperately need a high school curriculum with a greater emphasis on their transitional needs (Dowdy et al., 1990). Success in college depends on how effectively high schools prepare students to include opportunities for students to take high level courses that will prepare them for the rigors of college or the workforce (Plucker, Zapf, & Spradlin, 2004). Change must be universal if all high school students are to be prepared for college and the workforce (Plucker et al., 2004). According to Washburn-Moses (2006), "Policymakers and school leaders need to listen to teachers' recommendations when planning for reform" (p. 29). The following special education teachers shared what they felt was needed to improve transition services at Michael J. Hawkins High School:

"More resources availability would be helpful in effectively assisting our students with disabilities in transitioning from high school to adulthood."

"Better resources and tighter relationship with the community to get more stakeholders involved - also exposure to possible career paths."

"Also, parent support group and services so that parents realize the importance of the transition process."

"The district should continue to address as often as possible professional development needs of counselor, teachers and support staff in the area of transitional planning for students with disabilities."

To facilitate educational and vocational planning that will allow a student to make a successful adjustment to work, postsecondary education, and community living. A comprehensive assessment of a student's skills, it is difficult to identify the needs that should be addressed in the student's transition from high school to adulthood.

Students of all ages should be exposed to some type of career education with their everyday subjects so that it is not seen as a separate entity (Benning, Bergt, & Sausaman, 2003). In addition, the following special teachers suggested that Michael J. Hawkins High School provide:

"More hands on activities and field trips to actual work places, interviewing actual workers and having more guest speakers. Transitioning is important because education is useless if it does not have practical applications."

"Mandatory life skills classes."

Middle school students should be provided with a foundation of career awareness and career exploration experiences (Luzzo & MacGregor, 2001). The need for career education at the middle school level is necessary to lay the foundation for future career development and should be embedded into the curriculum (Benning et al., 2003). "IDEA requires that transition planning begin at the earliest age appropriate" (NCSET, 2002, p. 1). Two special education teachers agreed that transition services should begin before a student starts 11th grade:

"Transition services need to start earlier than 11th and 12th grade."

"Begin preparing these students before their junior and senior year to be successful in career, vocation, and post-secondary school life. Special education teachers/in class support should be more involved with the IEP implementation of the students with disabilities."

I think the work that has been done this year with DVR is a step in the right direction. Our students need life coaches that are assigned to them as freshmen. We need to develop closer relationships with businesses such as Wal-Mart, hotels, and motels: positions in which many of our students can actually work and train for advancements.

"IDEA requires that parents and students be involved in all aspects of transition planning and decision-making" (NCSET, 2002, p. 1). Two guidance counselors commented:

"As a school, we need to educate students, parents with services provided. Parents should have workshops, in-services and other services pertaining to opportunities for their child. Brochures, pamphlets and websites would be informational."

Students with disabilities are required to take the same courses as the mainstream population. This is fine for the student with the ability to succeed within an inclusion setting. But for the students with more severe academic issues they need to be allowed to take classes that allow them to learn hands on life skills. They need more ability appropriate shops that they could work through and then transition into a like job. There should be a school store that prepares them to go out into society, where they can learn all aspects and then transition once ready into an actual job.

The administrator participant implied: "Increase exposure to Career Technical Education. Having students take 3 levels of CTE courses, Reading programs, Life Readiness/Social Skills curriculum and meaningful interaction/communication of DVR."

Researchers have found that special education programs do not appear to individualize instruction, curriculum is often watered down or nonexistent, and service delivery models are unfocused and fragmented (Fuchs & Fuchs, 1994; Winzer, 2000, as cited in Gillis, 2006, p. 21). The New Jersey Core Curriculum Content Standards (NJCCCS) Career Education and Consumer, Family, and Life Skills standards identify key skills that students must meet upon graduation to include career awareness and planning, employability skill, critical thinking, self-management, interpersonal communication, character development and ethics, consumer and personal finance, and safety. Unfortunately, many teachers have difficulties meeting the requirements to teach Career Education and Consumer, Family and Life Skills because this is not a core-content subject and has to be taught whenever possible. According to NCSET (2004),

> It is critically important to increase the number of secondary special education teachers who can ably support students with disabilities through the process of transition to adult life. However, few institutions of higher education offer preservice training programs providing specialized emphasis on secondary education and transition services. (p. 15)

The ultimate goal for transition services is to provide practical information and activities to increase the probability of success for the MJHHS students transitioning from high school to adulthood. These services would also provide recommended courses, skills, and academic activities that students should participate in to be successful in high school as well. Alignment of the high school curriculum content with the skills and knowledge students will be expected to know when entering college can help prepare students for success in college or the workplace (Plucker et al., 2004). Students must be involved and engaged in any process regarding their education. This allows them an opportunity to take ownership in their overall education experience. Consider student engagement in the selection and development of reform initiatives (Zapf, Spradlin, & Plucker, 2006).

IMPLICATIONS AND RECOMMENDATIONS

Although the literature, laws, and needs of the students with disabilities point to the necessity of transition planning, many students with disabilities are not receiving it.

Clearly, the implementation of the transition planning process at the Michael J. Hawkins High School was hindered by staff and faculty perceptions and lack of administrative support. The following implications are based on the findings of this study.

Many of the special education teachers, guidance counselors, CST members, and administrators lack the necessary training to implement an effective transition planning process at MJHHS. Due to the lack of training it was difficult to collaborate with all the stakeholders involved in the implementation and monitoring of transition planning. The lack of effective student participation could have also been due to the lack of parental involvement at the IEP meetings. Many parents are unaware of the need of transition planning because they do not attend these meetings, therefore, are not able to ensure that their child participates in transition planning.

The following recommendations for the MJHHS were based on my findings and are needed to ensure that IDEA transition services mandates are implemented from the IEPs to the classrooms for secondary students with disabilities:

1. Provide professional development for special education teachers, guidance counselors, CST, and administrators regarding the implementation and monitoring of transition services and IEPs and incorporating transition services into the school curriculum.
2. Create small learning communities (SLC) to increase awareness and collaboration of all stakeholders involved in the implementation and monitoring of transition services.
3. Provide workshops for parents to increase parental involvement in transition services.
4. Create procedures to monitor and evaluate student overall preparedness for life after high school.

LIMITATIONS OF STUDY

This study was conducted with a limited number of participants. Other variables, such as School Improvement Grant (SIG) initiatives, Regional Achievement Center (RAC) initiatives, perception of special education, constant changing of staff members, faculty and administrators at the

MJHHS, the validity of student answers, assumptions that all respondents answered truthfully, unconscious influences by the researcher—I had previous knowledge and experience working with transition planning, and student mobility between various schools within the school district may have influenced or deterred the implementation of the transition planning process. Additionally, this research study did not include the perception of general education teachers and parents.

Another limitation of this study concerned the relationship of the researcher to the participants. As the researcher, I needed to develop a relationship with the participants where the participants could be candid and frank with me. I overcame this limitation by empowering the participants and building trust with the participants. The participants should not be inhibited by the researcher observing them and questioning them. Patton (2002) recommends a goal-free evaluation, which means that the fieldwork and the data collected for assessment are from a wide range of sources and outcomes. Next, Patton suggests that the researcher compare the collected data and the outcomes with what the participant needs. I followed Patton's suggestion for my study.

Lastly, the fact that I was using action research for my method of inquiry was yet another limitation. The research process is dependent on the practitioner's knowledge and training in transition planning. Therefore, the researcher needed to keep in mind that the study results might prove to be incomplete or invalid. The main criticism of action research is that attempting to do a good deed and find a remedy to a problem, does not necessarily mean that the good act transfers into good social research. Consequently, a practitioner needs to be aware of these issues when using action research (Bloor & Wood, 2006). To counter this limitation, I used a mixed methods approach to collect data.

CONCLUSION

For many high school students with special needs, transition services were not being implemented and monitored as mandated by Individuals with Disabilities Education Act (IDEA), therefore, the probability for a successful transition from high school to adulthood for these students was severely jeopardized. The literature review explored the reasons why a "results-oriented" transition planning process must be developed and implemented to ensure that the Individuals with Disabilities Education Act (IDEA) transition services mandates are implemented from the Individualized Education Plans (IEPs) to the classrooms for secondary education students with disabilities at Michael J. Hawkins High School.

REFERENCES

American School Counselor Association (ASCA). (2010). The professional school counselor and students with special needs position statement. Retrieved from http://asca2timberlakepublishing.com//files/Special%20Needs.pdf

Anderson, D., Kleinhammer-Tramill, P. J., Morningstar, M. E., Lehmann, J., Bassett, D., Kohler, P., ... Wehmeyer, M. (2003). What's happening in personnel preparation in transition? A national survey. *Career Development for Exceptional Individuals, 26*(2), 145–160.

Ankeny, E. M., Wilkins, J., &Spain, J. (2009). Mothers' experiences of transition planning for their children with disabilities. *Teaching Exceptional Children, 41*(6), 28–36.

Asselin, S., Todd-Allen, M., & deFur, S. (1998). Transition coordinators. *Teaching Exceptional Children, 30*, 11–15.

Bakken, J. P., & Obiakor, F. E. (2008). *Transition planning for students with disabilities: What educators and service providers can do.* Springfield, IL: Charles C Thomas.

Bangser, M. (2008). Preparing high school students for successful transitions to postsecondary education and employment. Retrieved from http://www.betterhigh schools.org/docs/ PreparingHSStudentsforTransition_073108.pdf

Bassett, D. S., & Kochhar-Bryant, C. A. (2006). Strategies for aligning standards-based education and transition. *Focus on Exceptional Children, 39*(2), 1–19.

Bassett, D., & Smith, T. E. C. (1996). Transition in an era of reform. *Journal of Learning Disabilities, 29*(2), 161–166.

Benitez, D. T., Morningstar, M. E., & Frey, B. B. (2009). A multistate survey of special education teachers' perceptions of their transition competencies. *Career Development for Exceptional Individuals, 32*(1), 6–16.

Benning, C., Bergt, R., & Sausaman, P. (2003). Improving student awareness of careers through a variety of strategies. Thesis: Action Research Project (ERIC ED481018) Chicago, IL: Saint Xavier University and Skylight Field-based Master's Program. Retrieved from http://www.eric.ed.gov/ERICDocs/data/ericdocs2sql/content storage_01/0000019b/80/1b/6d/93.pdf

Benz, M. R., Lindstrom, L., Unruh, D., & Waintrup, M. (2004). Sustaining secondary transition programs in local schools. *Remedial and Special Education, 25*(1), 39–50.

Blalock, G., Kochhar-Bryant, C. A., Test, D. W., Kohler, P., White, W., Lehmann, J., Bassett, D., & Patton, J. (2003). The need for comprehensive personnel preparation in transition and career development: A position statement of the division on career development and transition. *Career Development for Exceptional Individuals, 26*, 207–226.

Bloor, M., & Wood, F. (2006). *Keywords in qualitative methods: A vocabulary of research concepts.* London, England: SAGE.

Bolman, L., & Deal, T. (2008). *Reframing organizations.* San Francisco, CA: Jossey-Bass.

Boscardin, M. L. (2005). The administrative role in transforming secondary schools to support inclusive evidence-based practices. *American Secondary Education, 33*(3), 21–32

Brooke, V., & McDonough, T. J. (2008) The facts ma'am just the facts: Social security disability benefit programs and work incentives. *Teaching Exceptional Children.* https://doi.org/10.1177/004005990804100107

Brooke, V., Revell, G., & Wehman, P. (2009). Quality indicators for competitive employment outcomes: What special education teachers need to know in transition planning. *Teaching Exceptional Children, 41*(4), 58–66.

Burgstahler, S. E., & Kim-Rupnow, W. S. (2001). Transition from high school to postsecondary education and employment for students with disabilities. Center on Disability Studies Media Center, Phase II Findings Brief #12 (MS#27b (1)-H01).

Carter, E. W., Trainor, A. A., Sun, Y., & Owens, L. (2009). Assessing the transition-related strengths and needs of adolescents with high-incidence disabilities. *Exceptional Children, 76*(1), 74–94.

Clark, G. M. (1996). Transition planning assessment for secondary-level students with learning disabilities. *Journal of Learning Disabilities, 29*(1), 91–92.

Conderman, G., & Katsiyannis, A. (2002). Instructional issues and practices in secondary special education. *Remedial and Special Education, 25*(3), 169–179.

Condon, E., & Callahan, M. (2008). Individualized career planning for students with significant support needs utilizing the discovery and vocational Profile process, cross-agency collaborative funding and social security work incentives. *Journal of Vocational Rehabilitation, 28*, 85–96.

Conley, D., & Venezia, A. (2003, April 21–25). *High school transitions: State of the art and views of the future.* Paper presented at the Annual Meeting of the American Educational Research Association, Chicago, IL. Retrieved from http://www.eric.ed.gov/ERICDocs/data/ericdocs2sql/content_storage_01/0000019 b/80/1 b/1c/26.pdf

Cooney, B. F. (2002). Exploring perspectives on transition of youth with disabilities: Voices of young adults, parents, and professionals. *Mental Retardation, 40*(6), 425–435.

Cresswell, J. W. (2009). *Research design: Qualitative, quantitative, and mixed methods approach.* Thousand Oaks, CA: SAGE.

Cushing, L. S., & Parker-Katz, M. (2012). *Transition for urban youth with disabilities leaving secondary education.* Chicago, IL: Research on Urban Education Policy Initiative, University of Illinois at Chicago.

Deemer, S. A., & Ostrowski, M. (2010). Students' perceptions of a program for exploring postsecondary options. *American Secondary Education, 38*(3), 79–94.

deFur, S. (2003). IEP transition planning—From compliance to quality. *Exceptionality, 11*(2),115-128.

Denison, G. L. (2001, April 19–21). *An active self-determination technique: Involving students in effective career planning.* Paper presented at the Annual Meeting of the Council for Exceptional Children, Kansas City, MO. Retrieved from http://www.eric.ed.gov/ERICDocs/data/ericdocs2sql/content_storage_01/0000019 b/80/19/23/52.pdf

Dowdy, C. A., Carter, J. K., & Smith, T. E. C. (1990). Differences in transitional needs of high school students with and without learning disabilities. *Journal of Learning Disabilities, 23*(6), 343–348.

Eisenman, L. (2003). Theories in practice: School-to-work transitions-for-youth with mild disabilities. *Exceptionality, 11*(2), 89–102.

Federation of Families SC. (n.d.). Transition planning. Retrieved from http://fedfamsc.org/transition-training/middle-to-high-school/

Field. S., & Hoffman. A. (2002). Preparing youth to exercise self-determination: Quality indicators of school environments that promote the acquisition of knowledge, skills and beliefs related to self-determination. *Journal of Disability Policy Studies, 13*, 113–118.

Fuchs, D., & Fuchs, L. S. (1994). Inclusive schools movement and radicalization of special education reform. *Exceptional Children, 60*, 294–309.

Garrison-Wade, D. F. (2012). Listening to their voices: Factors that inhibit or enhance postsecondary outcomes for students with disabilities. *International Journal of Special Education, 27*(2), 1–13.

Gaylord, V., Johnson, D. R., Lehr, C. A., Bremer, C. D., & Hasazi, S. (Eds.). (2004). *Impact: Feature issue on achieving secondary education and transition results for students with disabilities, 16*(3). Minneapolis, MN: University of Minnesota, Institute on Community Integration.

Glomb, N., Lignugaris-Kraft, B., & Menlove, R. R. (2009). The USU mild/moderate distance degree and licensure program: Where we've been and where we're going. Retrieved from http://digitalcommons.usu.edu/cgi/viewcontent.cgi?article=1014&context=sped_facpub

Guy, B., Shin, H., Lee, S.-Y., & Thurlow, M. L. (1999). *State graduation requirements for students with and without disabilities* (Technical Report 24). Minneapolis, MN: University of Minnesota, National Center on Educational Outcomes.

Hoppe, S. E. (2003). Improving transition behavior in students with disabilities using a multimedia personal development: Check and connect. *TechTrends, 48*(6), 43–46.

Hulett, K. (2007). *Legal aspects of special education.* Upper Saddle River, NJ: Pearson Education.

Hurley, D., & Thorp, J. (2002). Decisions without direction: Career guidance and decision-making among American youth. Retrieved from http://ww.ferris.edu/htmls/administration/president/CI/report.pdf

Johnson, D. R., Sharpe, M., & Stodden, R. (2000a). The transition to postsecondary education for students with disabilities. *IMPACT, 13*(1), 2–3. Minneapolis, MN: University of Minnesota, Institute on Community Integration.

Johnson, D. R., Stodden, R. A., Emanuel, E. J., Luecking, R., & Mack, M. (2002). Current challenges facing secondary education and transition services: What research tells us. *Exceptional Children, 68*(4), 519–531.

Johnson, D. R., & Thurlow, M. L. (2003). *A national study on graduation requirements and diploma options* (Technical Report 36). Minneapolis, MN: University of Minnesota, Institute on Community Integration, National Center on Secondary Education and Transition and National Center on Educational Outcomes.

Katsiyannis, A., deFur, S., & Conderman, G. (1998). Transition services—Systems change for youth with disabilities? A review of state practices. *The Journal of Special Education, 32*(1), 55–61.

Knott, L., & Asselin, S. B. (1999). Transition competencies: Perception of secondary special education teachers. *Teacher Education and Special Education, 22*(1), 55–65.

Lee, S. H., Wehmeyer, M. L., Palmer, S. B., Soukup, J. H., & Little, T. D. (2008). Self- determination and access to the general education curriculum. *The Journal of Special Education, 42*, 91–107.

Leone, P., & Garfinkel, L. (2003, May 28). National center on secondary education transition (NCSET). Transcript on Conference Call Presentation at the University of Maryland.

Levine, P., Marder, C., & Wagner, M. (2004). Services and supports for secondary school students with disabilities. A special topic report of findings from the National Longitudinal Transition Study-2 (NLTS2).Retrieved from http://www.nlts2.org/reports/2004_11/nlts2_report_2004_11_ch2.pdf

Levinson, E. M., & Palmer, E. J. (2005). Preparing students with disabilities for schoolto-work transition and postschool life. *School Counseling 101*, 11–15.

Lindstrom, L., Paskey, J., Dickinson, J., Doren B., Zane, C., & Johnson, P. (2007). Voices from the field: Recommended transition strategies for students and school staff. *Journal for Vocational Special Needs Education, 29*(2), 4–15.

Luzzo, D. A., & MacGregor, M. W. (2001). Practice and research in career counseling and development–2000. *The Career Development Quarterly, 50*(2), 60–91.

Marshak, L. E., Dandeneau, C. J., Prezant, F. P., & L'Amorneaux, N. A. (2009). *The school counselor's guide to helping students with disabilities*. San Francisco, CA: Wiley, John & Sons.

Martínez, R. S., & Humphreys, L. A. (2006). The best choice: Choosing effective accommodations for students with disabilities requires administrators, teachers, and parents to work together to evaluate the students' individual needs. Retrieved from http://www.nasponline.org/resources/principals/AcademicAccomodations forStudentsWithDisabilties.pdf

McLaughlin, M. J., & Nolet, V. (2004). *What every principal needs to know about special education*. Thousand Oaks, CA: Corwin Press.

Miller, R., Lombard, R., & Corbey, S. (2007) *Transition assessment, planning transition and IEP development for youth with mild and moderate disabilities*. New York, NY: Pearson Education.

Milsom, A. S. (2002). Students with disabilities: School counselor involvement and preparation. *Professional School Counseling, 5*(5), 331–338.

Mithaug, D. E., Horiuchi, C. N., & Fanning, P. N. (1985). A report on the Colorado statewide follow-up survey of special education students. *Exceptional Children, 51*, 397–404.

Morningstar, M. E., Kim, K., & Clark, G. M. (2008). Evaluating a transition preparation program: Identifying transition competencies of practitioners. *Teacher Evaluation and Special Education, 31*(1), 47–58.

National Association of Special Education Teachers (NASET). (2007). Transition services. Retrieved from http://www.naset.org/transervices4.0.html

National Center for Education Statistics. (2006). *Profile of Undergraduates in U.S. Post Education Institutions: 2003–2004*, U.S. Department of Education, Retrieved from http://nces.ed.gov/fastfacts

National Center on Secondary Education and Transition (NCSET). (2002). Parent brief: Promoting effective parent involvement in secondary education and transition. Retrieved from http://www.ncset.org/publications/viewdesc.asp?id=423

National Center on Secondary Education and Transition (NCSET). (2004). Current challenges facing the future of secondary education and transition services for youth with disabilities in the United States. Retrieved from http://www.ncset.org/publications/discussionpaper/

National Joint Committee on Learning Disabilities. (1994). Secondary to postsecondary education transition planning for students with learning disabilities. Retrieved from http://www.ncd.gov/newsroom/publications/2000/pdf/transition_11-1-00.pdf

Naugle, K., Campbell, T. A., & Gray, N. D. (2010). Post-secondary transition model for students with disabilities. Retrieved from http://files.eric.ed.gov/fulltext/EJ914269.pdf

Neumark, D. (2004). The effects of school-to-career programs on postsecondary enrollment and employment. Retrieved from http://web.ppic.org/content/pubs/report/R_504DNR.pdf

New Jersey Department of Education (NJDOE). (2006). Chapter 14 special education New Jersey administrative code title 6a education. Retrieved from http://www.state.nj.us/education/code/current/title6a/chap14.pdf

New Jersey Department of Education (NJDOE) Special Education. (2010). Program improvement: Transition from school to adult life. Retrieved from http://www.nj.gov/education/specialed/transition/

New Jersey Department of Education (NJDOE). (2011). Christie administration announces up to $55 million in school improvement grant funds to help improve nine low performing schools. Retrieved from http://www.state.nj.us/education/news/2011/0727sig.htm

Overton, T. (2009). *Assessing learners with special needs, an applied approach* (6th ed.). Upper Saddle River, NJ: Pearson Education.

Patton, M. Q. (2002). *Qualitative research and evaluation methods* (3rd ed.). Thousand Oaks, CA: SAGE.

Plucker, J. A., Zapf, J. S., & Spradlin, T. E. (2004). Redesigning high schools to prepare students for the future. Center for Evaluation and Education Policy, *Education Policy Briefs, 2*(6), 1–12.

Policy Information Clearinghouse. (1997). Students with disabilities and high school graduation policies. *Policy Update, 5*(6). Alexandria, VA: National Association of State Boards of Education.

School of Human & Health Sciences, University of Huddersfield. (2007). Themes and codes. Retrieved from http://hhs.hud.ac.uk/w2/research/templateanalysis/technique/themesandcodes.htm

Sitlington, P. L., Neubert, D. A., Begun, W. H., Lombard, R. C., & Leconte, P. J. (2007). *Assess for success* (2nd ed.). Thousand Oaks, CA: Corwin Press.

Smith, T. E., Gartin, B. C., Murdick, N. L., & Hilton, A. (2010). Role of parents, students, and school personnel in transition planning. Retrieved from http://www.education.com/reference/article/role-parents-students-transitionplanning/

Snell, M., & Brown, F. (2006). *Instruction of students with severe disabilities* (6th ed.). Columbus, OH: Pearson Merrill Prentice Hall.

Stodden, R. A., & Dowrick, P. (2000a). The present and future of postsecondary education for adults with disabilities. IMPACT, *13*(1), 4–5. Minneapolis, MN: University of Minnesota, Institute on Community Integration.

Stodden, R. A., & Dowrick, P. (2000b). Postsecondary education and employment of adults with disabilities. *American Rehabilitation, 24*(3).

Test, D. W., Aspel, N. P., & Everson, J. M. (2006). *Transition methods for youth with disabilities.* Upper Saddle River, NJ: Pearson Education.

Thurlow, M. L. (2005). Educating students with disabilities: Do you pass the test? Retrieved from http://www.nasponline.org/resources/principals/nassp_assess.pdf

Tucker, K. J. (2012). A descriptive study of educational professionals' knowledge of transition assessment for individuals with intellectual disabilities. Retrieved from http://repositories.tdl.org/ttu-ir/bitstream/handle/2346/46951/TUCKER DISSERTATION.pdf?sequence=1

U.S. General Accounting Office. (2003, July). *Special education: Federal actions can assist states in improving postsecondary outcomes for youth.* Washington, DC: Author.

Wagner, M., Cameto, R., & Newman, L. (2003). Youth with Disabilities: A changing population. A Report of Findings from the National Longitudinal Transition Study (NLTS) and the National Longitudinal Transition Study-2 (NLTS2).

Wasburn-Moses, L. (2006). Obstacles to program effectiveness in secondary special education. *Preventing School Failure, 50*(3), 21–30.

Wehman, P. (2011). *Essentials of transition planning.* Baltimore, MD: Paul H. Brookes.

Williams, B. T., & Katsiyannis, A. (1998). The 1997 IDEA amendments: Implications for school principals. *NASSP Bulletin, 82*(594), 12–17.

Young, A. (2007). Transition best practice: Who is responsible for preparing our educators to promote transition related best practice? *Journal of Developmental and Physical Disabilities, 19*, 41–50.

Zapf, J., Spradlin, T., & Plucker, J. (2006). Redesigning high schools to prepare students for the future. 2006 update. *Center for Evaluation and Policy, Education Policy Brief, 4*(6), 1–12.

Zigmond, N. (2006). Twenty-four months after high school: Paths taken by youth diagnosed with severe emotional and behavioral disorders. *Journal of Emotional & Behavioral Disorders, 14*(2), 99–107.

CHAPTER 9

JUST THE BATHWATER, NOT THE BABY

Presenting an Alternative Framework to Inclusive Education in the Global South

Maya Kalyanpur
University of San Diego

Working as a special education professional and international consultant in inclusive education to the government Ministry of Education in Cambodia, I met a family with a 12-year-old blind daughter, Phalla, who had never been to school because her parents believed her blindness made her incapable of learning. However, in conversations with her, I noticed that she was bright and eager to learn and, with my Ministry colleagues, began to try to persuade the parents to send her to school. We explained that the Ministry of Education had just developed a collaborative pilot initiative with a local nonprofit agency to enroll students with visual impairments at the local school and provide them with the necessary supports to ensure their academic success in inclusive settings. It was the first such effort in the country—surely the parents would want to avail of such an opportunity! Besides, Phalla had the right to an education. But the parents sounded reluctant. How could Phalla learn

Comprehensive Multicultural Education in the 21st Century:
Increasing Access in the Age of Retrenchment, pp. 173–191
Copyright © 2019 by Information Age Publishing
All rights of reproduction in any form reserved.

anything if she was blind and started to study so much later than her siblings, they asked. They pointed out that, at 12, she would be older than her classmates and would be teased. No, she was useless, they said, she couldn't even help to plant rice!

As we listened to the family, we realized that what the family wanted for Phalla was for her to contribute in some way to the family income. Perhaps there would be good outcomes for her by going to school and being a good student, but there would be better outcomes for both her and her family if she could help to reduce their burden of poverty. And although we believed that Phalla had the right to an education, to this family and community, the group prerogative was more important than her individual right. So, together, this family of rice farmers and the special education professionals set about to develop a modification that would allow her to plant rice. I learned that there are two steps involved in planting rice. In the first step, the seed is sown at random, even thrown in, where Phalla could be involved if she used small sweeps of her hand to keep the seed within the rice bed. But in the second step, the transplanting, each plant must be placed manually in neat rows at equal intervals, a back-breaking task undertaken by women because of their manual dexterity. But if she couldn't see the rows and measure these distances, how could she help to transplant the rice? The device that the group came up with was low-cost and used local materials: two sticks that would be placed by a sibling at two ends of a row and connected by a string that had knots at the same distance at which the shoots should be transplanted. By running her hand along the string, Phalla would know where to place the new shoot; when she came to the end of the row, her sibling would just move the stakes to the next row. The family was delighted with this simple device and, at the end of our visit, even said they might consider enrolling Phalla in the school once the planting season was over!

To me, this anecdote exemplifies the messiness of international development work. My colleagues and I went in hoping we could enroll another student with disabilities in school—a clearly measurable outcome set by international standards that would allow us to assess easily the success of targets met as the numbers of enrolled students with disabilities increased. Instead, we came away with only the assurance that this idea would be considered. And yet, while few donors would be likely to fund a program based on this outcome, we had achieved much more. Rather than focusing on the deficits of the family culture which perceived a blind girl as being incapable of benefitting from an education, we worked with the family to build her potential to be a contributing member of society with economic worth. This change in their perception of her earning potential then allowed them to justify investing in an education for her.

This chapter questions the international aid agenda's assumption that notions of individual rights, inclusion and equality, on which the structure of inclusive education is based, are universally applicable. The intention is not to decry these notions, which indubitably have merit, and throw out the baby, idiomatically speaking, but to consider throwing out just the bathwater of the deficit model by recognizing the value of more nuanced, less Western-centric alternatives and the possibility of local strengths. What does social inclusion and inclusive education mean in developing countries, and to what extent do these understandings align with international standards on inclusive education for children with disabilities? This chapter is organized into three sections. In the first section, it presents the historical context to international inclusive education. In the next sections, it first examines the problematic aspects of assumptions of universality and uncritical applications and then explores some of the research that identifies possibilities for alternative frameworks.

HISTORICAL CONTEXT TO INCLUSIVE EDUCATION

In 2000, the World Education Forum in Dakar, Senegal, set the goal of achieving Education for All (EFA) by 2015 towards including within the educational mainstream all traditionally excluded and marginalized groups, such as girls, poor children, ethnic minorities and children with disabilities. The same year, the World Bank, while presenting the Millennium Development Goals as a means of implementing this goal, argued that disability, being both a cause and a consequence of poverty, needed to be targeted specifically in any development efforts (Braithwaite, Carroll, Mont, & Peffley, 2008).

The goal of EFA must be understood within the larger context of globalization and international development in a postcolonial world. In the assumption that poverty in the newly independent nations could be eliminated if they were developed along the lines of the industrialized countries, the model of economic development that had proved so successful for the latter has become the template for growth (Todaro & Smith, 2011). World nations are ranked along an index of "human development" measuring quality of life that ranges from "very high" to "low human development" (United Nations Development Programs [UNDP], 2010). To enable countries on the low end of the scale to move up, developed countries, consisting mostly of former colonial powers and also known as the global North, contribute monetarily through international development agencies (IDAs) and technically through an international technical assistance network, to recipient developing countries, most of which were former colonies, also known as the global South.

However, several postcolonial critical theorists (e.g., Breidlid, 2011; Cole, 2012; Connell, 2011; Grech, 2011) assert that this structure reproduces old patterns of colonial exploitation in a form of neocolonialism under the veneer of international assistance, what Cole (2012) has called the "white savior industrial complex." The belief that Western scientific knowledge is "the right path to development" and that local cultural beliefs are barriers rather than strengths (Dalal, 2002; Miles, 2002) has created a culture of "policy borrowing" (Mukhopadhyay & Sriprakash, 2011; Nguyen, Elliott, Terlouw, & Pilot, 2009; Pather, 2007; Steiner-Khamsi, 2014) whereby concepts that have emerged from the resource-rich North are being applied within completely different sociopolitical and economic Southern contexts (e.g., UNESCO, 2004). As Breidlid (2013) points out, the heavy dependence of countries in the global South on financial and technical aid from IDAs precludes their ability to "question the educational discourse imposed from the North" (p. 75) while the IDAs themselves continue to perpetuate the hegemonic one-size-fits-all approach, what Goodley (2011) refers to as the "MacDonaldization of education" (p. 144). In the disability and special education field, in particular, an international framework for policies, legislation and service provision has developed, a "geodisability knowledge production" (Campbell, 2015) based on best practice and values that prevail in the North that the global South is expected to adopt (Kalyanpur, 2015; Shakespeare, 2012). These policies and programs include the 1994 Salamanca Statement on Principles, Policy and Practice in Special Needs Education and a Framework for Action to promote inclusive education, the 2008 UN Convention on the Rights of Persons with Disabilities (UNCRPD), community-based rehabilitation and the International Classification of Functioning, Disability and Health (ICF) (for extended analyses, see Goodley, 2011). The mandates identified inclusive education, or the education of children with disabilities with nondisabled students in the same school and classroom settings with appropriate supports to enable them to succeed academically and socially, as the most ethically, financially and pedagogically sound approach towards achieving the EFA goal.

This assumption of so-called universal standards has resulted in a deficit model which focuses on the limitations based on these external parameters and an "epistemological silence" (Grech, 2011) which denies the possibility of alternative frameworks for how disability is perceived. Descriptive analyses of inclusive education systems in countries such Brunei, Zimbabwe, and Vietnam present their implementation as "lagging behind" many European and American contexts (Fitzgerald, 2010). In their analysis of the application of the "international orthodoxy" of inclusive education in Lesotho, Urwick, and Elliott (2010) concluded that despite government and donor support, "the grand inclusion program of the 1990s, fuelled by the rhetoric of human rights, had little chance of taking hold" (p. 146) because it failed to consider its financial implications for the resource-strapped country within the context of a limited pool of trained personnel, limited physical infrastructure, and lack of basic assistive devices for children with disabilities. Similarly, in a study of inclusive education policy and practice in Papua New Guinea, Le Fanu (2013) found that, by failing to tap into teachers' existing ability to respond to the needs of children with disabilities or to engage in an attempt to change parents' reluctance to send their child with disabilities to school and the community's negative perceptions about the employability of people with disabilities, the top-down approach employed by both donors and government left the teachers feeling inadequate about their pedagogical knowledge and led to no change in school enrollment figures for children with disabilities. As Grech (2011) notes, the international standards' prescriptive individualistic, rights-based platform and the resource-rich model of service provision often have little relevance in the collectivist and resource-strapped contexts that prevail in the global South.

Instead, scholars recommend the need for moving away from a perception of deficit and eliciting local perceptions and understandings or "indigenous knowledges" (Breidlid, 2013) by adopting a strengths-based or an assets lens, based on the premise that responses to disability tend to be embedded in or emerge from that specific cultural, historical, political, social, and economic context (Addlakha, 2013; Connell, 2011; Grech, 2011; Rao, 2015). Their argument is that disability is a social construction. Using an assets lens helps identify and acknowledge these nuances rather than bringing in a priori assumptions of who is disabled and what supports they might need in any given context based on parameters established in a universal standard. The definition of inclusive education with the international development framework does not translate easily into contexts that are resource-strapped or more collectivist. As Terzi (2004) points out, labeling students as disabled to provide supports brings a dilemma of difference: does labeling these students truly serve a positive purpose or it is more harmful because of the stigmatizing effect of calling a child disabled? For instance, Korea followed the U.S. policy of requiring labels in order to receive services to find out that parents preferred not to receive services to avoid having their child stigmatized by a label (Kalyanpur & Harry, 2012).

PROBLEMATIC ASPECTS OF ASSUMPTIONS OF UNIVERSALITY

Assuming the universal applicability of the international standards brings an element of a "top-down" approach with the understanding that recipients of monetary assistance follow the IDAs' guidelines specifying how policies are to be developed and programs implemented, narrowing the role of national governments to that of policy borrower (Mukhopadhyay & Sriprakash, 2011; Steiner-Khamsie, 2014). Often, this stipulation is tied in to how the monies are to be spent, which constrains local governments further. In many cases, however, local governments themselves are eager to implement these international standards and best practices, regardless of their applicability to their own circumstances, because they see it as part of the development process in their endeavor to become developed like the global North. Policy borrowing occurs at two levels at least. At the top level, this consists of the expectation that all countries will ratify international legislation, such as the UNCRPD, and national governments enacting legislation and policies that are based almost completely on international standards. The Indian government, for instance, has enacted several laws to reach the EFA goal including the 1995 Persons with Disabilities Act and the 2009 Right to Education Act. At the next level, IDAs support governments to implement programs and practices defined in the international standards. For instance, the Global Partnership for Education (GPE) funded the Cambodian government $57 million over a three-year period to provide programmatic support to the Ministry of Education. The monies were spent largely towards constructing 650 new, wheelchair accessible schools, training teachers and school leaders on current best instructional and administrative practices, and providing need- and merit-based scholarships to students (Kalyanpur, 2014).

In addition to financial support, IDAs also provide technical support whereby experts in the field from the global North, and in most recent years, from more developed countries in the global South, bring their expertise towards this programmatic implementation in less developed countries. The role of the international consultant as facilitator and conduit of expertise is often one of the most problematic aspects of this situation (for an extended analysis, see Kalyanpur, 2014). For one, by the time an instructional strategy or concept developed by an IDA in Geneva or Paris passes through the international and national consultants, and national, provincial and district trainer of trainers before reaching a remote village teacher in, say, Cambodia, it is considerably distorted much like in the game of "telephone" (Kalyanpur, 2011). Consultants often overlook the conceptual meanings embedded in technical terms which may get lost in translation: These distortions can be as petty as the creative respelling of "Down Syndrome" to "donsinraum" to the considerably larger problem of the creation of a disability category classification system that was not grounded in local perceptions of disability (Kalyanpur, 2014) For another, the duration of stay of the international consultants in the beneficiary country varies greatly, from the duration of the project, for example 3 years in the case of the GPE project in Cambodia, to the duration of a specific task such as a week-long teacher training workshop (Kalyanpur, 2014). The latter, often referred to as "the 10-day consultant" is the more numerous, which is not conducive to two-way learning for both consultant and beneficiary. Although all consultants, we must assume, are well-intentioned, the reality of these short stays is that, in addition to the barriers imposed by the assumption of universal applicability, there is little time to investigate and understand local strengths and alternative frameworks. Many come in with the deficit lens, seeing only what the beneficiary country is "not doing," unaware of the deeply embedded values in their professional recommendations. Here we examine some complications that emerge from value differences in certain fundamental concepts of (a) the role of the child, (b) the meaning of community, and (c) the meaning of inclusive education.

The Role of the Child

While the outcome of inclusive education is laudable, we must remember that it emerges from contemporary western sensibilities in countries which benefitted from the inequities of protectionism and colonialism. For instance, child labor was widespread in the early days of industrialism in the west: In the 1820s, about half of cotton textile workers in the US were under 16 and British children were working between 12.5 and 16 hours per day (Chang, 2003). Similarly, the Declaration of the Rights of the Child, sometimes known as the Geneva Declaration of the Rights of the Child, an international document promoting child rights and first proposing the concept of the child as having rights, was adopted by the League of Nations less than a century ago in 1924. Thus, the role of the child as a student evolved over an extended period of time as the countries of the now developed world themselves developed. Even so, access to education was still primarily the bastion of the elite and aristocratic: in Europe, working class children had to pay four pence a week to learn to read, another four pence to learn to write and a further four pence if they wished to learn to add (Moberg, 1951). In the United States, the concept of universal primary education emerged in the mid-19th century from the need to create a common curriculum amidst the competing values of immigrant communities (Bellah, Madsen, Sullivan, Swidler, & Tipton, 2007); rural school calendars aligned with the harvest and planting seasons, so that students could help on the farm and not miss school, while urban schools were open for 11 months so parents could work knowing their children were safe and learning English. In other words, the west had the benefit of several centuries to consolidate its economic status and had less need of child workers at the point when child rights and the child's role as student came into being.

In trying to impose the standards of universal primary education and inclusive education in developing countries, the international aid agenda often tends to ignore this reality of the historical development of today's developed world (Chang, 2003). For instance, in 1956, the newly independent postcolonial Cambodian government quickly adopted UNESCO's recommendation to implement universal primary education; till then, education in the all-French curriculum was accessible only to the elite class which was being groomed for administrative positions in the colonial government (Ayres, 2004). The new government instituted Khmer, the national language as the medium of instruction although the content of the curriculum remained the same, retaining its colonial focus, and kept the original school calendar. As a result, rural children, who constituted the majority of the school-going population, were largely disadvantaged, not only by the fact that the education they received was not relevant to their needs, but also because they were forced to miss school during harvest and planting seasons, causing them to fall behind and eventually drop out—even as recently as 2010, the Cambodian government identified rural school dropout as a seemingly intractable problem (Kalyanpur, 2011).

The perception of the child as a potential earner for the family as opposed to a student continues to impact children's access to education, and even more so for children with disabilities, as we saw in the opening vignette. In a study on school dropout in Cambodia, Robertson (2006) found that parents understood that education was important for children to acquire the basic literacy and numeracy skills; therefore, they were willing to send their children to school up to Grade 3, after which they assumed the children had acquired sufficient skills to navigate their world as adults and could now contribute to the family income. Seeking to learn to what extent the construction of Cambodian children's prosthetic legs, based on Western use and lifestyles, was congruent for their Cambodian lifestyle and uses, Hussain and Sanders (2012) noted that the children often mentioned that having a prosthetic leg meant they could not climb a tree. Their initial thought was that this barrier was related to the children's social integration in that they could not join their friends in play, and later came to the realization that it was, in fact, related directly to their economic integration: in not being able to climb a tree, they could not *work* and lacked income-earning capacity, compounding their isolation.

The Meaning of Community

The women's rights movement, starting with the Seneca Falls women's rights convention in 1848, that occurred concomitantly with the child's rights movement, and the unique individualism that emerged from the homesteader lifestyle during the settlement and acquisition of North American territory (Bellah at al., 2007) has resulted in an American macroculture that is more individualistic than collectivist (Kalyanpur & Harry, 2012). The notion of individual rights is not only imbedded into the American political structure through, for example, the Constitution and the Bill of Rights, but also is part of the cultural capital of every American. Friedman relates the story of a homeless man who, when urged by a policeman to move into a shelter for the night for fear he might freeze to death, refused on grounds that he knew his rights and he had the right to choose where he slept (Friedman, 1990, as cited in Kalyanpur & Harry, 2012). In its more benevolent aspect, rights offer protections to all citizens—protections that can be demanded and enforced. The Civil Rights movement sought redress for all marginalized groups, including children with disabilities; subsequent legislation ensured access to appropriate, individualized education as well as parents' rights to participate in the educational decision-making process. This rights-based platform expects parents to advocate on behalf of their child and expects professionals to respond to parents' advocacy efforts on the basis of the legal framework of rights. However, at its extreme, this embedded knowledge also has created a litigious society. Often parents feel forced to sue school districts to ensure that their child receives appropriate serviced and some school districts have even been found to spend more funds on legal fees than they would have providing the actual service to the child.

The rhetoric of rights has become a major platform of the international aid agenda, with the twin goals of democratization and decentralization (Stiglitz, 2007). However, in the more collectivist social networks in many countries in the global South, this rights agenda does not sit easily. For one, there is little enforcement of legislation. In Cambodia, for instance, despite legislation mandating a quota system for hiring people with disabilities, violations tend to go unpunished (Aide et Action, 2014). While similar legislation in India has increased employment for adults for disabilities, many corporations tend to prefer to pay the fine for being below the requisite hiring quota than actually hire people with disabilities. For another, the collectivist approach creates a hierarchy where the community is considered to be higher than the individual. A study of a self-advocacy group for adults with disabilities in India found that the primary goals of advocacy were less individualistic and more societal, focusing on seeking to change public attitudes to become more accepting and the built environment to become more accessible, with the group's activism being couched in the language of reciprocity and societal responsibility (Kalyanpur, 2009). Similarly, studying the perspectives of Indian parents whose children with disabilities were attending inclusive schools, Kalyanpur and Gowramma (2007) noticed that, despite legislation, parents did not assert themselves, demand services, or claim their rights and that both parents and teachers justified inclusion based on local cultural values of acceptance and cooperation, rather than on rights. In Cambodia, parents of children with severe disabilities spoke about "dhamma" or duty as the impetus for both their efforts to seek services and the professionals' responsibility to provide these services (Ayala Moreira, 2011). By the same token, the Bangladeshi families in East London in Hillier and Rahman's (2002) study felt a sense of parental disempowerment from the "legal flavor" all services for children carry, and worried that their child might be taken away from them because they could be perceived as "not adequate to look after a child." In Rao's study (2015), the Bengali mothers in India appealed to the neighborhood using extended kinship metaphors of aunty and daughter-in-law to create a sense of community and social inclusion for their children with disabilities.

The Meaning of Inclusive Education

One aspect where the dissonance between international and indigenous understandings is perhaps the most significant is in the meaning of the term "inclusive education". Scholars note that while inclusive education in the global North is understood primarily in terms of children with disabilities or students with special educational needs (SEN), in most countries in the global South, it is perceived as the inclusion of all traditionally marginalized children, such as girls, poor children, and children from lower castes (Kalyanpur, 2009; Peters, 2004; Singal, 2006). Further, children with disabilities tend to be the last group included within the educational system (World Health Organization (WHO) & World Bank, 2011), and when children with disabilities are included, it is often in special schools or similarly segregated settings, all of which are considered to be inclusive (Kalyanpur, 2009; Singal, 2006). This is because the movement towards inclusive education in the west emerged from a history of segregation with institutions and special schools that proved to offer inferior quality education, a legacy which is lacking in the global South. Inclusive education in the west was possible because of this heritage of specialized resources particularly with regard to trained personnel, allowing students with disabilities to receive appropriate individualized services within the general education classroom to the maximum extent possible. In the global South, any effort to include children with disabilities within the educational system however segregated is considered inclusive education because this group of children has traditionally been excluded from any schooling at all (Kalyanpur, 2009; Singal, 2006).

There is another paradox that emerges from this dissonance in meaning. Inclusive education in the west has tended to favor students with mild or moderate levels of disability as being the more easily integrated within the general education setting than students with more severe disabilities. These categories include learning disability, behavior disorders and mild intellectual impairment, and are often referred to as "soft categories" because their etiology is subjective and based on teachers' perceptions of what is considered academically or behaviorally unacceptable in a student. These three groups constitute 85% of all students with disabilities, with learning disabilities alone making up over 50%, while conditions with clear medical etiologies like visual or hearing impairments, cerebral palsy, and spina bifida are considered low incidence categories and students may or may not receive an education in an inclusive setting, depending upon the level of severity. In other words, students with more severe needs are more likely to be accommodated in segregated settings. Conversely, in most developing countries, any initiatives to start providing services for children with disabilities inevitably brings to the forefront children with clearly visible impairments, which are usually more severe. Students with relatively invisible conditions like mild intellectual impairments or learning disabilities are unidentified because the process of identification is inextricably tied in to academic performance. Such students would either not be in school at all or have dropped out soon after experiencing school failure. In other words, these categories of disability deemed low incidence in the global North, by virtue of their visibility and/or severity are, in fact, high incidence categories in the global South and the inverse is true of high incidence categories, again because of their low visibility and strong correlation with academic difficulties. As a result, the international standard for inclusive education becomes less effective in situations where large numbers of children continue to be out of school: the children with disabilities who are most identifiable and have the more significant needs because their condition is most visible cannot be accommodated within the parameters of inclusive education because there are insufficient numbers of trained special education teachers and general education teachers to meet these significant needs.

The resource-rich expectations for effective inclusive education can be problematic for resource-strapped countries. To be effective, inclusive education in the global North requires that students with disabilities receive services that are appropriate and individualized to their needs so that they can be academically successful. This can involve implementing instructional strategies that respond to differences in students' learning styles, often referred to as differentiated instruction (UNESCO, 2005). In the United States, legislation mandates each aspect of this service provision, from prescribing the assessment process that would determine the presence of a disability to identifying the various services, known as accommodations and modifications, that the student, now deemed disabled, would need to receive; these services are entered into a legal document, called an individualized education plan. Again, these processes and strategies assume the presence of a corpus of highly trained specialized professionals and small classroom sizes which would allow such individualized attention to each student. In most countries in the global South, there is a limited number, and even a lack of, specialized professionals such as physical, occupational or speech therapists to provide these supplementary services (Kalyanpur, 2016). The expectation that general education teachers, even if trained in differentiated instruction and similar strategies, implement them in classrooms with class sizes of sixty and more students and few, if any, material resources, is also unrealistic.

As we have seen, applying policies and programs that have emerged from environments in the global North to contexts which have very different economic, cultural and social traditions can be problematic and render the transfer less effective. In the next section, we examine some of the alternative frameworks that practitioners or researchers who may be engaging in international work as consultants could consider in their action.

ALTERNATIVE FRAMEWORKS: IMPLICATIONS FOR PROFESSIONALS

The postcolonial context of international aid has continued the imposition of the Western one-size-fits-all epistemologies with rather unfortunate consequences, most significant of which is the subversion of alternative frameworks that might emerge from and therefore be more suited to local contexts (Breidlid, 2013; Stiglitz, 2007; Kalyanpur, 2014). As Breidlid (2013) states, it is increasingly "necessary for indigenous and Western knowledge systems to coexist (and create) a situation where the hegemonic knowledge system talks to the dominated one and acknowledges the urgency of addressing issues that the dominant epistemology seems unable or unwilling to tackle" (p. 47). The existence of indigenous knowledge systems does not suggest a binary divide of modern versus tradition, western versus non-western. The intention, which relates back to the need for care in ensuring that we are throwing out only the bathwater and not the baby as well, is to move away from the hegemony of Western-centric epistemology by eliciting and considering indigenous knowledges and developing alternative frameworks that could combine the best aspects of both traditions. Equally significant is the use of an assets rather than a deficit lens that recognizes the strengths embedded in these local epistemologies. What is at stake is the need to learn about the beliefs and value systems that underlie these alternative explanations for parenting and child development, health and disability, and help-seeking practices. For instance, while the western health belief system separates the corporeal from the spiritual aspects, attributing all causes of ill health to a physical component, most non-Western health or healing traditions perceive the two aspects as intricately linked; differences in beliefs on the causes of specific conditions then impacts the type of treatment or help that is sought. In

Fadiman's (2012) study of the collision of two belief systems, while the American doctors prescribed a regimen of anticonvulsants for a young Hmong girl with a seizure disorder to counteract what they perceived as a neurological condition, the Hmong parents sought the services of a shaman and conducted an animal sacrifice to exorcise the evil spirit which they believed resided in their daughter. As a result of the two knowledge systems remaining disparate, the mother was charged with negligence and her daughter placed in foster care, leading eventually to the young girl's death. This outcome might have been prevented if all the participants had engaged in a dialogue to share their values, recognize the contradictions and work towards a mutually acceptable solution.

This section presents three approaches that have been used successfully in international contexts: the cultural-historical activity theory (CHAT), participatory action research (PAR), and the capabilities approach (CA). All three have built on Freire's (1970) concept of conscientization, through which a catalyst, such as an international consultant, engages in a dialogue with the dominated groups to raise awareness of the inequities of continued postcolonial hegemony, and Bhabha's (1996) theory of cultural hybridity by which the process of conscientization creates a third space that questions entrenched knowledge systems and creates new possibilities.

Botha (2011, as cited in Breidlid, 2013) offered the cultural-historical activity theory (CHAT) as a conceptual framework for using mixed methods to analyze the inherent contradictions in an activity. As

> a tool to mobilize differences between knowledge systems, (CHAT) rep-resents a space where indigenous peoples can name and practice their knowledge-making processes and relate them to Western knowledge.... On a micro level, it implies creating dialogues across traditional barriers and knowledge systems by breaking down the skewed power relationships and redistributing power (opening) up spaces for sustainable change. (Breidlid, 2013, p. 49)

The intention is that researchers or practitioners, such as international consultants, will deliberately and consciously engage in a reflective dialogic process with participants in a shared activity, such as a training workshop, to identify the contradictions in the Western and indigenous knowledge systems to focus on the root causes of the problem and create solutions based on these contradictions. Breidlid provides the example of the application of CHAT in developing a system of interventions for HIV/AIDS in Zambia, involving the governmental education sectors as well as the traditional leadership structure. The traditional leaders' power basis turned them into gate keepers and role models who took on the responsibility to go into communities and openly discuss issues related to sexuality, HIV/AIDS prevention and the need for changing cultural practices.

A similar approach that has also been applied successfully in international contexts is participatory action research (PAR), the purpose of which is "to disrupt the hegemony of positivist social science and academic knowledge over popular knowledge and community participation, (whereby) participants interrogate and transform unjust and unsustainable relations and the social structures in which they are embedded" (Lange, 2009, p. 123). Here, all participants are considered researchers, collectively engaging in a reflective process to create new knowledge including setting the agenda of the inquiry, participating in data collection and analysis and controlling the use of the outcomes (McTaggart, 1997). For instance, by applying PAR, the developers of a critical experiential learning model in a nursing education program in Thailand recognized the importance of incorporating Satipatthana, a Buddhist form of mindfulness, into the curriculum to make it more culturally relevant to local needs (Chuaprapaisilp, 1997).

Emerging from economic theory and philosophy, the capabilities approach (CA) is based on an understanding of functioning, or what is, and capabilities, or what could be, in each human (Sen, 1992; Terzi, 2005). Its basic premises are that (a) the freedom to achieve well-being is of primary moral importance, (b) achieving this well-being must be understood in terms of capabilities or freedoms that people have to do what they aspire to do and be who they want to be, and (c) agency, or what a person can do to realize any these goals, is constrained by the available social, political, and economic opportunities. According to Sen (1992), education is a basic capability with the capacity for expanding further capabilities, incorporating instrumental value, or benefits like career opportunities and better life prospects, as well as intrinsic value, or the possibility to engage and fully participate in social life. CA also acknowledges the intersectionality of disability with other factors, such as gender, or socioeconomic status; for instance, the outcomes of an education for students with disabilities will be different for poor and affluent children, or for boys and girls (Norwich, 2014; Terzi, 2004, 2005). Hammad and Singal (2015) applied CA in their study of the outcomes of education on women with disabilities in Pakistan and found that although high levels of education resulted in increased status for the young women within their family due to their higher earning capacity, it did not increase opportunities for close friendships or improve their marriage prospects. They concluded that while education enhances individual agency, the deeply-held societal prejudices about disability, over which the participants had little or no control constrained the further expansion of their capabilities to attain that significant marker of being a woman in Pakistani society, that of wife and mother.

In the field of international inclusive education, these approaches could be applied to elicit indigenous knowledge by engaging in dialogue with the key stakeholders: people with disabilities and their families whose lived realities in the global South serves to ground and inform services. International consultants need to understand the existence of multiple realities or alternative frameworks, what Super and Harkness (2009) call parental ethnotheories, or parents' belief systems on child development and understanding how children learn, societal expectations and goals for children, and for parenting styles. The child's developmental niche, which is composed of the physical and social environment, culturally-regulated child-rearing practices, and the psychology of the individual caregivers, determines which qualities, most prized within a culture, most children acquire. Comparing parenting practices between Anglo and Bangladeshi families in the United Kingdom, for instance, Brooker (2003) found that the Anglo mothers' view of learning as transmission was less overt and couched in terms of play through games and activities or playacting chores, while the Bangladeshi families' was more overt, with structured sessions for learning Arabic, English, and Bengali through repetition and memorization, and actual chores. On the other hand, Anglo routines were more compartmentalized by strict bedtimes for children, while the Bangladeshi families had more fluid routines for bedtimes and mealtimes. Interestingly, while the Bangladeshis' more overt learning structure prepared their children better for school than the Anglos' less overt play-based learning, the structured routines of the Anglo families was more compatible with school expectations than the Bengali families' fluid routines. The study moves us away from misperceptions of "right" and "wrong" ways of parenting.

Similarly, Kalyanpur and Harry (2012) noted the profound differences that perceptions of independence could have on educational goal-setting in the United States. While Anglo-American professionals might insist on independence, for instance, in terms of self-reliance by living on one's own in a setting removed from the nuclear family, for a young adult with disabilities, parents from culturally diverse backgrounds might emphasize interdependence and the skill of getting along as the more important goal to adulthood, especially if living within an extended family network were the more normative milestone. Within an international context, these differences in parental ethnotheories suggest that international consultants must first identify the values embedded in their own practice and recognize how they differ from that of the families. This stance moves away from the prevailing top-down approach and creates a sense of democratization of stakeholder engagement. In the opening vignette, we recognized that our value of Phalla's right to education was different from Phalla's family's value that she had a duty to contribute economically to the family. Together, we responded to their needs of providing a simple device, a basic accommodation, to allow her to enhance her capabilities.

CONCLUSION

International development in the current context of globalization has
become fraught with underpinnings of neocolonialism whereby a Western-
centric epistemology has been and continues to be imposed on the global
South, silencing local or indigenous knowledges. This has led to a distor-
tion of outcomes far removed from the original intention of policies and
practices. In the field of disability and inclusive education, the implementation of the international standards has yielded similar contradictions and
dilemmas. It behooves researchers or practitioners who may be providing
technical assistance as international consultants to countries in the global
South to be more mindful of the assumptions embedded in their practice and elicit local knowledge. A variety of methodological frameworks,
including cultural-historical activity theory (CHAT), participatory action
research (PAR), and capabilities approach (CA) to understand parental
ethnotheories on disability and inclusive education are available that could
be applied to initiate a dialogue among all participants, between consultant
and recipients, towards creating a new, shared knowledge.

REFERENCES

Addlakha, R. (Ed.). (2013). *Disability studies in India: Global discourses, local realities.*
New Delhi: Routledge.

Aide et Action. (2012). *Identifying barriers to employment of youth with intellectual disabilities in Cambodia: Determining strategies and service provisions for increasing
workforce participation.* Phnom Penh, Cambodia: Author.

Ayala Moreira, R. (2011). *Intellectual disability in rural Cambodia: Cultural perceptions
and families' challenges.* Phnom Penh, Cambodia: New Humanity.

Ayres, D. M. (2004). *Anatomy of a crisis: Education, development and the state in Cambodia, 1953–1998.* Chiang Mai, Thailand: Silkworm Books.

Bellah, R. N., Madsen, R., Sullivan, W. M., Swidler, A., & Tipton, S. M. (2007).
Habits of the heart: Individualism and commitment in American life. New York,
NY: Harper & Row.

Bhabha, H. K. (1996). Culture's in-between. In S. Hall & P. Du Gay (Eds.), *Questions
of cultural identity* (pp. 53-60). London, England: SAGE.

Braithwaite, J., Carroll, R., Mont, D., & Peffley, K. (2008) *Disability and development
in the World Bank: FY2000–2007.* Social Protection & Labor Series paper.
Washington, DC: The World Bank.

Breidlid, A. (2013). *Education, indigenous knowledges and development in the global
South: Contesting knowledges for a sustainable future.* New York, NY: Routledge.

Brooker, L. (2003). Learning how to learn: Parental ethnotheories and young children's preparation for school. *International Journal of Early Years Education,
11*(2), 117–128.

Campbell, F. K. (2015). The terrain of disability law in Sri Lanka: Obstacles and possibilities for change. In S. Rao & M. Kalyanpur (Eds.), *South Asia and Disability Studies: Redefining boundaries and extending horizons* (pp. 76–102) New York, NY: Peter Lang.

Chang, H.-J. (2003). *Kicking away the ladder: Development strategy in historical perspective*. London, England: Anthem Press.

Chuaprapaisilp, A. (1997). Participatory action research: Improving learning from experience in nurse education in Thailand. In R. McTaggart (Ed.), *Participatory action research: International contexts and consequences* (pp. 247–263). Albany, NY: State University of New York Press.

Cole, T. (2012). *The white savior industrial complex. The Atlantic.* Retrieved from http://www.theatlantic.com/international/archive/2012/03/the-white-savior-industrial-complex/254843/

Connell, R. (2011). Southern bodies and disability: Re-thinking concepts. *Third World Quarterly, 32*(8), 1369–1381.

Dalal, A. K. (2002). Disability rehabilitation in a traditional Indian society. Asia Pacific *Disability Rehabilitation Journal, 13*(2), 17–26.

Fadiman, A. (2012). *The spirit catches you and you fall down: A Hmong child, her American doctors, and the collision of two cultures.* New York, NY: Farrar, Straus & Giroux

Fitzgerald, K. W. (2010) Enhancing inclusive educational practices within secondary schools in Brunei. *Journal of the International Association of Special Education, 11*(1), 48–55.

Freire, P. (1970). *Pedagogy of the oppressed.* New York, NY: Bloomsbury

Goodley, D. (2011). *Education: Inclusive disability studies.* In D. Goodley (Ed.), *Disability studies: An interdisciplinary introduction* (pp. 138–156). London, England: SAGE.

Grech, S. (2011). Recolonising debates or perpetuated coloniality? Decentring the spaces of disability, development and community in the global south. *International Journal of Inclusive Education, 15*, 87–100.

Hammad, T., & Singal, N. (2015). Disability, gender and education: Exploring the impact of education on the lives of women with disabilities in Pakistan. In S. Rao & M. Kalyanpur (Eds.), *South Asia and disability studies: Redefining boundaries and extending horizons* (pp. 197–223). New York, NY: Peter Lang.

Hillier, S., & Rahman, S. (2002). Childhood development and behavioral and emotional problems as perceived by Bangladeshi parents in East London. In S. Hillier & D. Kelleher (Eds.), *Researching cultural differences in health* (pp. 38–68). London, England: Routledge.

Kalyanpur, M. (2009) Cultural variations on the construct of self-advocacy in the context of India. In M. Alur & V. Timmons (Eds.), *Crossing boundaries and sharing ideas: Inclusion education* (pp. 331–341). Thousand Oaks, CA: SAGE.

Hussain, S., & Sanders E. B.-N. (2012). Fusion of horizons: Co-designing with Cambodian children who have prosthetic legs, using generative design tools. *CoDesign, 8*(1), 43–79.

Kalyanpur, M. (2011). Paradigm and paradox: Education for All and the inclusion of children with disabilities in Cambodia. *International Journal of Inclusive Education,* doi:10.1080/13603116.2011.555069

Kalyanpur, M. (2014). Distortions and dichotomies in inclusive education for children with disabilities in Cambodia in the context of globalization and international development. *International Journal of Disability, Development and Education, 61*(1), 80–94. doi:10.1080/1034912X.2014.878546

Kalyanpur, M. (2015). Mind the gap: The evolution of special education policy and practice in India in the context of globalization. In S. Rao & M. Kalyanpur (Eds.), *South Asia and disability studies: Redefining boundaries and extending horizons* (pp. 49–72). New York, NY: Peter Lang.

Kalyanpur, M. (2016). Inclusive education policies and practices in the context of international development: Lessons from Cambodia. *Journal of International Education Research and Development Education, 39*(6), 16–21.

Kalyanpur, M., & Gowramma, I. P. (2007). Cultural barriers to South Indian families' access to services and educational goals for their children with disabilities. *Journal of the International Association of Special Education, 8*(1), 69–82.

Kalyanpur, M., & Harry, B. (2012). *Cultural reciprocity in special education: Building reciprocal family-professional relationships.* Baltimore, MD: Brookes.

Lange, E. A. (2009). Reconceptualizing participatory action research for sustainability education. In D. Kapoor & S. Jordan (Eds.), *Education, participatory action research, and social change: International perspectives* (pp. 123–136). New York, NY: Palgrave Macmillan.

Le Fanu, G. (2013). The inclusion of inclusive education in international development: Lessons from Papua New Guinea. *International Journal of Educational Development, 33*, 139–148. http://dx.doi.org/10.1016/j.ijedudev.2012.03.006

McTaggart, R. (Ed.). (1997). *Participatory action research: International contexts and consequences.* Albany, NY: State University of New York Press.

Miles, M. (2002). Community and individual responses to disablement in South Asian histories: Old traditions, new myths? *Asia Pacific Disability Rehabilitation Journal, 13*, 1–16.

Moberg, V. (1951). *The emigrants.* New York, NY: Simon & Schuster.

Mukhopadhyay, R., & Sriprakash, A. (2011). Global frameworks, local contingencies: policy translations and education development in India. *Compare: A Journal of Comparative and International Education, 41*(3), 311–326.

Nguyen, M., Elliott, J., Terlouw, C., & Pilot, A. (2009) Neocolonialism in education: Cooperative learning, Western pedagogy in an Asian context. *Comparative Education, 45*(1), 109–130

Norwich, B. (2014). How does the capability approach address current issues in special educational needs, disability and inclusive education field? *Journal of Research in Special Educational Needs, 14*(1), 16–21. doi:10.1111/1471-3802.12012

Pather, S. (2007) Demystifying inclusion: implications for sustainable inclusive practice. *International Journal of Inclusive Education 11*(5), 627–643.

Peters, S. (2004). *Inclusive education: An EFA strategy for all children.* Washington, DC: World Bank.

Rao, S. (2015). Just a member of the neighborhood: Bengali mothers' efforts to facilitate inclusion for their children with disabilities within local communities. In S. Rao & M. Kalyanpur (Eds.), *South Asia and disability studies: Redefining boundaries and extending horizons* (pp. 229–251) New York, NY: Peter Lang.

Robertson, K. (2006). *Why grade 3? A study on primary school dropout in Kampot province, Cambodia*. Phnom Penh, Cambodia: Voluntary Service Overseas.

Sen, A. (1992). *Inequality reexamined*. Oxford, England: Clarendon Press.

Shakespeare, T. (2012). Disability in developing countries. In N. Watson, A. Roulstone, & C. Thomas (Eds.), *Routledge handbook of disability studies* (pp. 271–284). London, England: Routledge.

Singal, N. (2006). Inclusive education in India: International concept, national interpretation. *International Journal of Disability, Development and Education, 53*(3), 351–369.

Steiner-Khamsi, G. (2014). Cross-national policy borrowing: Understanding reception and translation. *Asia Pacific Journal of Education, 34*(2), 153–167. doi:10.1080/02188791.2013.875649

Stiglitz, J. E. (2007). *Making globalization work*. New York, NY: W.W. Norton & Co.

Super, C. M., & Harkness, S. (2009). Culture and infancy. In G. Bremner & T. D. Wachs (Eds.), *Blackwell handbook of infant development* (pp. 182–191). Oxford, England: Blackwell.

Terzi, L. (2004). The social model of disability: A philosophical critique. *Journal of Applied Philosophy, 21*(2), 141–157.

Terzi L. (2005). Beyond the dilemma of difference: The Capability Approach to disability and special educational needs. *Journal of Philosophy of Education, 39*(3), 443–459.

Todaro. M. P., & Smith, S. C. (2011). *Economic development* (11th ed.). Edinburgh, Scotland: Pearson.

United Nations Development Programs [UNDP]. (2011). *Human development report 2011: Sustainability and equity: A better future for all*. New York, NY: Palgrave Macmillan.

UNESCO. (2004). *Changing teaching practices: Using curriculum differentiation to respond to students' diversity*. Paris, France: Author.

Urwick, J., & Elliott, J. (2010). International orthodoxy versus national realities: Inclusive schooling of children with disabilities in Lesotho. *Comparative Education, 46*(2), 137–150.

World Health Organization (WHO) & World Bank. (2011). *World report on disability*. Washington, DC: Author.

CHAPTER 10

ENGAGING BIRACIAL STUDENTS IN HOLISTIC LEARNING SPACES WITH A GENDERED PERSPECTIVE

Ashley N. Patterson
The Pennsylvania State University

James L. Moore III
The Ohio State University

Scholars, thought leaders, and practitioners of multicultural education implore the American educational system to fulfill its responsibility of meeting the needs of all its students. Generally speaking, multicultural education offers a critical teaching framework for engaging and instructing diverse students who are often pushed to the margins by mainstream, negative classifications of race and racial identity. Across the nation, many cultural meanings exist in school systems, based on identify markers that often deny students access to "equal opportunities to learn" (Banks, 2010, p. 3). Students are "othered," according to their socioeconomic status, language usage, abilities, gender, sexuality, citizenship status and their race,

Comprehensive Multicultural Education in the 21st Century:
Increasing Access in the Age of Retrenchment, pp. 193–213
Copyright © 2019 by Information Age Publishing

and as Banks (2010) explains, this othering is repeatedly a by-product of the oppressive characteristics of U.S. social institutions (e.g., schools) that are systematically retained for the advantage of some and disadvantage of others.

Race has long been recognized as a social construct, based on individuals' apparent physical traits, but it remains one of the most pervasive but conspicuous identity markers to denote difference in the nation. As a result, multicultural education scholars frequently concern themselves with how educators translate this difference into deficit school practices (Banks & Banks, 2010). In society at large, phenotypic traits, such as skin color and hair texture, tend to yield heavy reliance on the ways that people mark racial differences. Whether consciously or unconsciously learned, these traits are not easily hidden during face-to-face interactions with others, but are vivid and distinguishing characteristics (Spickard, 1992), which is one reason the salience of race has endured. Another reason is that race continues to be socially constructed as an integral and necessary component of American society (Omi & Winant, 1994; Mills, 1997). The social history of race in this country is largely built upon dubious conceptions of *Blackness* and *Whiteness*, specifically related to the two being antithetical to one another. The often oversimplified, binary nature in which race is presented minimizes the visibility of students who can or do claim allegiance at once to both racial identities, Blackness and Whiteness. To date, the needs and perceptions of Black-White biracial[1] students are included only sparingly within the multicultural education literature (e.g., Cortés, 1999; Ford, Whiting, & Goings, 2016; Harris, 2002; Root, 2004; Dutro, Kazemi, & Balf, 2005). Additional examination of educational issues affecting this group of students should be undertaken in order to truly interrogate the marginalization of those who are othered.

Within the cultural framework of America, race is a significant marker of identity that people use to uphold the social-political system that empowers some and opresses others (hooks, 2004). It is also an important variable used to measure social outcomes. Yet, there is considerable ambiguousness about race and its significance (Wilson, 1996). Race alone does not adequately describe, depict, explain, and predict the complexity of one's identity. Instead, it often presents an inaccurate or incomplete representation of the person—absent of other important identity constructs, such as gender. Andersen and Collins (2004) acknowledged the close linkage of race and other variables. In particular, intersectionality theory (Crenshaw, 1989) recognizes the interplay of race and gender. Many problems frequently occur when individuals fail to recognize how the two variables intersect. In the case of biracial males, it is critical that multicultural educators understand "the stereotyped ascription of compounded personal and group traits onto an individual perceived to be a member of a forbidding and alien "other' (e.g., threatening Black men)" (Johnson & Rivera, 2015). Although space limitations do not allow full coverage of the topic, popular and scientific literature on intersectionality highlights the interplay of *race* and *gender* and how the two variables work together.

In this chapter, we explore both the challenges and opportunities associated with creating holistic learning spaces for biracial students across racial and gender lines. While the importance of considering race among the threads that weave together an educational setting has long been established, the specific consideration of biracial students within these contexts has often been ignored or either conflated with or presented in opposition to their monoracial peers. Using an intersectional lens that considers the important ways in which gender plays a role in perceptions of and interactions with biracial students, we consider implications of educators' dispositions and approaches and classroom practices that have the potential to recognize biracial students as whole beings made up of physical, psychological, cognitive, and spiritual components, capable of academic and social success. We begin by providing a working definition of holistic learning spaces and a description of the context within which we situate our commentary before articulating approaches that we believe serve as foundation for holistic learning spaces attune to the needs of biracial students.

A holistic approach to including biracial students in a learning space demands they are considered in their entirety, as multifaceted and complex individual human beings. The term holistic means "characterized by comprehension of the parts of something as intimately interconnected and explicable only by reference to the whole" (Holistic, 2015). The caveat that the parts can only be referenced in relationship to the whole is paramount; in application, the phrase "holistic learning space" emphasizes an environment within which an individual is recognized and engaged as a complete, whole person, and not a sum of one's many parts. For biracial individuals, the establishment of such an environment can lead to achievement of Patterson's (2013) interpretation of wholeness as "the ability to feel comfortable in your skin regardless of your surroundings because your true, complete self is active" (p. 149).

Education scholars, including Palmer (1983/1993), Miller (1996), Miller (2000) and Kessler (2000), have outlined the importance of holistic education, building upon the foundational understanding that "healthy human development requires emotional security and the ongoing experience of feeling valued by and connected to others" (Koegel, 2003, p. 11). The basis of a holistic pedagogical approach includes seeing each learner as a unique individual and fostering knowledge of self as a gateway for enhancing additional avenues of learning. Mayes, Cutri, Rogers and Montero (2007) discuss a holistic approach to multicultural education in particular. The authors insisted that all students be recognized as whole beings, comprising their various physical, psychosocial, cognitive, ethical, and spiritual components. Furthermore, the authors indicate the importance of bridging understandings of identity and pedagogy, explaining that educators should both "honor the fact that every student is a complex person" and "design their curricula and instruction accordingly" (p. 4).

Addressing one part of the educational context (e.g., the self-understandings of those who share the space) without considering the other (e.g., the academic content students interact with in the space) does not provide a complete understanding of the context and, thus, cannot prepare practitioners to create holistically engaging learning spaces. As we continue, we are guided by an understanding that, in order for educational spaces to effectively engage biracial students in a holistic manner, they should both recognize the wholeness of students and be rich in academic content.

HISTORICAL CONTEXT OF SIGNIFICANCE

The 2000 United States Census marked the first time that Americans were able to identify themselves as belonging to more than one race. Since that time, the number of Americans choosing to racially identify in this way has notably increased. While the Census reported 6.8 million residents who identified as belonging to two or more races in 2000, in 2010, 9 million people identified in this way, making it the largest growing racial subpopulation (Jones & Bullock, 2012). Considering individuals identifying their two races as White and Black specifically, this group grew by over a million at a rate of 137%, constituting the largest and fastest growing disaggregated group within the two or more races category and totaling 1.8 million (Jones & Bullock, 2012). In predicting the growth of the school-age component of the "two or more races" subpopulation, the National Center for Education Statistics (NCES, 2016) estimates the group will experience a growth rate of 34% between 2012 and 2025.

Though the steady increase of the Hispanic student population has garnered significant media and academic attention (e.g., Carreira & Beeman, 2014; Cohn, 2016; Gándara & Contreras, 2010; Klein, 2015; Sáenz & Ponjuan, 2011; Vega & Moore, 2016), NCES predicts its growth in the same time frame at 21%. As the number of mixed-race school-age children continues to increase, the multicultural education field will need to provide educational practitioners with more and nuanced insight into working with this population. In spite of the rapidly changing U.S. classroom landscape, there remains little educationally-based academic work focused around issues pertaining to the multiracial student population in particular. Educators and educational researchers alike must engage in the work now that will prepare holistic learning spaces for students entering them in the near future. Before we move forward with suggestions for how to do so, we provide contextual information for the importance of considering the needs of mixed race students and Black-White biracial students in particular both at the macro-historical and micro-individual levels.

Contestations concerning the humanity of Black people in the U.S. have been in place since they were brought to this country and enslaved by White Americans who colonized these lands. Kant (1775/1997), Hegel (1822/1997) and Hume (1885) are among respected intellectuals of the time who provided "data" that served as "scientific" explanation of the Black person's inferiority. Though the biological foundation of race has long been disputed, the fact that it is socially constructed and impacts our daily lives in any given number of ways allows the concept to live on as a reality (West, 1993/2001; Mills, 1997). In the United States, the social construction of race is tied to the politics of being Black or White, identities that are placed at opposite ends of a dichotomy. A twofold function of these racial politics dictates that, one, White people do not have to claim a race and, two, anyone deemed non-White is required to make such a claim.

The history of biracial individuals in the United States is intertwined with the one drop rule. This application of the concept of hypodescent automatically associates persons with mixed racial ancestry with the category of the race enjoying the least cultural or sociopolitical capital (Spickard, 1992). The "one drop rule" phrasing references the colloquialism, "It only takes one drop of Black blood to make someone Black." This rule has been played out on America's legal and social stages over the past three centuries (see Virginia's Racial Integrity Act of 1924 [Wolfe, 2015] or the ruling in the 1983 *Susie Guillory Phipps vs. the State of Louisiana* [Jaynes, 1982] case for such examples) and continues to carry weight though it is no longer a legally sanctioned order. The origins of the one drop rule were fueled by efforts of Whites to oppress and disenfranchise Blacks (Spickard, 1992). Many of the first biracial Americans were born as a result of the rapes of enslaved mistresses by their enslavers. A maintenance of the system of slavery required White fathers to be released from legal and social responsibility for these offspring and, as a result, the children were racially categorized along with their enslaved Black mothers. The socially dominant narrative that biracial children simply could not be successfully absorbed into the White world was thus born. This narrative served to reinforce the ideology behind the rule of hypodescent and the common image of the "tragic mulatto," the biracial individual that will be equally unable to find solace in her White heritage or in her Black background (Hickman, 1997).

The fairly recently emerged multiracial movement pushes back against some of these ideals that have characterized the United States' biracial population for centuries now. After the 1967 ruling in the *Loving vs. Virginia US*

Supreme Court case established the federal legalization of interracial mar-riage, families of multiracial children and multiracial individuals began to organize in a grassroots manner, forming support groups and more formal nonprofit organizations throughout the country as early as the late 1970s and continuing into the early 1990s (Wardle, 2013). Many of the concerns focused on the day-to-day well-being of multiracial families and children, but some agendas featured political goals such as the revision of the U.S. Census to allow for either a multiracial or a "check all that apply" racial option on the document (Douglass, 2003). The check all that apply option prevailed and was introduced on the 2000 U.S. Census.

Within the movement, a universal consensus as to whether a collective multiracial identity is an attainable or desirable goal has not been estab-lished (Douglass, 2003), and it has also experienced opposition from those outside of the movement (Wardle, 2013). What cannot be argued, however, is that the population of people living in America who chose to identify in this way is both sizeable and growing. As the biracial or multiracial popula-tion continues to grow and define itself, Black-White biracial individuals remain an important part of the national conversation, constituting the largest combination of two or more races on the 2000 and 2010 U.S. Cen-suses (Jones & Bullock, 2012). A juxtaposition of the continued prevalence of individuals in the nation with one Black and one White parent to the lack of academic literature dedicated to the needs of this population sup-ports the topic and objectives of this chapter. In addition to establishing historical context, it is important to consider the implications of this work at the individual level.

INDIVIDUAL CONTEXT OF SIGNIFICANCE

Identity development is a vital part of the individual growth process and a set of experiences that are especially vivid for young people. Given the racialized nature of U.S. society, racial identity is a necessary component of a holistic identity development process. While studies have shown that some biracial individuals adopt a monoracial Black identity (Khanna & Johnson, 2010; Renn, 2004; Rockquemore & Brunsma, 2002), this is not true of other biracial persons. Regardless of the accuracy of the supposi-tion, however, many biracial individuals are regularly assumed to be among the Black community by those, including educators, with whom they inter-act on an everyday basis. In order for biracial persons to be holistically engaged in educational contexts, their identities—as they are conceived by the individual—should be acknowledged and sustained. How one sees himself or herself typically affects an individual's life in innumerable ways, including the ways he or she navigates the many facets of the world of education. It is worth noting that, self-understanding also impacts social interactions with peers and adults, interpretation of school curricula, and educators' willingness to take risks in a learning setting.

Patterson's (2015) study considered the educational experiences of biracial individuals, across PK–12 to higher education settings. Data culled from a larger study are used to support for the approaches offered in the following section. The qualitative narratives analyzed were gathered from 12 memoirs published by biracial individuals and over 50 YouTube videos posted by individuals who identified themselves as having one Black parent and one White parent. Applying a thematic analysis (Braun & Clarke, 2006), Patterson identified four broad thematic findings, which were used to characterize the experiences of the study's informants, including individual relationships with biraciality both influence and are influenced by the specific educational contexts within which those relationships develop; specific aspects of the learning space itself (e.g., teachers and curricula) are influential components of how biracial students engage in the educational context; peers with whom the learning space is shared are also influential components of engagement; and the nature of the relationship between the home context and the school context is another influential component of the ways biracial individuals conceptualize each space and their places within them.

In the second phase of the study, Patterson (2015) interviewed eight biracial higher education students with whom she shared the thematic findings from the first phase. The participants responded with input about the degree to which the conclusions drawn in the first phase of the study matched their own experiences. In both study phases, informants recounted experiences illustrating ways in which their schooling were not holistically engaging. For instance, Christine (this and all interview participant names are pseudonyms), a college student at a small, private Midwestern institution, recalled a classroom within which a science professor listed her among a group of brown items in an effort to guide students toward identifying the relationship between light waves and color (personal communication, February 4, 2016). The student felt a momentary sense of disbelief as she processed the casualness with which the professor dehumanized and objectified her in front of a classroom of peers. Another informant, Derrick, remembered an elementary school experience in which he shared with his class that his grandmother had been a childhood friend of Anne Frank before the Holocaust. His teacher responded by sternly demanding that he "stop lying," the indication being that a student she perceived to be Black could not have familial relations to a European Jew (personal communication, February 17, 2016). Though his pride may have been salved when he brought in a copy of a documentary featuring his grandmother to prove his story the next day, the broken trust was beyond remedy. A number of other stories similar to those of the aforementioned informants make a strong case for educators to purposefully create learning spaces that allow for the holistic engagement of biracial students.

Though neither of these experiences were explicitly tied to notions of gender, a closer look reveals the way race and gender can work together to create a doubly binding oppression. The fracturing of Christine's self in terms of race was obvious as she was reduced to the status of an object because of her skin color. Coupled with the fact that the comment listing her among objects considered to be desirable and stimulating (e.g., coffee and cocoa) came from a male instructor as she sat in a course within a male-dominated STEM field, the educational space was unwelcoming for Christine both in terms of her race *and* her gender. The quickness with which Derrick's teacher dismissed his contribution as a lie is referential of the archetype ascribed to Black males as untrustworthy individuals.

Effective educational settings allow for individuals to learn how to navigate the world around them and how to be successful within it. Some of the lessons that yield these understandings are explicit and intentionally taught, others are subtle, and absorbed subconsciously. One premise of this chapter is to move fellow educators closer to the goal of establishing educational classrooms that foster the most enriching and engaging learning experiences for all students, regardless of the differences that they bring to our classrooms. Through the provision of an approach that focuses the interests of biracial individuals in a holistic manner, it is likely that this chapter can pave the way both for researchers to inquire empirically about the topic and for educational practitioners to consider and later make intentional decisions about the learning spaces that they co-occupy and co-create alongside biracial students.

SUGGESTIONS FOR NEW APPROACH

Before we offer our suggestions for approaches to be undertaken, we first acknowledge that classrooms of any level and of any composition are complex, complicated spaces. We do not argue that adopting these approaches alone would be the singular catalyst for holistic engagement of biracial students within learning spaces. Rather, we offer these approaches as a starting place, meaning the implementation of these suggestions should be a part of a larger process of ensuring educational spaces have a social justice foundation and a process that spans beyond the classroom and into policy spheres. As Ball and Tyson (2011) note, the conversation about teaching from a multicultural education standpoint should begin somewhere, and this chapter is an example of such a location. They further suggest that knowledge be tied to educational practice and that connections be made between teacher training and the classrooms these teachers establish and maintain. The authors also emphasized that educators need skills for working with marginalized students and that the voices of marginalized students must be included in the work that serves to inform educational practitioners. With this in mind, multicultural teacher training should encourage preservice and in-service teachers to abandon their habitual ways of thinking (Senge, Scharmer, Jaworski & Flowers, 2004) by changing the ways they automatically or subconsciously think about members of marginalized groups (Ball & Tyson, 2011). With this guidance in mind, we offer the following approaches to be taken up by educational practitioners who seek to establish holistic learning spaces with biracial students in mind. We also offer approaches that biracial students can take up in those spaces (see Table 10.1).

Table 10.1.
Suggestions for Engaging Biracial Students in Educational Spaces

Suggestions for Educational Practitioners	Suggestions for Biracial Students
1. Help to build of a "safer space" in which one's racial identity is neither questioned nor assigned.	1. Participate in dialogue.
2. Establish as component of that safer space an invitation to engage open, honest questioning, and discussion where dialogue is required.	2. Engage in reflection.
3. Be deliberate in choosing academic content that is reflective of student's identities.	3. Question images and experiences that do not suggest one's wholeness as an individual.
4. Be hyper aware of behaviors that may influence biracial individuals to think of themselves as "naturally" or "necessarily" challenged.	4. Own your right to evolve.
5. Raise consciousness of differences in a way that does not work to label the student as abnormal without making assumptions.	5. Consider your micro- and macro-contexts
6. Develop skills for identifying and intervening upon subtle acts of aggression or isolation.	
7. Acknowledge the power of perception.	
8. Remember that everything does not have to be about race, but it is important to be aware of its social effects.	

Source: Adapted from Patterson (2015).

SUGGESTIONS FOR EDUCATIONAL PRACTITIONERS

1. Help to Build of a "Safer Space" in Which One's Racial Identity Is Neither Questioned Nor Assigned

The term *safe space* is used to connote a number of different things in K–12 educational contexts. It is important to acknowledge that creating a classroom learning environment that is absolutely and universally safe for all students is a challenge and that opportunities for improvement are always possible. Thus, educational vulnerability cannot be altogether averted; any time students are called upon to share or display a piece of themselves, a degree of vulnerability is necessarily involved in the process. A safer space, however, allows biracial students to feel supported in taking these risks that ultimately result in individual and collective growth. This is not to say that critical discussions on identity should not be had in classrooms, rather the insistence is with the fact that individuals be provided autonomy in naming themselves racially and that their choices be deemed legitimate on a de facto basis.

The freedom to racially self-name is a part of the healthy development process of biracial students (Renn, 2004; Rockquemore & Brunsma, 2002). The actual terms used to name oneself are far less important than the ways in which the self-naming process is received. Scott Minerbrook (1996) noted the appreciation that he felt, when he entered a learning space that embraced and encouraged the autonomy of his self-naming: "Boarding school was the first place that had ever given me that option—of how I wanted to identify myself and who I wanted to be my friends" (p. 161). Without the pressures of an environment that constrained his self-understanding, Minerbrook was able to interpret his growth opportunities as unlimited. In contrast, CelestialBeautyFly (2013) remembered in a YouTube post a situation in an elementary classroom that stunted her identity growth and left her to feel as if she was being pathologized.

As a part of the classroom activity, students were invited to stand up to indicate their race as it was called by the teacher. In an attempt to accurately represent herself in what she saw as a "very logical" manner, CelestialBeautyFly (2013) stood up both when White was called and when Black was called. In response, the teacher asked, "Honey, don't you know what you are?" CelestialBeautyFly recalled the anger and confusion of her internal reaction to the teacher's comment: "Like that's supposed to be funny? Like I was having some kind of identity crisis?" A safer learning space would have embraced CelestialBeautyFly's identity choice instead of causing her to think that it required intervention.

2. Establish as Component of That Safer Space an Invitation to Engage Open, Honest Questioning and Discussion Where Dialogue Is Required

A safe classroom space allows biracial students the freedom to try out new ways of understanding themselves and the world around them, with room to change, when ready. Psychosocial growth is achieved through self-exploration, and the classroom provides a rich opportunity composed of multiple viewpoints within which to do so. As for requiring dialogue, social interaction comes in a variety of forms—sometimes in the form of vocalized speech, sometimes in the form of silence, but always through some level of connection with others (Kinloch & San Pedro, 2014)—all of which should be respected and considered legitimate. Hence, students and educators should be encouraged to interact with each other and with their own thoughts but in a setting that encourages honest sharing with understanding as the goal. Reflecting on a classroom experience in which these had not been the goals of the interaction, Devin Hughes (2012) noted, "It would have been different if the atmosphere in the room was one of curiosity, but the air was thick with judgment" (p. 45). An interrogation of difficult topics is an important means for expanding consciousness and biracial individuals should be provided the space to both contribute to and benefit from such conversations.

3. Be Deliberate in Choosing Academic Content That Is Reflective of Students' Identities

Multicultural scholars have long heralded the importance of students being able to see themselves reflected in the curriculum (Banks & Banks, 2010; Ford, 2011; Ford, Moore, & Harmon, 2005). This holds for biracial students as well. In some instances, this may involve including topics around biraciality in the classroom discussion (e.g., Dutro, Kazemi, & Balf, 2005). It may also include providing students the opportunities to interact with topics related to each of their racial heritages. Mark Whitaker (2011) relished in the curriculum to which he was exposed once enrolling in boarding school. He explained:

> At George School, for the first time in my life, I was reflecting on my racial identity ... I was reading *Native Son*, by Richard Wright, and James Baldwin's *Go Tell It on the Mountain*, with their bracing portraits of what it was like to be black in places like the South Side of Chicago and Harlem. Although written in a previous generation, they raised powerful questions about whether any black American, of any shade or upbringing, could be untouched by racism, conscious or unconscious. (p. 161)

Access to this information about his Black heritage that was previously unknown to him opened the doors for Whitaker to explore his own identity. As holistic education scholars argue, students themselves should also serve as sites of meaning-making (Miller, 2000). In a similar instance, informant Derrick found the opportunity to write a paper elucidating upon his perception of his parent's social lives in a high school sociology class to be "a really positive experience" and "the first time that [he] talked about what was important to [him]" in an educational setting. Regardless of the embraced identity, students should have ongoing opportunities to engage meaningful classroom content as a part of their school curriculum.

4. Be Hyper Aware of Behaviors That May Influence Biracial Individuals to Think of Themselves as "Naturally" or "Necessarily" Challenged

This goal can be accomplished in a number of ways. Education practitioners can foster movement toward this objective by providing positive examples of biracial individuals, including topics related to biraciality in the curriculum and incorporating biraciality within the umbrella term of *diversity*; and engaging in self-reflection about one's thoughts and beliefs about race. It is also important to note that biracial students retain a lot of the agency necessary to achieving this goal. Though there is little doubt that some biracial students experience school challenges related to their racial identity as many youth of many racial backgrounds do, it is vital that an assessment of such challenges not be blindly assigned to student members of this group. With this in mind, we have been mindful and deliberate to address room for growth within learning spaces instead of presenting biracial students as requiring intervention.

5. Raise Consciousness of Differences in a Way That Does Not Work to Label Them as Abnormal

Though the specific composition of the classroom's diversity is typically outside of the control of the educator, diversity always exists in some form. It is important that, when highlighted, instructors do not make a spectacle of the differences present in the classroom in a way that makes some differences appear to be assigned a more positive value than others. While it is a natural human instinct to want to categorize things, biracial individuals defy categorization in a number of ways. By encouraging open dialogue and sharing, educators may avoid what may otherwise feel like a necessity to make assumptions about how a biracial student feels, how that student self-identifies or what that student wants to come out of a particular situation.

6. Develop Skills for Identifying and Intervening Upon Subtle Acts of Aggression or Isolation

Increasingly, tools for combating bullying in school are more widely emphasized and focused upon (e.g. American Educational Research Association, 2013; Smith, 2014; Schott & Sondergaard, 2014). Many of Patterson's (2015) informants recalled situations in which the incidents that made them feel uncomfortable at school were subtle and were often either not observed or not interrupted by school professionals. These types of negative interactions must be afforded the same attention as more easily observed incidents as their impactful influence can be much clearer than the incidents themselves are salient. Remembering her high school years, ladycthebeauty (2013) said, "I just didn't have a good high school experience when it comes to feeling accepted by my peers." Outside of three close friends, ladycthebeauty remembers girls being mean to her. Cafeteria times were especially difficult as she explained:

> I remember, you know, getting my lunch and everything and then I'm coming out of the line and I'm looking across the cafeteria and girls are just, like, mad doggin', you know. Basically just giving me body language that they don't want nothing to do with me. I remember that happening a lot in high school. So, I wasn't necessarily teased, I was just not invited.

Though she was not being physically or verbally intimidated, and she reiterated at the end of her statement that she "wasn't necessarily teased," these regular cafeteria experiences (and any other similar experiences the details of which she did not share) were enough to cause ladycthebeauty to characterize her overall high school experience as one lacking acceptance by her peers. In another illustration of an absence of teasing that ultimately results in feelings of ridicule, Tiffany Jones (2014) described an uncomfortable classroom experience. For example, she states,

> This is where White people do this thing in a way when they don't necessarily tease you for something, but you can definitely end up feeling ashamed. So, definitely when my friend was reading out loud in history class from the book and read "the River nigger" instead of "the River Niger," that stands out as a time I was embarrassed.

Though Tiffany Jones specifically characterizes the example she provides as *not* being an example of teasing, she notes that it results in feelings of embarrassment as overt teasing often does. In a holistic learning space, it becomes the responsibility of the educator to look out for and to mediate such troubling situations.

7. Acknowledge the Power of Perception

An individual's perception is that individual's reality. This fact surfaced in several informants' comments. For example, Scott Minerbrook (1996) remembered his elementary school teacher by stating:

> Mrs. Rosen never stopped shouting. That was how she controlled us. But it seemed to me that she spoke differently when she talked to the white students, and this made me dislike her even more than I disliked Mrs. Daniloff. (p. 99)

It seemed to Minerbrook that the teacher exhibited preferential treatment to White students over Black students. As this perception later constituted his truth, he began to dislike her even more than another teacher of whom he was not fond. In an example of perceived positivity in interpreting an adult's actions, Mark Whitaker (2011) remembered attending a school with a Black Portuguese principal. He recalled, "Mr. Holbert always winked and smiled when he saw me in the hallway, and I took it as a secret signal that we had a special bond and that he was looking out for me" (p. 107). Whitaker did not mention having had any special introduction to his principal or having any connection to him outside of the educational setting. The only connection he made obvious was their shared racial otherness, hence the "special bond" he referred to was likely their racial similarity. Consequentially, this point of connection influenced his perception that Mr. Holbert was sending him a "secret signal" of support and acceptance in his winks and smiles.

As an educator, acknowledging the power of perception may mean that students' speech or actions are understood in a manner contrary to one's intentions. While educators may not have the opportunity to directly alter a student's perception, they always have the ability to alter their own speech and actions so that these communication modes are better aligned with intent. A major part of this process may include critical self-reflection on the part of the educational practitioner.

8. Remember That Everything Does Not Have To Be About Race, But It Is Important To Be Aware of Its Social Effects

There are a number of identity factors at play at all times. Students' racial identity markers are not always forwarded. For instance, students may feel most closely connected to their gender or language identities depending on the situation at hand. Each encounter with biracial students requires its own separate assessment to determine if race is playing a fore grounded role in the exchange or if it is affecting the situation in a less obvious manner.

SUGGESTIONS FOR BIRACIAL STUDENTS

1. Participate in Dialogue

We do not mean to suggest here that biracial students take on a burdensome responsibility of educating peers and adults about all things biracial, but we do encourage an embrace of the fact that each unique individual has a perspective to share and if she chooses not to, it will not be heard. Thus, this urging applies to academic conversations and social situations alike.

2. Engage in Reflection

Taking time to think about and to examine experiences can be a fruitful process. Paying close attention to the feelings aroused by certain situations as they happen can provide rich information as the situation is revisited at a later time with a goal of understanding it differently or more completely. It can also be helpful to think of one's experiences in relation to other local happenings and national or even global events. As Phillip noted, taking time out during his middle school years to be alone with his thoughts "laid the foundation for the deep introspection and reflection about society and where [he] fit in" (Jones, 2009). As a result, Phillip came to "consider [himself] a deep and thoughtful person about these issues," though he expressed skepticism as to whether he would have that self-image if he had not deliberately engaged in reflective practice. The reflection process may help some experiences and/or perceptions be more clearly understood and may help to identify others as requiring additional follow-up so that clarity can be achieved.

3. Question Images and Experiences That Do Not Suggest One's Wholeness as an Individual

Notions about biraciality like that of the tragic mulatto/a are still at work in our society in some subtle and some obvious ways. If biracial students encounter situations that challenge their self-understanding or otherwise result in unease, and, even if the origin of the unease is elusive, it is important to take a moment to interrogate the details of the circumstance at play.

Doing so may develop resistance against situations that may otherwise go unnoticed or unchallenged.

4. Own Your Right to Evolve

Changing the ways we think about ourselves and the world are natural parts of growth as human beings. Identity is a fluid entity, and it is also very personal. While outside influences certainly impact self-understanding, ultimately, only the individual can think for herself or himself. For example, Christine's racial self-identity went largely unchallenged during enrollment in diverse K–12 schools and, as a result, she rarely considered its implications. Upon attending a college where approximately 92% of her peers are White, Christine felt compelled by interactions with peers and faculty to examine her racial self-understanding, an ongoing process. She noted, "More recently, I find pride in both my races, but I'm still trying to figure out how to respond to that" (personal communication, February 4, 2016). Though reaching a clear and conclusive end may be an elusive component of the personal evolutionary process, it is important to understand that how one thinks about and projects oneself to the world can—and are allowed to—change with time.

5. Consider Your Micro- and Macro-Contexts

Though input from others does not necessarily have to change one's own understandings, it is important to be apprised of the multitude of viewpoints that are available. Though they a crucial part of one's life and experiences, those with whom one has close proximal contact—parents, siblings, family, teachers, peers—represent only a portion of the perspectives there are to be had. It may be helpful to engage with texts and other information-sharing forums (e.g., social media, affinity groups, internet sources, published texts, narrative literature) in order to develop a more globalized picture of how others conceptualize their biraciality and how these understandings affect their school experiences.

CONCLUSION

The approaches offered here help to position biracial students as agents in their own educational experiences. While teachers are saddled with a great deal of responsibility for creating and maintaining a classroom culture that is conducive to holistic engagement, a classroom would not a classroom be without the students that populate it. Thus, the students themselves must also take active responsibility for the nature of the contexts within which they learn. Many of the educational practitioner-directed texts currently available focus on the duties of the teacher, rarely mentioning the role of the students in the process other than the implied response to educate the teacher about their needs. Rather, each of our offered approaches upholds a holistic engagement focus, and in doing so, necessarily places students at the classroom's core.

Creating holistic learning spaces involves considering each student in the classroom as a united conglomerate of all of the characteristics that result in their individuality without reducing them to a collection of disconnected features (e.g., race, socioeconomic status, gender, sexuality, ability, home language, etc.). This viewpoint is closely aligned with a culturally sustaining pedagogical approach (Paris, 2012) by which a pluralistic educational setting that endorses the importance of a multitude of cultures and ways of knowing is sought. For such an environment to be realized, each of its members must actively engage in the process of learning oneself so that all can learn from one another. This goal can be facilitated if those who share a learning space are each welcomed in their wholeness. Such an environment effects the comfort that can nurture individual growth as well as academic pursuits.

This work adds a specific perspective to the multicultural education conversation. Additionally, the lens of this contribution is novel. By explicitly linking the topic of biraciality to educational spaces, this chapter is moving toward an approach to understanding the experiences of biracial individuals that has not yet been established within the field. The viewpoint offered here provides concrete, applicable, actionable next steps. The suggestions are not overly theoretical or overly general, but rather conceptualized for the purpose of practicality and grounded in input from biracial students. The heart of any educational space is its students; students themselves should be the continued focus as educational practitioners envision and create learning environments that holistically meet their needs and foster their growth.

NOTE

1. We use *biracial* as a term noting the race of individuals with one Black-identified and one White-identified parent. Further, we use this term for the purpose of signifying the group of individuals we are referencing in this chapter, with acknowledgement that not all who could be classified as such would choose the same racial title for themselves. We also use the term *biraciality* throughout this chapter to indicate the plethora of identities related to one's biracial status. Akin to recognition that *blackness* cannot be utilized as a universal descriptor of the self-understanding of every Black

individual, biraciality is used to indicate the identity of a broad group, but with recognition that individuals within that group embody the meaning of the term in varied ways.

REFERENCES

American Educational Research Association (AERA) (2013). *Prevention of bullying in schools, colleges, and universities: Research report and recommendations*. Washington, DC: American Educational Research Association.

Andersen, M. L., & Hill, C. P. (2004). *Race, class, and gender: An anthology*. Belmont, CA: Wadsworth/Thomson Learning.

Ball, A. F., & Tyson, C. A. (2011). Preparing teachers for diversity in the twenty-first century. In A. F. Ball & C. A. Tyson (Eds.), *Studying diversity in teacher education* (pp. 399–416). Lanham, MD: Rowman & Littlefield.

Banks, J. A. (2010). Multicultural education: Characteristics and goals. In A. Banks & C. A. M. Banks (Eds.), *Multicultural education: Issues and perspectives* (7th ed., pp. 3–32). New York, NY: John Wiley & Sons.

Banks, J. A., & Banks, C. A. M. (Eds.). (2010). *Multicultural education: Issues and perspectives* (7th ed.). New York, NY: John Wiley & Sons.

Braun, V., & Clarke, V. (2006). Using thematic analysis in psychology. *Qualitative Research in Psychology, 3*(2), 77–101.

Carreira, M. M., & Beeman, T. (2014). *Voces: Latino students on life in the United States*. Santa Barbara, CA: ABC-CLIO.

CelestialBeautyFly. (2013, March 11). Mixed girl tag part 1 [Video file]. Retrieved from https://www.youtube.com/watch?v=zEmegeWfjJE

Cohn, D. (2016). It's official: Minority babies are the majority among the nation's infants, but only just. *Pew Research Center*. Retrieved from: http://www.pewresearch.org/fact-tank/2016/06/23/its-official-minority-babies-are-the-majority-among-the-nations-infants-but-only-just/

Cortés, C. (1999). Mixed-race children: Building bridges to new identities. *Reaching Today's Youth: The Community Circle of Caring Journal, 3*(2), 28–31.

Crenshaw, K. W. (1989). Demarginalizing the intersection of race and sex: A black feminist critique of antidiscrimination doctrine, feminist theory, and antiracist politics. In J. James & T. D. Sharpley-Whiting (Eds.), *The Black feminist reader* (pp. 208–238). Malden, MA: Wiley Blackwell.

Douglass, R. (2003). The evolution of the multiracial movement. In M. P. P. Root & M. Kelley (Eds.), *Multiracial child resource book: Living complex realities* (pp. 14–16). Seattle, WA: MAVIN Foundation.

Dutro, E., Kazemi, E., & Balf, R. (2005). The aftermath of 'you're only half': Multiracial identities in the literacy classroom. *Language Arts, 83*(2), 96–106.

Ford, D. Y. (2011). *Multicultural gifted education* (2nd ed.). Waco, TX: Prufrock Press.

Ford, D. Y., Moore, J. L., III, & Harmon, D. A. (2005). Integrating multicultural and gifted education: A curricular framework. *Theory Into Practice, 44*, 125–137.

Ford, D. Y., Whiting, G. W., & Goings, R. B. (2016). Biracial and multicultural gifted students: Looking for a grain of rice in a box of sand. In J. L. Davis & J. L. Moore III (Eds.), *Gifted children of color around the world: Diverse needs, exemplary practices and directions for the future* (pp. 121–135). Bingley, England: Emerald Group Publishing Limited.

Gándara, P., & Contreras, F. (2010). *The Latino educational crisis: The consequences of failed social policies*. Cambridge, MA: Harvard University Press.

Harris, H. L. (2002). School counselors' perceptions of biracial children: A pilot study. *Professional School Counseling, 6*(2), 120–129.

Hegel, G. W. F. (1997). Geographical bases of world history. In E. C. Eze (Ed.), *Race and the enlightenment: A reader* (pp. 109–149). Cambridge, MA: Blackwell. (original work published 1822)

Hickman, C. (1997). The devil and the one drop rule: Racial categories, African Americans and the U.S. Census. *Michigan Law Review, 95*(5), 1161–1265.

Holistic. (2015). In *Oxford Dictionaries*. Retrieved from http://www.oxforddictionaries.com/us/definition/american_english/holistic

hooks, b. (2004). *The will to change: Men, masculinity, and love*. New York, NY: Simon & Schuster.

Hughes, D. C. (2012). *Contrast: A biracial man's journey to desegregate his past*. Highland Park, IL: Writers of the Round Table Press.

Hume, D. (2014). Of national characters. In E. F. Miller (Ed.), *Essays moral, political and literary* (Vol. 1). Indianapolis, IN: Liberty Fund, Inc. (Original work published 1885). Retrieved from http://www.econlib.org/library/LFBooks/Hume/hmMPL21.html

Jaynes, G. (1982, September 30). Suit on race recalls lines drawn under slavery. *The New York Times*. Retrieved from: https://www.nytimes.com/1982/09/30/us/suit-on-race-recalls-lines-drawn-under-slavery.html

Johnson, R. G., & Rivera, M. A. (2015). Intersectionality, stereotypes of African American men, and readdressing bias in the public affairs classroom. *Journal of Public Affairs Education, 21*(4), 511–522.

Jones, N. A., & Bullock, J. (2012). *The two or more races population: 2010*. Retrieved from http://www.census.gov/prod/cen2010/briefs/c2010br-13.pdf

Jones, T. [mulattodiaries]. (2009, August 16). Mulatto diaries #107 Phillip interview. [Video file]. Retrieved from https://www.youtube.com/watch?v=N6PymmviDRY&index=18&list=UUWpOb7OTotlAR0-FSgkpUeg

Jones, T. [mulattodiaries]. (2014, February 10). The mixed girl tag [Video file]. Retrieved from https://www.youtube.com/watch?v=TC11SSdfxwQ&list=UUWpOb7OTotlAR0-FSgkpUeg

Kant, I. (1997). On the different races of man. In E. C. Eze (Ed.), *Race and the enlightenment: A reader* (pp. 38–48). Cambridge, MA: Blackwell. (Original work published 1775)

Kessler, R. (2000). *The soul of education: Helping students find connection, compassion and character at school*. Alexandria, VA: Association for Supervision and Curriculum Development.

Khanna, N., & Johnson, C. (2010). Passing as black: Racial identity work among biracial Americans. *Social Psychology Quarterly, 73*(4), 380–397.

Kinloch, V., & San Pedro, T. (2014). The space between listening and story-ing: Foundations for Projects in Humanization (PiH). In D. Paris & M.T. Winn (Eds.), *Humanizing research: Decolonizing qualitative inquiry with youth and communities* (pp. 21–42). Thousand Oaks, CA: SAGE.

Klein, I. (2015). In 10 years, America's classrooms are going to be much more diverse than they are now. *The Huffington Post*. Retrieved from: http://www.huffingtonpost.com/2015/05/07/classroom-demographics-2025_n_7175760.html

Koegel, R. (2003). The heart of holistic education: A reconstructed dialogue between Ron Miller and Rob Keogel. *ENCOUNTER: Education for Meaning and Social Justice, 16*(2), 11–18.

ladycthebeauty. (2013, August 11). Mixed girl tag [Video file]. Retrieved from https://www.youtube.com/watch?v=D8bN_9Hu6QM

Mayes, C., Cutri, R. M., Rogers, P. C., & Montero, F. (2007). *Understanding the whole student: Holistic multicultural education*. Blue Ridge Summit, PA: Rowman & Littlefield Education.

Miller, J. (1996). *The holistic curriculum*. Toronto: OISE Press.

Miller, R. (2000). *Caring for new life: Essays on holistic education*. Brandon, VT: Foundation for Educational Renewal.

Mills, C. W. (1997). *The racial contract*. Ithica, NY: Cornell University Press.

Minerbrook, S. (1996). *Divided to the vein: A journey into race and family*. New York, NY: Houghton Mifflin Harcourt.

National Center for Educational Statistics. (2016). *Enrollment and percentage distribution of enrollment in public elementary and secondary schools, by race/ethnicity and region: Selected years, fall 1995 through fall 2025*. [Data table]. Retrieved from http://nces.ed.gov/programs/digest/d15/tables/dt15_203.50.asp

Omi, M., & Winant, H. (1994). *Racial Formation in the United States: From the 1960s to the 1990s*. New York, NY: Routledge.

Palmer, P. (1993). *To know as we are known: Education as a spiritual journey*. San Francisco, CA: Harper San Francisco. (Originally published in 1983)

Paris, D. (2012). Culturally sustaining pedagogy: A needed change in stance, terminology, and practice. *Educational Researcher, 41*(3), 93–97.

Patterson, A. N. (2013). Can one ever be wholly whole?: Fostering biracial identity founded in spirit. In C. B. Dillard & C. L. Okpaloaka (Eds.), *Engaging culture, race and spirituality: New visions*, (pp. 144–166). New York, NY: Peter Lang.

Patterson, A. N. (2015). *Exploring experience, influence and personal truths: Biraciality and educational spaces* (Doctoral dissertation). Retrieved from ProQuest. (3710339)

Renn, K. A. (2004). *Mixed race students in college: The ecology of race, identity and community on campus*. Albany, NY: State University of New York Press.

Rockquemore, K. A. & Brunsma, D. L. (2002). *Beyond Black: Biracial identity in America*. Thousand Oaks, CA: SAGE.

Root, Maria P. P. (2004). Multiracial families and children: Implications for education research and practice. In J. A. Banks & C. A. M. Banks (Eds.), *Handbook of research on multicultural education* (2nd ed., pp. 110–126). San Francisco, CA: Jossey-Bass.

Sáenz, V. B., & Ponjuan, L. (2011). *Men of color: Ensuring the academic success of Latino males in higher education*. Institute for Higher Education Policy. Retrieved from http://www.ihep.org/sites/default/files/uploads/docs/pubs/brief_men_of_color_latinos.pdf

Schott, R. M., & Sondergaard, D. M. (2014). *School bullying: New theories in context*. New York, NY: Oxford University Press.

Senge, P., Scharmer, C. O., Jaworski, J., & Flowers, B. S. (2004). *Presence*. New York, NY: Doubleday.

Smith, P. K. (2014). *Understanding school bullying: Its nature and prevention strategies*. Thousand Oaks, CA: SAGE.

Spickard, P. R. (1992). The illogic of American racial categories. In M. P. P. Root (Ed.), *Racially mixed people in America* (pp. 12–23). Thousand Oaks, CA: SAGE.

Vega, D., & Moore, J. L., III. (2016). Where are all the Latino males in gifted programs? In J. L. Davis & J. L. Moore III (Eds.), *Gifted children of color around the world: Diverse needs, exemplary practices and directions for the future* (pp. 87–103). Bingley, England: Emerald Group Publishing Limited.

Wardle, F. (2103). *Pushback of the pushback (critiquing the recent attacks on the multiracial movement and multiracial people)*. Retrieved from http://csbchome.org/?p=45

West, C. (1993/2001). *Race matters*. Boston, NA: Beacon Press.

Whitaker, M. (2011). *My long trip home: A family memoir*. New York, NY: Simon & Schuster.

Wilson, W. J. (1996). *When work disappears: The world of the new urban poor*. New York, NY: Alfred A. Knopf.

Wolfe, B. Racial Integrity Laws (1924–1930). (2015, November 4). In *Encyclopedia Virginia*. Retrieved from http://www.EncyclopediaVirginia.org/Racial_Integrity_Laws_of_the_1920s.

CHAPTER 11

LAW AND DISORDER

Classroom Management, Discipline, and the Promise of Multicultural Education

Brandi N. Hinnant-Crawford
Western Carolina University

C. Spencer Platt
University of South Carolina

Dorian Wingard
Western Carolina University

"I am the law-and-order candidate," President Trump declared during his acceptance speech at the Republican National Convention (Nunberg, 2016, para. 1). "Law and order" is a term that has been used by politicians for years, and it is one that begs two questions: Who is enforcing the law, and who needs order? Historians and political writers have reported that President Trump was recycling Richard Nixon's playbook, and that "law and order" is coded language. Azari (2016) for instance, explained law and order could be defined as "disdain for those who question tradition

Comprehensive Multicultural Education in the 21st Century:
Increasing Access in the Age of Retrenchment, pp. 215–236
Copyright © 2019 by Information Age Publishing
All rights of reproduction in any form reserved.

215

and support for the use of force to keep order" (para. 10). Nunberg (2016) argued that Trump's cry for law and order was to create the perception of a new crisis, and that it "weaves together assaults by those he calls radical Islamic terrorists, inner-city thugs and illegals" (para. 11). The political cry for law and order in 1968 and in 2016 was a rallying call for what Nixon called the "silent majority;" and was used to "represent a complex ecosystem of anxieties" (Zeitz, 2016, para. 21). Zeitz (2016) explains in 1968, when law and order was used:

> the Silent Majority [was] also worried about the general breakdown of civil order and authority ... [younger] Americans were far more accepting than their parents of premarital sex, same-sex relationships and cohabitation between unmarried couples.... Young people were less willing to conform in dress, grooming or manners to what society *deemed normative* [emphasis added]. (para. 12)

In other words, terms like "law and order" are coded messages for his base. These messages are about crime and punishment but they are also very much about race, ethnicity, sexuality, and a social order in American life. The images often conjured up are of the 1950s as an ideal time period in American life in comparison to the turmoil and radical changes that followed in the 1960s and subsequent decades. However, during this same time period (1950s) dejure, Jim Crow segregation was still the law of the land.

Despite the undeniable browning of the United States, the normative remains White, middle class, Christian, heterosexual, and cisgender. "Law and order" has made its way into our schools as well; the cry for "safe and orderly" schools unconsciously considers some youth and their behaviors as normative and others as those who need to be surveilled and policed. In this chapter, we examine the literature on classroom management and discipline and how some practices may marginalize children not deemed "normative" in the name of "law and order."

Education, as an institution, influences outcomes and practices of public institutions and can reproduce inequality and injustice (Rector-Aranda, 2016). However, education can also challenge and reduce these same injustices and inequalities. Yet, in order to challenge and reduce, the inequity and injustice must first be acknowledged as problematic. Majoritarian stories are "bundles of presuppositions, perceived wisdoms and shared cultural understandings persons of the dominant race bring to the discussion of race" (Delgado & Stephanic, 1993, p. 462). Majoritarian stories gain power through their invisibility, as they are often taken at face value and assumed to be free of value judgments. In the case of school discipline, policies and outcomes might be viewed as color-blind, objective, neutral and free of bias despite racial disparities in outcomes. Viewing schooling and policies through this color-blind lens allows one to see only the flaws in the student but offers little critique of institutions and systems with regard to accountability for failing those students (Rector-Aranda, 2016).

We argue that disorder is perpetuated through school discipline practices in two ways: (1) by interrupting opportunities to learn and (2) by further marginalizing our most vulnerable students. As we describe the current state of school discipline, we illustrate how [?] disorder ensues when ostensibly neutral discipline policies are enacted through human fallacy, leaving them susceptible to perversion and tainted by the implicit biases and deficit ideologies held by educational actors. The sad irony is that in the name of "law and order" disorder persists, evidenced by disproportionality in suspensions and office referrals, as educators punish what the school culture deems as nonnormative. We also offer, for the reader's consideration, multicultural education as a tool for bringing order to the current state of disciplinary chaos.

Preeminent multicultural education scholar, James Banks (1993), posits that there are five dimensions of multicultural education: content integration, knowledge construction, prejudice reduction, equity pedagogy, and cultivating an empowering school culture and climate (p. 5). A great deal of scholarship focuses on content integration, knowledge construction, prejudice reduction, and equity pedagogy, with great reason. While these dimensions are not mutually exclusive, the last dimension, cultivating an empowering school culture and climate, is harder to tackle, and often outside the scope of the work of curriculum scholars. Yet, school culture and climate are as critical to academic achievement as the teacher and the curriculum; when a culture is not conducive to learning—learning is less likely to occur. In this chapter, we argue multicultural education is an essential component for establishing classroom cultures and school environments that facilitate optimal opportunities for learning. Specifically, we examine multicultural education and its relationship to classroom management and school discipline.

DECADES OF DISORDER: HISTORY OF DISPROPORTIONALITY IN DISCIPLINE

Many believe that it is unfortunate that Black, Brown, and LBGTQ youth are disproportionately suspended, expelled, and disciplined in schools, but that these actions are disciplinary reactions to disruptions and are necessary to preserve the educational environment of all students. School discipline, much like the criminal justice system, is perceived to be neutral, color-blind, objective, straightforward, and dispassionate regarding justice and discipline. In other words, if one population of students receives more discipline and harsher discipline in schools, then it is because of their own behavior. However, the facts reflect a very different, more complex reality, even in settings where the official policy is one of zero tolerance for disruption. The Civil Rights Divisions in both the U.S .Department of Justice and U.S. Department of Education bore witness to the complex reality that is school discipline. In 2014, a joint dear colleague letter was issued by the U.S. Department of Justice and U.S. Department of Education on the subject of nondiscriminatory administration of school discipline that stated: "in our investigations we have found cases where African American students were disciplined more harshly and more frequently because of their race than similarly situated White students. In short, racial discrimination in school discipline is a real problem" (U.S. Department of Education & U.S. Department of Justice, 2014, p.4).

The issue for Black students is twofold. It is the discriminatory, subjective manner in which they are given harsher discipline than similarly situated White students and it is the over reliance on out of school suspension and expulsion and the ripple effect that causes [that causes what?] in the student's academic life. We might imagine that out of school suspension is used for the most dangerous students and the most serious offenses, but we would be incorrect (Simson, 2014).

For more than four decades, researchers have noted the disproportionality of disciplinary consequences for different subgroups of students. Students of color, particularly African Americans, LGBTQ students, and students with disabilities have empirical data illustrating their increased likelihood to experience exclusionary discipline practices. Suspensions and expulsions deprive students of their opportunity to learn. Unlike after school detention or other punitive responses to behavior problems, suspensions and expulsions increase the likelihood of student exposure to a host of negative consequences. For example, Skiba, Arrendo, and Williams (2014) explicate:

> Out of school suspension and expulsion are associated with short-term negative outcomes, such as academic disengagement and depressed academic achievement that may cascade over time, ultimately, increasing a student's risk for contact with law enforcement and involvement in the juvenile justice system. (p. 557)

Similarly, the American Academy of Pediatrics (2003) explains the potential for health and psychological risks that may come from exclusionary discipline practices in a 2003 policy statement. To complicate the matter, suspensions and expulsions as disciplinary practices have been on the rise (Skiba, Arredondo, & Williams, 2014; Stone & Stone, 2011). Scholars have found that in the United States "the rate at which students across the country were suspended and expelled from schools almost doubled, from

3.7% (1.7 million) suspended in 1974 to 6.6% (over 3 million) suspended in 2009–2010" (Skiba, Arredondo, & Williams, 2014, p. 550). Suspensions and expulsions are not reserved for the most problematic and severe school behaviors and disruptions; increasingly it has become a preferred disciplinary action of administrators.

Removal from the school setting is problematic for all children, but that problem is exacerbated when the most vulnerable children bear the brunt of such a practice. When examining the Office of Civil Rights Data (2014) on suspensions, it is evident that students experiencing suspension is not proportionate to the enrollment of students in U.S. public schools (see Figures 11.1 and 11.2). That is, certain groups (e.g., African Americans) are disproportionately represented in these numbers.

The Civil Rights Data Center explained in the 2013–2014 school year, Black preschool children were 3.6 times more likely to receive an out of school suspension and Black K–12 students were 3.8 times more likely to receive a suspension (U.S. Department of Education, 2016). Furthermore, Black girls were the only demographic of girls that were suspended at disproportionate rates. Native American, LatinX, Hawaiian, and multiracial boys were also suspended disproportionately (U.S. Department of Education, 2016). In addition to students of color, students with disabilities (served under IDEA) were twice as likely to be suspended in grades K–12, though their preschool suspension rates were not disproportionate (U.S. Department of Education, 2016).

The evidence of the disproportionality has been studied quite a bit, quantitatively, examining incidences of referrals, suspensions and expulsion. The multivariate analyses have been quite useful in testing hypotheses for why the disproportionality exists. Disproportionality in and of itself is not indicative of individual or systematic bias; it is the multivariate analyses that have allowed scholars to test various theories about why the disproportionality exists and if it is a sign of differential behavior patterns along subgroup lines.

Students of Color

Students of color is one of subgroups most explored in the empirical literature on school suspension. Most of the literature on students of color has focused on Black students, as Skiba and associates explain, "Over representation of African American students in discipline has been documented extensively for nearly 40 years" (Skiba, Arredondo, & Williams, 2014, p. 557). Yet, the overrepresentation of students of color in exclusionary discipline practices, while disproportionate, is not limited to African Americans. Losen and Gillespie (2012) found:

Public School Enrollment by Race/Ethnicity 2013-2014

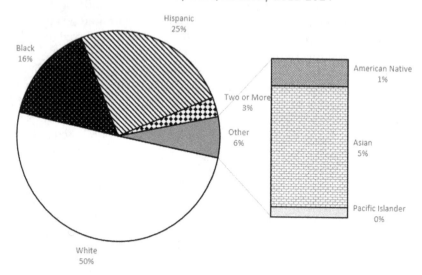

Figure 11.1. 2013–2014 U.S. Public School Enrollment by Ethnicity from OCR Data.

Students with 1 or More Susepensions by Race/Ethncity 2013-2014

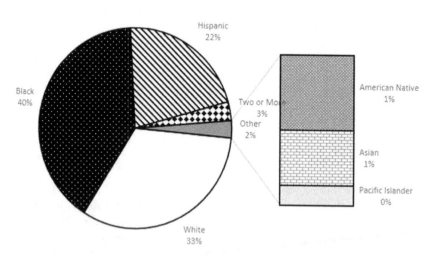

Figure 11.2. Students Suspended in 2013–2014 by Ethnicity, OCR Data.

> Suspension rates show that 17%, or 1 out of every 6 Black school-children enrolled in K–12, were [sic] suspended at least once. That is much higher than the 1 in 13 (8%) risk for Native Americans; 1 in 14 (7%) for Latinos; 1 in 20 (5%) for Whites; or the 1 in 50 (2%) for Asian Americans. (p. 6)

Deficit ideologies that fuel school decisions creating such disproportionality is often the etiology for counterproductive, discipline-focused school ecosystems. The qualitative consequence of such disproportionality is that it adversely impacts their community and family stabilization. West (2005) reminds educators that our students are not blind to conditions of inequity and inequality facilitated by agents of school culture and climate.

The multivariate analyses, often using logistic transformations with suspension as the outcome, have given scholars the most insight on the nature of the problem. In a nationally representative sample, logistic regression revealed both African Americans and Latinos were more likely to receive referrals and be suspended (Skiba, Horner, Chung, Rausch, May, & Tobin, 2011). At the elementary school level, Latinos were underrepresented in terms of referrals to the office and African Americans were twice as likely as whites to receive office referrals. At the middle school level Latinos were overrepresented in referrals and African Americans were four times as likely to receive a referral. In terms of suspensions, the study found Latinos being twice as likely as Whites and African Americans four times as likely at the middle school level (Skiba et al., 2011).

In addition to Black students and LatinX students, Native Americans have been found to be overrepresented in discipline procedures and Asian American to be underrepresented (Skiba et al., 2014, p. 550).

LGBTQ Students

Lesbian, gay, bisexual, transgender, and queer (LGBTQ) youth also disproportionately feel the impact of exclusionary discipline practices. Because most large datasets do not yet collect this demographic information, less large scale analyses have been conducted on this subgroup of students. However, the data that is available about this group of students is quite concerning.

Himmelstein and Bruckner examined the relationship between three measures of nonheterosexuality and suspensions, expulsions, arrests, and convictions within the criminal justice system. Their logistic regressions revealed that, "nonhetereosexual adolescents had between 1.25 and three times greater odds than their heterosexual peers of experiencing sanction" (Himmelstein & Bruckner, 2011, p. 54). They concluded nonheterosexual youth are more likely to be punished for risky behaviors than they are to receive the support they need.

Qualitative research on LGBTQ youth and discipline is just as disturbing. In a study of LGBTQ youth experiences with participants from Arizona, California, and Georgia, focus groups and interviews reveal differential treatment. For example, Snapp and associates found that sanctions for public displays of affections (PDA) and dress code (particularly when someone dresses outside gender norms) were given more to LGBTQ students (Snapp, Hoenig, Fields & Russell, 2015). Furthermore, they discussed the problematic nature of zero-tolerance policies by explicating, "When LGBTQ youth respond to bullying by fighting back, they are often blamed and punished for their own victimization" (Snapp, Hoenig, Fields, & Russell, 2014, p. 69). Last but not least, they found some instances where administrators would "out" students when reporting incidents to their parents. Depending on the parents, that could risk a child's livelihood.

Students With Disabilities

In addition to students of color and LGBTQ students, students with disabilities are disproportionately excluded from school due to behavioral infractions. Losen and Gillespie (2012) found that "For all racial groups combined, more than 13% of students with disabilities were suspended. This is approximately twice the rate of their non-disabled peers" (p. 7). This rate is compounded by race, wherein one in four African Americans with disabilities has been suspended at least once from school (Losen & Gillespie, 2012).

Students with disabilities are protected from exclusion from school with manifestation determination, meaning it is only lawful to suspend a student once it has been determined that their behavior is not a manifestation of their disability (Hallahan, Kauffman, & Pullen, 2009). Losen and colleagues' examination of suspension data found that students identified as emotionally disturbed or as having a specific learning disability were more likely to be suspended.

Emotional and behavioral disorders are often characterized by two types of behaviors: internalizing and externalizing. Internalizing is considered "Acting-in behavior" and can lead to conditions such as depression, anxiety, or withdrawing from peers (Hallahan et al., 2009, p. 268). On the other hand, externalizing behaviors or "acting-out behavior" can be "aggressive or disruptive behavior that is observable as behaviors directed towards others" (Hallahan et al., 2009, p. 268). These are more likely to be punishable.

When examining disproportionality and students with disabilities, one must understand the disproportionality that comes with placement into special education categories (which is explored in greater detail in the Rush and Robinson chapter in this volume). Harry and Klinger (2007) explain that special education categories with the largest degree of disproportionality are those based upon "clinical judgement" compared to categories based on "biologically verifiable conditions" where disproportionality rarely exists (p. 17). They go on to explain that the history of disproportionality in special education can be tied to forced integration where students of color "were subject to low expectations and intense efforts to keep them separate from the white mainstream" (p. 17). Two teachers may observe the same child and one may describe the child as hyperactive, impulsive and a daydreamer; whereas the other might describe the same child as energetic, spontaneous, and imaginative. And, one could argue, the different attributes ascribed are colored by the describers perceptions of the child and the groups in which that child holds membership—especially when those groups are different than what the describer considers normative. Losen and associates caution that:

> Blacks are overidentified in these two categories that consistently predict increased suspensions and underidentified for autism, the category that consistently predicts lower suspension rates for both Black and White students. In other words, this pattern of categorical over and underidentification may have a net disparate impact on Black students ... the empirical trends combined with predictive values by category also raise the question of whether there is an unlawful racially disparate impact connected to the disparities in identification by disability category. (Losen, Hodson, Ee & Martinez, 2014, p. 15)

It is critical when examining students with disabilities in judgement categories not to underestimate the way race and special education identification coalesce.

THE ETIOLOGY OF DISORDER

Much of the positivist research on disproportionality has tried to test theories about the causes of disproportionality. Three commonly explored theories revolve around the relationship of race and poverty, difference in behaviors, and theories related to cultural dissonance between students and the school.

One common assumption is that the racial disparity in discipline incidences is the result of socioeconomic disparity and that students "overexposed to the stressors of poverty, are more likely to be under socialized with respect to school norms and rules" (Skiba et al., 2011). However, in their study of disciplinary data in an urban district, after controlling for socioeconomic status, Skiba and associates (2002) found the practical significance of race (measured by effect size) on office referrals per student, suspensions per student, proportion of referrals suspended, and number of days suspended remained largely unchanged. This means that ***poverty failed to explain the racial disparities in discipline.*** A similar study investigating multiple variables that may lead to disparities in discipline, examined the poverty level of the school, finding that "higher school rates of eligibility for free and reduced lunch at school were not significantly related to the probability of out-of-school suspensions" and were actually inversely related to expulsions (Skiba, Chung, Trachok, Baker, Sheya, & Hughes, 2014, p. 660). Unfortunately, that same study did find the proportion of Black students in a school was highly predictive of the likelihood for out-of-school suspensions. In fact, the scholars clarify:

> This is not simply a matter of higher rates of suspension in poor urban schools with higher concentrations of African American students. Simultaneous entry of a number of individual and school characteristics in the multivariate model means that in rich and poor schools alike, regardless of one's gender, one's school achievement level, or the severity of one's behavior, simply attending a school with more Black students substantially increases one's risk for receiving an out-of-school suspension. (Skiba et al., 2014, p. 661)

Race of the student and racial composition of the school are both factors that predict the likelihood of experiencing suspension.

A second hypothesis often explored in multivariate analyses of discipline is whether the disparities are the consequence of differences in behavior. When examining the disproportionality among gender, it was found that boys do commit more infractions than girls. However, when examining race, the same study found White students were more likely to be suspended for clear-cut offenses such as smoking and obscene language, whereas *black students were more likely to be suspended for more subjective behaviors such as excessive noise and disrespect* (Skiba, Michael, Nardo, & Peterson, 2002). While there is an understanding that exclusionary discipline is reserved for dangerous offences, Stone and Stone (2011) found that in the 2007–2008 school year in Maryland, more that 37% of suspensions were for "disrespect, insubordination, and disruption" or subjective behaviors (p. 12). A multivariate analysis of data from Denver Public Schools revealed, "Black, Latino, and Multiracial students were often punished more harshly than white students for the same offenses" (Anyon et al., 2014, p. 383). Taken together, these studies illustrate behavior is not the source of the disparity in disciplinary practices.

Theories of cultural dissonance are often tested as explanations for the disproportionality in discipline. Such theories take on different names in the literature such as racial threat, which is borrowed from criminology, and cultural synchrony, which is uniquely educational. Gordon (1999) gives a useful foundation for understanding how cultural dissonance can impact education; he explicates:

> It is in the relationship between social institutions and the learner that high degrees of dissonance can result in failure to learn or a distortion of the learning process. In a society with tremendous cultural diversity and a culturally hegemonic educational system, dissonance between what is learned in personal interaction with the significant other [in the family] may come into conflict with demands and expectations of the social institution [in this case the school]. (p. 42)

Again, the institution has a culture that is deemed normative, and the non-normative must be surveilled and policed. In the United States, that norm is White, middle-class, heterosexual, cisgendered, and Christian.

The racial threat hypothesis, featured prominently in the work of Welch and Payne (2010), "suggests that as the proportion of blacks increases in relation to whites, intensified measures of control will proliferate in response to the perceived growing threat derived from closer proximity to minorities" (p. 29). Punitive actions are invoked to maintain "dominance of the majority" (p. 29). While the racial threat hypothesis was borrowed from criminal justice and responses to crime, Payne and Welch tested the hypothesis in reference to punitive discipline in schools, and found it to be a plausible explanation. As the proportion of Black students in a school increased, so did the likelihood for punitive punishment including suspensions (Welch & Payne, 2010, 2012).

Using different language, and slightly different methods, Blake et al. (2016) had similar findings. Instead of only examining the makeup of the student body, Blake and associates examined the make-up of the faculty as well as the student body, and how similar or dissimilar they were. They found the greater the congruence the lower the risk for discipline. They explain, "the cultural synchrony hypothesis asserts that educators' negative evaluations of Black students are fueled by stereotypes of Black adults, who are depicted in the media as violent, threatening, hypersexualized, and in need of socialization" (p. 80).

The evidence that supports both racial threat and cultural synchrony theory are concerning for a number of reasons. The first and most obvious reason is that the demographic makeup of U.S. schools and the teachers within them are vastly different. Boser (2011) found that only 17% of U.S. teachers are teachers of color, making 83% of U.S. teachers, White. In his state by state analysis and creation of a diversity index (that measures the percentage point difference between the percent of non-White teachers and the percent of non-White students), he found no states' teachers perfectly mirrored its students. This is why teachers must be prepared to work with students who are outside what they deem as normative.

THE CASE FOR MULTICULTURAL EDUCATION

The current high levels of racial disproportionality in school discipline is a reflection of teachers not understanding and incorporating the cultural values, orientations, experiences of African, Latino, Asian, and Native Americans into curriculum and instruction. Multicultural curriculum content and teaching techniques make it easier for teachers to maintain classroom environments that are conducive to learning, and build positive relationships with ethnically, racially, socially, and linguistically diverse students. (Gay, 2006, p. 343)

In the *Handbook on Classroom Management*, noted multicultural scholar Geneva Gay reaffirms the cultural synchrony/racial threat hypothesis and offers multicultural education as a preventative solution for discipline disproportionality. Classroom management is a realm of actions teachers employ to cultivate an environment that is conducive to learning. Classroom management includes everything from classroom rules to daily rituals to the physical design of the space. Two components of classroom management are student socialization and disciplinary interventions (Brophy, 2006). Student socialization deals with communicating expectation of behavior and trying to influence behavior. Disciplinary interventions are actions used to improve behavior once an issue has become evident. Like Brophy's (2006) typology of socialization and intervention, Gregory, Bell, and Pollock (2016) recommend educators employ principles of conflict prevention and principles of conflict intervention. Principles of conflict prevention include: supportive relationships, academic rigor, culturally relevant and responsive teaching, and bias-free classrooms and respectful school environments (Gregory et al., 2016, p. 41). On the other hand, principles of conflict intervention include: inquiry into the causes of conflicts, problem solving approaches to discipline, inclusion of student and family voice in understanding causes and solutions, as well as plans to integrate students after a conflict has occurred (Gregory et al., 2016, p. 41).

Often, like other aspects of education such as curriculum, classroom management is viewed as a culture-free enterprise. Yet, scholars of multicultural education know that:

Discrimination occurs when teachers do not recognize that behavior is culturally influenced; when they devalue, censure, and punish behaviors of non-mainstream groups; and when they fail to see that their management practices alienate and marginalize some students, while privileging others. (Weinstein, Curran, & Tomlinson-Clark, 2003, p. 270)

Educators often fail to realize that their understanding of appropriate behavior is based upon behavioral patterns of groups they deem as normative. In the body of work that advocates for culturally responsive classroom management (CRCM), Weinstein, Tomlinson-Clark, and Curran explain (2004):

> European American teachers, for example, are generally accustomed to a "passive-receptive" discourse pattern; they expect students to listen quietly while the teacher is speaking and then respond individually to teacher-initiated questions. When some African American students, accustomed to a more active, participatory pattern ("call-response") demonstrate their engagement by providing comments and reactions, teacher may interpret such behavior as rude and disruptive. Similarly, teacher who do not realize how strongly Pacific Islanders value interpersonal harmony may conclude that these students are lazy when they are reluctant to participate in competitive activities. In addition, teachers may be shocked when Southeast Asian students smile while being scolded if they are unaware that smiles are not meant as disrespect, but as an admission of guilt and an effort to show that there are no hard feelings. (p. 26)

The examples Weinstein and associates illustrate that unintentional bias that can be present in teacher judgements of student behaviors. However, even behaviors that seem more sinister may be misinterpreted. Kinloch (2017) articulates youth of color, and we would speculate other marginalized groups as well, may enact performances of resistance to protect themselves in a school environment that has proven to be hostile to them. She explains:

> I use the phrase performances of resistance to refer to a mode of communication or a particular, directed way of responding to the negative gaze, the degrading treatment, and the hurtful assumptions many youth of color receive from others, peers and adults alike. They engage in performances of resistance (e.g. eye-rolling, sharp verbal responses, silence, a seemingly disinterested disposition, absence, etc.) as a way to protect and safeguard themselves from harmful, potentially painful, damaging forms of interaction they often encounter from others who might misread, misunderstand, ridicule, and denigrate them. (p. 27)

Knowing that students of color are more likely to be reprimanded and punished for subjective behaviors than their White peers, it is necessary for educations committed to equity and justice to explore how multicultural education can be used to prevent compounded marginalization through discipline.

The research on CRCM is quick to explain that it is "a frame of mind, more than a set of strategies of practice" (Weinstein, Tomlinson-Clark,

Curran, 2004, p. 27.) Like most educational practice it begins with being reflective and acutely aware of what is happening in the classroom. Sociologist Amanda (2009) describes an incident where a well-intentioned teacher and administrator named every Black boy in the classroom as having been referred to the office throughout the course of the year. Lewis, posed the question, "Even sweet, gentle, Larry?" a boy who liked to read during recess. Lewis problematizes the incident, saying not only was it disturbing that they named every child in the demographic, but that they did not even realize what they had done or the pattern among the students with office referrals. Teachers cannot be blind to patterns in discipline any more than they should be blind to patterns in achievement. They have to be willing to "see color," "see sexuality," "see differently abled" individuals in order to protect them from and try to dismantle systematic or unintentional discrimination.

Weinstein, Tomlinson-Clark, and Curran (2004) outline five components of CRCM, the first of which is identify work, or "recognition of one's own ethnocentrism and biases" (p. 27). First and foremost, many White Americans have not explored the concept of whiteness and are unaware that what they consider "normative" is not normative for other individuals. And we know the great majority of the teaching force is middle-class and white. Teachers must grapple with their own assumptions about children and families. Conceptions of innocence must be explored by classroom teachers. There is empirical evidence that shows adults view children of color as less innocent than White children; it is irresponsible to think teachers perceptions of children would be different than other adults without opportunities to interrogate such beliefs (Goff, Jackson, Di Leone, Culotta, & DiTomasso, 2014). But beyond perceptions of the children, teachers must evaluate their perceptions of the children's communities and families. For example, teachers must "consider the possibility that a lack of direct involvement reflects a differing perspective about parental responsibility, rather than a lack of commitment to their children's education" (Weinstein, Curran, & Tomlinson-Clark, 2003, p. 273). Teachers cannot begin to transition from deficit ideologies to asset based views of children if they never examine their own assumptions and ethnocentric worldviews.

This task is not solely for White teachers. Teachers of all backgrounds must interrogate what they believe about themselves as well as what they believe about others. They need to explore the history of marginalization in education systems to understand the mistrust students may have of their intentions. They must also move from a deficit gaze to a assets based understanding of what each student brings to the classroom. This cannot be accomplished in a workshop, but is lifelong work; hence the assertion that this approach to classroom management is more a frame of mind than an actual set of strategies.

In addition to the identity work required, teachers must advance their "knowledge of students cultural backgrounds" (Weinstein, Tomlinson-Clark, & Curran, 2004, p. 27). They cannot make assumptions about where children come from based on stereotypes or deficit based reading material such as Ruby Payne's *Framework for Understanding Poverty*. A student is a teacher's biggest resource in learning about his or her background. Communication must flow in two directions. Teachers should be willing to share about themselves as well; it humanizes them.

Beyond knowing their students, teachers must be scholars of the contexts of their students' lives and education (Weinstein, Tomlinson-Clark, Curran, 2004). Teachers cannot be apolitical or keep their heads in the sand; to the contrary, culturally responsive classroom managers have to be aware of the sociopolitical and economic context in which schooling happens. Last but not least teachers need to be willing to use appropriate strategies and committed to building caring classroom communities (Weinstein, Tomlinson-Clark, & Curran, 2004, p. 27).

Creating a Welcoming and Inclusive Classroom Environment

Despite the illusion of neutrality, education is a political enterprise. Teachers transmit messages to students with their dress, the way their classroom looks, and what aspects of the curriculum they choose to focus. The space, layout, and decoration in the classroom is the first way we communicate expectations. Teachers must ask, do my displays and walls communicate a welcoming and inclusive environment? Are tables and chairs arranged to optimize interaction and collaboration or do they promote competition and individualism? While physical space is a critical part of classroom management, simply having posters of persons of color or "Bienvenido" on the door, does not make the space inviting. Do not trivialize or oversimplify what it means to create a welcoming environment.

It is important that students know what is expected of them in terms of behavior. Designing classroom norms and expectations is an important part of establishing the classroom culture at the beginning of the year. Teachers may find that establishing classroom rules collectively is a great way for students to have voice in and input in their classroom environment. Weinstein and colleagues suggest having three to six classroom rules and no more; using the law of diminishing returns—too many rules may lead to fewer rules being followed. While this is usually a task done at the beginning of the year, it should be revisited throughout the year. As students transfer in or new behaviors develop, it makes sense to have [?] a living document that can be revised or amended to meet the needs of the environment at the time.

230   B. N. HINNANT-CRAWFORD, C. S. PLATT, and D. WINGARD

In diverse classrooms, it is critical to "make certain that students understand what the norms mean in terms of specific behavior" (Weinstein, Curran, & Tomlinson-Clark, 2003, p. 271). Activities like role playing different behaviors so students can see what is expected, juxtaposed to what is unacceptable, is a clear way to ensure that despite cultural understandings of appropriate behavior everyone is on the same page. In addition to making time to teach about expected behaviors, time is not wasted clarifying one's approach to communication. Weinstein, Curran, and Tomlinson-Clark (2003) argue that instead of making assumptions that students will know what you mean, it is best to "Provide students with explicit lessons on how nondirective verbal interactions are actually 'code' for direct commands" (p. 272). Being explicit about expectations and why those expectations are important are an essential part of classroom management.

Physical setting and expectations are just two facets of many things teachers can do to create a caring environment. Weinstein and her colleagues caution, "Caring also involves communication of high expectations and holding students accountable for high quality work" (Weinstein, Curran, & Tomlinson-Clark, 2003, p. 272). Sometimes, deficit ideologies lead well-meaning educators to have lower expectations of marginalized students, even those identified as gifted (Ford, 1998). While CRCM scholars do not use the term, the literature on CRCM describes the behaviors of "warm demanders" (Irvine & Fraser, 1998; Ware, 2006). Described as disciplinarians, care-givers, and the embodiment of loco parentis, warm demanders view student success as a non-negotiable. Irvine and Fraser (1998) give the example of Ms. Irene Washington, who after chastising student Darius explains, " I know if I don't reach him, or if I retain him, I may lose him to the streets this early [first grade]. That's what I'm here for—to give him opportunities—to get an education and confidence" (para. 4). The no-nonsense attitude accompanied by undeniable care, allows warm demanders to experience a great deal of pedagogical success as well (Ware, 2006), in part because they establish an environment conducive to learning.

Caring environments go beyond the behaviors of the teacher. Educators must be clear that bullying, especially that rooted in difference, is unwelcome in the classroom and school community. CRCM scholars suggest integrating expectations of tolerance and acceptance using curriculum:

> Students can read fiction that relates to the topic of harassment; conduct surveys about bullying; depict their feelings about name calling and put downs through drawings and paintings; have open meeting on name-calling, teasing, and bullying, and discuss appropriate and inappropriate responses. (Weinstein, Curran, & Tomlinson-Clark, 2003, p. 273)

If a teacher is reading a book about an LGBTQ protagonist and is not particularly knowledgeable on LGBTQ issues, this presents an opportunity to ask members of that community to be guests in the class for discussions—further exemplifying the classroom commitment to inclusion. (Teachers should not expect students who are members of that community to serve as the ambassador for the class; that is unfair.) As teachers make curricular decisions about what to read, what to watch, and what research questions to explore, they have a chance to reinforce expectations about desirable behaviors in the classroom and to demonstrate their unwavering pursuit of a welcoming and caring environment.

RESTORATIVE JUSTICE, TRANSFORMATIVE DISCIPLINE, AND ALTERNATIVES TO EXCLUSION

Even in environments most conducive to learning, the occasional behavioral infraction can occur. In such instances, it is best that teachers and administrators respond in ways that do not diminish a student's opportunity to learn. Ladson-Billings (1995) declared, "but that's just good teaching" to describe culturally relevant pedagogy; one could argue the same for employing CRCM techniques. In fact, evidence suggests, pedagogical interventions that help teachers respond to the individual needs of students have positive impacts on discipline outcomes, even when equitable discipline was not the goal of the intervention (Gregory, Hafen, Ruzek, Mikami, Allen, & Pianta, 2016). We can never underestimate the transformative power of good teaching.

One alternative approach to discipline that is becoming popular is restorative justice. In 2017, restorative justice was adopted to replace suspensions in Chapel Hill-Carrboro Schools. With its origins in indigenous American and African communities, restorative justice seeks to restore harmony in a community once a violation has occurred. Payne and Welch (2015) explain, "within the restorative justice model, student misbehavior is viewed as a violation of a relationship, either one between the offender and victim or one between the offender and the overall school community" (p. 540). Restorative justice uses a variety of strategies including peer mediation, student conferences, and restitution. Goad (2017) reports "A big part is restorative circles, where the wronged and accused come together to discuss how to deal with an offense, or where a whole class can get together to discuss something" (para. 5). Restorative justice can be viewed as " an opportunity to build students' capacity to consider how their behavior is impacting the greater [?] school community" (Payne & Welch, 2015, p. 541). Despite its potential, research shows restorative justice is less likely to be adopted as a strategy in schools with larger percentages of Black students (Payne & Welch, 2015). Because???

For all its praise and the preference for it to punitive practices, restorative justice is not without critique. Erica Meiners (2016) argues that:

> RJ [restorative justice] places the responsibility to create peace in schools on students (and teachers). This definition of the problem not only places the burden on young people but also strategically creates a focus on particular forms of violence. Interpersonal violence or harm enacted by young people is made visible, and systemic or structural violence—hyper-racialized school policing—is rendered invisible. (p. 113)

She goes on to say that so-called "peace rooms" are not markedly different from detention halls. And while some restorative justice programs embed character education and anger management to help students better cope with the realities of life (i.e., poverty, family issues, etc.), Meiners (2016) suggests, "these practices of accommodation that often name structural violence but refuse to engage and remake systems are ... forms of domination" seeking to fix the person instead of the system (p. 115). She advocates for transformative justice, which can be considered, "in opposition to punitive justice systems" (p. 121). Transformative justice raises the question of whether or not justice can occur or restoration is possible in "contexts where structural inequality is the norm" (p. 121).

Exclusionary discipline remains a problem for students of color, LGBTQ students, and students with disabilities. We recognize discipline is only one area where these students are marginalized. However, as we try to cultivate real communities where marginalized groups have voice and choice in their learning—restorative justice may be a viable alternative for the immediate future, to allow students to have voice in their school environment. Transformative justice, however, remains the goal.

LARGE-SCALE DISORDER

In 2017, the update to the Booker Report found that Black males received sentences that were 19.1% longer than white males with similar offences. Furthermore, a history of violence did no more to explain the variance in criminal sentencing than poverty explained school disciplinary decisions; in other words, justice is not blind. Race matters.

Just as the rate of in school] suspensions, out of school suspensions and expulsions have increased over time, "in less than thirty years, the U.S. penal population exploded from around 300,000 to more than 2 million (Alexander, 2012, p. 6). While most of the increase in incarceration is due to drug related offenses, Alexander (2012) writes, the drug war was declared when drug use was actually in decline. Furthermore, she argues, "The stark racial disparities [in incarceration] cannot be explained by rates of drug crime. Studies show that people of all colors *use and sell* illegal drugs at remarkably similar rates" (p. 7). The disparity is not in the crime; it is in the punishment. Should not the sentences be similar?

Since the late 1980s, or for roughly 30 years, schools have increasingly relied on zero tolerance policies and exclusionary disciplinary policies, i.e., suspensions and expulsions (Simson, 2014). The disparities are in the punishment rather than the infractions. We argue that schools are alienating and pushing students out of schools and into a waiting prison pipeline but the students who are being pushed out are often students of color, students with disabilities, and LBGTQ students. The lives of Black, Brown, gay, lesbian, transgender, and differently abled youth must matter as much to schools as White lives. The disorder to LGBTQ communities, differently abled youth and communities of color that is caused in the name of "law and order" must be problematized and stopped.

The disorder that is evident in our school disciplinary practice is simply a microcosm of the larger societal problem that criminalizes what it sees as nonnormative. Yet, instead of mimicking society, schools can set the standard: a very different standard. Instead of reproducing inequality, schools can become sites that are the foundation of a liberatory, fair, just, and equitable new reality—if we have the will to make it so.

REFERENCES

Alexander, M. (2012). *The new Jim Crow: Mass incarceration in the age of colorblindness.* New York, NY: The New Press.

American Academy of Pediatrics (Committee on School Health). (2003). Policy statement: Out-of-school suspension and expulsion. *PEDIATRICS, 112*(5). 1206-1209.

Anyon, Y., Jenson, J. M., Altschul, I., Farrar, J., McQueen, J., Greer, E., Downing, B., & Simmons, J. (2014). The persistent effect of race and the promise of alternatives to suspension in school discipline outcomes. *Children and Youth Services Review, 44,* 379–386. http://dx.doi.org/10.1016/j.childyouth.2014.06.025

Azari, J. (2016, March 13). From Wallace to Trump, The evolution of "law and order". Retrieved November 28, 2017, from https://fivethirtyeight.com/features/from-wallace-to-trump-the-evolution-of-law-and-order/

Banks, J. A. (1993). Multicultural education: Historical development, dimensions, and practice. *Review of Research in Education, 19*(1), 3–49. doi:10.2307/1167339

Blake, J. J., Smith, D. M., Marchbanks III, M. P., Seibert, A. L., Wood, S. M., & Kim, E. S. (2016). Does student-teacher racial/ethnic match impact Black students' discipline risk? A test of the cultural synchrony hypothesis. *Inequality in School Discipline,* 79–98. doi:10.1057/978-1-137-51257-4_5

Boser, U. (2011). *Teacher diversity matters: A state-by-state analysis of teachers of color.* Washington, DC: Center for American Progress.

Brophy, J. (2006). History of research on classroom management. In C. M Everston & C. S. Weinstein (Eds.), *Handbook of classroom management: Research, practice, and contemporary issues* (pp. 17–42). New York, NY: Routledge.

Brown, D. F. (2004). Urban teachers' professed classroom management strategies reflections of culturally responsive teaching. *Urban Education, 39*(3), 266–289. doi:10.1177/0042085904263258

Delgado, R., & Stefancic, J. (1993). Critical race theory: An annotated bibliography. *Virginia Law Review, 79*(2), 461–516.

Ford, D. Y. (1998). The underrepresentation of minority students in gifted education: Problems and promises in recruitment and retention. *The Journal of Special Education, 32*(1), 4–14.

Gay, G. (2006). Connections between classroom management and culturally responsive teaching. In C. M. Everston & C. S. Weinstein (Eds.), *Handbook of Classroom Management: Research, Practice, and Contemporary Issues* (pp. 343–370). New York, NY: Routledge.

Gregory, A., Bell, J., & Pollock, M. (2016). How educators can eradicate disaparties in school discipline. In R. J. Skiba, K. Mediratta, & M. K. Rauch (Eds.), *Inequality in school discipline: Research and practice to reduce disparities* (pp. 39–58). New York, NY: Palgrave Macmillan.

Gregory, A., Hafen, C. A., Ruzek, E., Mikami, A. Y., Allen, J. P., & Pianta, R. C. (2016). Closing the racial discipline gap in classrooms by changing teacher practice. *School Psychology Review, 45*(2), 171–191. doi:10.17105/spr45-2.171-191

Gregory, A., Skiba, R. J., & Noguera, P. A. (2010). The achievement gap and the discipline gap. *Educational Researcher, 39*(1), 59–68. doi:10.3102/0013189x09357621

Goad, M. (2017, December 19). Chapel Hill-Carrboro school replacing suspensions with restorative conversations. *The Herald Sun*. Retrieved from https://www.heraldsun.com/news/local/education/article190535559.html

Goff, P. A., Jackson, M. C., Leone, D., Lewis, B. A., Culotta, C. M., & DiTomasso, N. A. (2014). The essence of innocence: Consequences of dehumanizing Black children. *Journal of Personality and Social Psychology, 106*(4), 526–545.

Gordon, E. W. (1999). *Education and justice: A view from the back of the bus*. New York, NY: Teachers College Press.

Hallahan, D.P., Kauffman, J. M., & Pullen, P. C. (2009). *Exceptional learners: Introduction to special Eeducation*. New York, NY: Pearson Education.

Harry, B., & Klingner, J. (2007). Discarding the deficit model. *Educational Leadership, 64*(5), 16–21.

Himmelstein, K. E., & Brückner, H. (2011). Criminal-justice and school sanctions against nonheterosexual youth: A national longitudinal study. *PEDIATRICS, 127*(1), 49–57.

Irvine, J. J., & Fraser, J. W. (1998). Warm demanders. *Education Week, 17*(35), 56–57.

Kinloch, V. (2017). 'You ain't making me write' Culturally sustaining pedagogies and black youths' performances of resistance. In D. Paris & H. S. Alim (Eds.), *Culturally sustaining pedagogies: Teaching and learning for justice in a changing world* (pp. 25–41). New York, NY: Teacher's College Press.

Ladson-Billings, G. (1995). But that's just good teaching! The case for culturally relevant pedagogy. *Theory into Practice, 34*(3), 159–165.

Lewis, A. (2008). Even sweet, gentle Larry? The continuing significance of race in education. In S. Green (Ed.), *Literacy as a civil right: Reclaiming social justice in literacy in literacy teaching and learning* (pp. 69–86). New York, NY: Peter Lang.

Losen, D. J., & Gillespie, J. (2012). *Opportunities suspended: The disparate impact of disciplinary exclusion from school.* Civil Rights Project/Proyecto Derechos Civiles.

Losen, D., Hodson, C., Ee, J., & Martinez, T. (2014). Disturbing inequities: Exploring the relationship between racial disparities in special education identification and discipline. *Journal of Applied Research on Children: Informing Policy for Children at Risk, 5*(2), Article 15, 1–20.

Meiners, E. R. (2016). *For the children? Protecting innocence in a Carceral State.* Minneapolis, MN: University of Minnesota Press.

Nunberg, G. (Host). (2016, July 28). Is Trump's Call For 'Law And Order' A Coded Racial Message? [Radio Broadcast Episode] https://www.npr.org/2016/07/28/487560886/is-trumps-call-for-law-and-order-a-coded-racial-message

Payne, A. A., & Welch, K. (2015). Restorative justice in schools: The influence of race on restorative discipline. *Youth & Society, 47*(4), 539–564. doi:10.1177/0044118x12473125

Rector-Aranda, A. (2016). School norms and reforms, critical race theory, and the fairytale of equitable education. *Critical Questions in Education, 7*(1), 1–16.

Simson, D. (2014). Exclusion, punishment, racism and our schools: A critical race theory perspective on school discipline [Review]. *UCLA Law Review, 61*(2), 506–563.

Skiba, R. J., Arredondo, M. I., & Williams, N. T. (2014). More than a metaphor: The contribution of exclusionary discipline to a school-to-prison pipeline. *Equity & Excellence in Education, 47*(4), 546–564. doi:10.1080/10665684.2014.958965

Skiba, R. J., Chung, C., Trachok, M., Baker, T. L., Sheya, A., & Hughes, R. L. (2014). Parsing disciplinary disproportionality: Contributions of infraction, student, and school characteristics to out-of-school suspension and expulsion. *American Educational Research Journal, 51*(4), 640–670.

Skiba, R. J., Horner, R. H., Chung, C., Rausch, M. K., May, S. L., & Tobin, T. (2011). Race is not neutral: A national investigation of African American and Latino disproportionality in school discipline. *School Psychology Review, 40*(1), 85–107.

Skiba, R. J., Michael, R. S., Nardo, A. C., & Peterson, R. L. (2002). The color of discipline: Sources of racial and gender disproportionality in school punishment. *The Urban Review, 34*(4), 317–342.

Snapp, S. D., Hoenig, J. M., Fields, A., & Russell, S. T. (2014). Messy, butch, and queer: LGBTQ youth and the school-to-prison pipeline. *Journal of Adolescent Research, 30*(1), 57–82. doi:10.1177/0743558414557625

Stone, D. H., & Stone, L. S. (2011). Dangerous & disruptive or simply cutting class; When should schools kick kids to the curb: An empirical study of school suspension and due process rights. *Journal of Law & Family Studies, 13*(1), 1–42.

U.S. Department of Education. (2016). *2013-2014 Civil Rights Data Collection A First Look: Key Data Highlights on Equity and Opportunity Gaps in Our Nation's Public Schools.* Washington, DC: Author. Retrieved from ocrdata.ed.gov

U.S. Department of Education, Office of Civil Rights, Civil Rights Data Collection. (2014). *2013–2014 Discipline Estimates by Discipline Type* [Data file]. Retrieved from https://ocrdata.ed.gov/StateNationalEstimations/Estimations_2013_14

U.S. Department of Justice/US Department of Education. (2014, January 8). *Nondiscriminatory Administration of School Discipline*. Washington, DC: U.S. Government Printing Office.

Ware, F. (2006). Warm demander pedagogy: Culturally responsive teaching that supports a culture of achievement for African American students. *Urban Education, 41*(4), 427–456.

Weinstein, C., Curran, M., & Tomlinson-Clarke, S. (2003). Culturally responsive classroom management: Awareness into action. *Theory into Practice, 42*(4), 269–276.

Weinstein, C. S., Tomlinson-Clarke, S., & Curran, M. (2004). Toward a conception of culturally responsive classroom management. *Journal of Teacher Education, 55*(1), 25–38.

Welch, K., & Payne, A. A. (2010). Racial threat and punitive school discipline. *Social Problems, 57*(1), 25–48.

Welch, K., & Payne, A. A. (2012). Exclusionary school punishment: The effect of racial threat on expulsion and suspension. *Youth Violence and Juvenile Justice, 10*(2), 155–171.

West, C. (2005). *Democracy matters: Winning the fight against imperialism*. New York, NY: Penguin.

Zeitz, J. (2016, July 18). How Trump Is Recycling Nixon's 'Law and Order' Playbook. *POLITICO*. Retrieved November 28, 2017, from https://www.politico.com/magazine/story/2016/07/donald-trump-law-and-order-richard-nixon-crime-race-214066

CHAPTER 12

OUR KNOWLEDGE, OUR WAY

The Indigenous Reclamation of Research

Sweeny Windchief (Tatanga Togahe),
Deb (Clairmont) LaVeaux, James M. Del Duca
(Chiluubé Akchiá), and William David Aderholdt
Montana State University

This chapter contributes to existing literature related to academic inquiry and subsequent dissemination of knowledge in a way that is accountable to Indigenous community ontologies. In order to accomplish this and be in alignment with Indigenous ontologies, we are obliged locate ourselves.

WHO WE ARE

As Indigenous[1] researchers making use of Indigenous research methodologies (IRMs), we are enabled to be who we are (Weber-Pillwax, 2001). Shawn Wilson (2008) suggests that an Indigenous methodology implies relational accountability, meaning the researchers are fulfilling the responsibilities of their relationships with the world around them. As researchers who endorse IRMs, we are obliged to locate our collective voice in an effort to communicate who we are, as well as to understand that we

Comprehensive Multicultural Education in the 21st Century:
Increasing Access in the Age of Retrenchment, pp. 237–254
Copyright © 2019 by Information Age Publishing

have a responsibility to give place and voice to others' relationships with what is real. San Pedro, Carlos, and Mburu (2016) state:

> in order to engage these conversations productively, we have to first understand our positions, our subjectivities, our assumptions, *and* [original emphasis] we need to know when we're asking "Why are you different?" that we really need to be asking of one another, "Who are you in relation to me, not in opposition to me?" (p. 18)

In this spirit we, the authors, want to introduce ourselves and encourage you to find a space for personal connection: we are learners and researchers, three doctoral students and one professor, who study IRMs and have a commitment to Indigenous community. In the interest of multicultural education, we must consider the accountability that comes with community constructed identities. Collectively we come from multiple identity constructs that include the Salish from the Confederated Salish and Kootenai Tribes, Italian, French, German, Scottish, English, Apsáalooke (through traditional adoption), Cherokee, Moroccan, and Fort Peck Assiniboine. Our cumulative voice includes our identities as grandparents, parents, stepparents, spouses, ex-spouses, partners, siblings, stepsiblings, children, and grandchildren. We have experience working both on and off reservation communities, in the Indian health service, counseling, teaching, and the military; finally, we are all participants in higher education. We truly believe that when we listen to our hearts, and act with honor and respect for others, our paths lead us to where we should be. For many reasons, we are honored to be part of this collaboration and offer to share what we have learned through researching how Indigenous peoples have experienced research.

We write as a collective. "We" as opposed to "I," moves us away from the standard individualistic vernacular of a western research paradigm and toward a shared perspective that reflects the collaborative nature of Red pedagogy and Indigenous ontology (Grande, 2015). Together we have decided to engage in scholarship that is useful to Indigenous communities. This is a project that provides insight that (1) originates with Indigenous people, (2) honors relationships, and (3) provides information that is intended to be used in a way that is generative as opposed to exploitative. In order to frame research in a way that is generative, we must develop a critical consciousness of the way that research is typically done, understanding that ethical misconduct from an Indigenous perspective may be different than misconduct from a non-Indigenous paradigm.

INTRODUCTION

The objective of this chapter is to illuminate research as it relates to Indigenous community. By implementing IRMs through a collective voice, and sharing research practices that are accountable to Indigenous peoples, we challenge the typical approaches of Western research. It is important to recognize that Western approaches are generally homogenous despite the various methods that have been established during its long history. In its most essential form, accepted Western research requires: a specific research problem, research questions based on a hypothesis, and hypothesis testing. In this process, the researcher determines the best method for use in answering the research question. Only after a method is deemed appropriate, does/do the researcher(s) identify a sample or population and begin collecting data. In order to prevent bias due to researcher impartiality, the researcher(s) attempt to maintain relational and emotional distance from the population. Often, once the research is completed, the researcher leaves the respondent community and has no further interaction with the people sampled. These standards are designed to minimize error by controlling for researcher bias.

While these standards are thought to establish objectivity in the results of typical western research methods, this conduct can be considered "helicopter research" for Indigenous communities. In other words researchers from outside the community fly in for a short time, gather their data, and fly away without subsequent contact. This lack of investment and sustained relationships leaves Indigenous respondents and their communities skeptical of outside researchers (LaVeaux & Christopher 2009). These types of research practices are not in alignment with multiple Indigenous communities or their corresponding ontologies. In an effort to avoid over-essentializing any one peoples' indigenous identity, we recognize that indigenous community realities and experiences are not the same. We choose however to focus on experiences that are shared among indigenous peoples as they relate to research. The purpose of this chapter is for Indigenous peoples to initiate and direct what research happens, how the process works to align with cultural values, and ultimately to practically benefit indigenous communities. The benefit of researchers better understanding Indigenous ways of being is key to better research, but the primary purpose of IRMs is to benefit Indigenous peoples. In order for well-intentioned researchers to better understand Indigenous tradition, community context, and people, IRMs are continuously being developed, improved upon and employed.

IRMs help researchers identify and utilize methods that are culturally appropriate for the Indigenous communities in which they work. When compared to non-Indigenous communities, the transfer of knowledge and information happens differently. In Indigenous communities, giving and receiving knowledge is considered a mutual process where all participants benefit, and mutually give consent, in the process. Knowledge is typically passed from person to person through story and conversation (Archibald, 2008). Often, knowledge passes from one to another, without being sought.

This is a communication of responsibility and is not to be taken lightly, however this falls outside the realm of academic research, but certainly illuminates the need for relationship and trust in the process of sharing knowledge, which can be lost in traditional academic research.

Not only do the listeners gain something from these transmissions, the storytellers (those collaborators sharing their knowledge) may find new meaning when sharing their stories as well. This is not to say that Indigenous knowledge is not without protection from plagiarism. Permission is (and should be) requested when wishing to share a story with others. When sharing a story, the storyteller will often share with those listening, how they received the knowledge and how they came to receive it. Given the complexities of knowledge being held by and for the collective, when sharing knowledge within an Indigenous paradigm earned trust is essential and one way of earning that trust is to be forthcoming in how you know what you know.

This chapter will also explore and provide examples of two highly important concepts: (1) generative research and (2) exploitative research. Generative research is a *creative* process that produces new value in the form of ideas, information, understandings and approaches that can then be used to benefit the community in practical ways. Exploitative research is an *extractive* process that takes valuable information from the community in order to benefit those not in the community. By consciously and carefully evaluating their research goals and methods to confirm that they are truly *generative* in relation to the Indigenous community, researchers will successfully avoid becoming unwitting agents of colonization and/or exploitation. Excerpts from conversations that occurred with members of Indigenous communities during a research study that utilized culturally appropriate methods will appear throughout the chapter.

LITERATURE REVIEW

Regarding Indigenous people(s) there is a history of ethical misconduct and a consequential distrust of researchers or institutions. A primary concern is that of researcher intent and beneficence, including Indigenous research participant consent (or refusal) to participate in research (Buchwald et al., 2006; Chawla-Sahota, 2012; Hiratsuka, Brown, Hoeft, & Dillard, 2012; Noe et al., 2007). Research has been conducted that suggests these experiences have influenced the motivation of Indigenous peoples to engage in research (Baldwin, 1998; Beauvais, 1998; Buchwald et al., 2006; Guillemin et al., 2016), however, few studies have utilized Indigenous methodologies (Kovach, 2010a) to gather and honor the stories of participants' experiences with respect to what research "looks like" within Indigenous spaces. Our decision to use Indigenous methodologies, particularly a conversational method (Kovach, 2010b), in this chapter is a deliberate act that honors the experiences of Indigenous peoples and accounts for the responsibility of passing-on shared knowledge.

Interpreting the Silence

The lack of academic literature in the area of how Indigenous peoples experience research, in a contemporary sense, suggests that, by-and-large, the academy has not been concerned with the qualitative experience or subjective outcomes of research from the point of view of the Indigenous people(s) being studied. It further suggests that researchers have almost uniformly been primarily focused on "the science" which is connected to contributions in their respective fields, and their own professional goals, rather than on the impact their research has on the population that they are studying. This impact has several overarching effects, including how some Indigenous communities have developed and refined their own Tribal Institutional Review Board and/or community specific regulations on what research can be conducted in their communities. These actions can be seen as enactments of tribal sovereignty. According to Lomawaima and McCarty (2002), Sovereignty is communities' rights "to self-government, self-determination, and self-education. Sovereignty includes the right to linguistic and cultural expression according to local languages and norms" (p. 284).

While Indigenous people are a favorite subject of academic inquiry, researchers typically neglect to ask the people being researched about their experience. Researchers often do not ask pertinent questions such as: How did it feel being researched? What were you expecting? What did you expect to gain for yourself or your community by cooperating with research? Was the experience generative? Was the experience negative? Would you be willing to be researched again? These questions call attention to the importance of seeing the respondents as people, receiving answers, responding appropriately, and modifying research methods and procedures accordingly.

Foundational information about why this is an important issue is provided in the literature. Grande (2004) and Smith (1999) each provide excellently detailed descriptions of the history and journey that Indigenous peoples have traveled, and how those experiences have influenced the current relationships that they (we) have with governments, education systems, and research. Telling the stories of these journeys is beyond the scope of this chapter, but we acknowledge the foundational works of those

242 S. WINDCHIEF ET AL.

who have worked to give voice to Indigenous communities' stories and experiences and problematize the objectification of Indigenous peoples.

Indigenous Values

In an illuminating article, Kirkness and Barnhardt (1991) developed the "Four R's" as a way to explain how institutions of higher education can better address the human resource and educational needs of First Nations students and communities. These "Four R's" are: respect, relevance, reciprocity, and responsibility. This is the respect of the person and Indigenous communities in teaching and practice. In order for information to be relevant to Indigenous students, it must build "upon their customary forms of consciousness and representation" (p. 4). Educators must understand the importance of relationship in their teaching and the cultural significance of a two-way flow of information rather than the western tradition of teaching as a one-way relationship. Lastly, obtaining education has different meaning for Indigenous students, as it opens access to influence and authority in a non-Indigenous context. This provides an excellent foundation for community-centered values as they pertain to education and we advocate that they be applied to research, particularly the research that informs K–20 education in policy and practice.

Archibald (2008) encourages us to search our own motives and methods, to ensure we do not repeat negative experiences and the negative legacy of outside researchers. In taking on this project, were we doing anything different from previous researchers who contributed to the legacy of mistrust among Indigenous communities? Were we being generative? We could, as Archibald, warns "stay by the fire and try to adapt qualitative methodology to fit an Indigenous oral tradition [but this] is also problematic because Indigenous theory does not drive the methodology" (p. 36). As a result, we asked our research collaborators to share their stories.

Archibald (2008) shares that "stories have a way of 'living', of being perpetuated both by the listener/learner's way of making meaning and by the storytellers, who have an important responsibility to tell stories in a particular way" (p. 112). There is a synergistic action between the story and storyteller, and couched in Indigenous tradition, little guidance is given by the teller as to the meaning of the story. The teller need only "breathe life" into the story leaving the hearer to make their own meaning of the story as it applies to their lived reality. This "ambiguity of information" may conflict with the western educational and qualitative research approaches, particularly those having specific guidelines for listening to, and making meaning of a story. In academic research, this is accomplished through the preapproved list of interview questions and prompts that must be submitted through an Institutional Review Board. In her suggestions for successful research within tribal communities, Indigenous researcher Tom-Orme (2014) joins others such as Wilson (2008) and Smith (1999), encouraging researchers to "present studies from a Native paradigm, and develop Native theories and methods that could more appropriately explain challenges in Native communities" (Tom-Orme, 2014, p. 152).

Our collective perspective and theoretical framework is the result of scholarship by Indigenous authors and makes specific use of Indigenous theories including: *Tribal Critical Race Theory* (Brayboy, 2005), *Red Pedagogy* (Grande, 2008), *Decolonizing Methodologies* (Smith, 1999), *Indigenous Storywork* (Archibald, 2008). These seminal works, when braided together, provide a framework that honors the lived realities of Indigenous people. "Stories are not separate from theory; they make up theory and are, therefore, real and legitimate sources of data and ways of being" (Brayboy, 2005 p. 430) and helps us center our work in hearing and honoring the stories of our participants. In *Red Pedagogy* (First Edition) Grande (2004) not only calls for an improvement upon the current educational paradigm but asks of scholars in the world of Indigenous intellectualism to struggle in finding answers. Linda Smith's (2002) seminal text *Decolonizing Methodologies* reminds us that this work is more than merely deconstructing Western scholarship, and that it is mindful of the damage that Western scholarship can do when it informs policy. We understand that that there are complex ways of engaging in, telling, listening to, and acting upon, stories that are shared through relationship (Archibald, 2008). Finally we want to illuminate how scholarship is strengthened as a result of understanding and making use of relationships with each other and among research collaborators (often referred to as respondents) in an Indigenous research paradigm, being mindful of axiology, epistemology, and ontology (Kovach, 2010a; Wilson, 2008).

By making use of an Indigenous research paradigm we challenge western assumptions of what it means to find the answer. We consider our community partners as research collaborators as opposed to "respondents," "informants" or "subjects" in an effort to make research a humanizing process (Paris & Winn, 2013).

AN INDIGENOUS METHODOLOGY

During our collective discourse it was suggested that the best way to learn about Indigenous research should be to talk directly to Indigenous people who have participated in research. Using Indigenous methodologies, decolonizing methodologies, our own learned Indigenous ontologies, and borrowing from published Indigenous research paradigms (Archibald,

2008; Grande, 2005; Smith, 2002; Wilson 2008), we coconstructed a research plan that would originate in, and integrate an Indigenous paradigm. A collaborative design emerged, and a plan to converse with American Indian and Alaska Native (AIAN) people who had participated in some type of research study using conversational methods was implemented. Kovach (2010b) explains that the conversational method "aligns with an Indigenous worldview that honors orality as a means of transmitting knowledge and upholds the relational which is necessary to maintain a collectivist tradition" (p. 42). This study utilized a conversational (qualitative) method to capture experiences from previous AIAN research participants.

The authors had unscripted and unrecorded conversations with research collaborators. These conversations were later documented and presented to the collaborators making sure that they accurately reflected the conversations and information from the conversations could be shared through publication. This action (sometimes referred to as "member checking") both respected Indigenous cultural protocol and ensured that the information to be shared was accurate and appropriate to share within public intellectual space. This practice guards against deficit perspectives becoming part of the research model. Deficit model research includes assumptions, usually based on stereotypes and biases both conscious and unconscious, that a person or population has a weakness, vulnerability, or somehow deviates from "normal."

If methodology is indeed using the appropriate method to find the answer to a particular question, then it is important to choose the most culturally appropriate method when working with any population. An appropriate (Indigenous) methodology shows the importance of earning, maintaining, and responsibly utilizing trust when working with Indigenous peoples. In order to establish trust and subsequent authenticity of voice, the authors identified a research collaborators as opposed to "data sources" or "subjects" with whom they had a previously established relationship to engage in conversation. One of the authors did not have a previously established relationship with someone who was both Indigenous and a previous research participant, and so they utilized a concept we will call "relationship by proxy" to be defined later in the chapter.

In the application of an Indigenous methodology we oppose "Western" notions of objectivity in research. In our collective discourse we want to reiterate that respondents are research collaborators, choosing to strengthen relationships. Too often people are referred to in traditional academic inquiry in dehumanizing ways. By employing an Indigenous research method we are working with Indigenous peoples and communities, not "units" to be examined, measured and objectified.

Indigenous methodologies in research explore the importance of relationship and trust between the researcher and the community in which research is being done as well as how knowledge can be received, recorded, and shared, in alignment with Indigenous communities' contexts in pragmatic ways. The authors share these conversations only after receiving permission from our research collaborators. With regard to confidentiality and in order to provide autonomy, the research collaborators in these conversations were offered the opportunity to choose a pseudonym, or use their real names, and are represented as, "Kennedy" (pseudonym), John, and Cheryl. The excerpts that they provided represent the lived experiences of North American Indigenous people who have been involved in research both in the capacities of researchers and research respondents.

RESEARCH COLLABORATORS

Our research collaborators provided a wealth of knowledge through their own lived experiences. All self-identify, and are identified by different Indigenous communities, as North American Indigenous people in different ways. They have been engaged in Indigenous research both as "subjects" of academic inquiry as well as performed academic research as professionals and scholars, thus they are "experts," though in alignment with Indigenous ontologies, they most likely would not verbalize this. We would like to introduce them to you.

Kennedy (pseudonym)—Kennedy has developed a unique perspective as a mentor for AIAN students through a summer research experience program. She has also been involved as a participant in (or more accurately a subject of) a student-led research study at an institution of higher learning, as well as conducted research within her own home community. Throughout her conversations and stories, she moved in and out of these identities, and shared a number of unique insights into research by, on, and within self identified American Indian/Alaska Native (AI/AN) communities.

John—John, working with other committed Apsáalooke community members as well as non-Indigenous researchers and professionals, secured major grant funding to upgrade the community water supply systems. He has now invested decades of his life contributing to the process of upgrading water distribution and sewer systems in Crow Agency, MT, and addressing other water related problems all over the reservation. John related that there was a strong feeling of resentment against nontribal members doing research, even if it was connected to matters of vital and pressing importance to tribal members. He is recognized by both his community and the scientific academe as a leader in conducting research and affecting change on his own reservation.

Cheryl—Cheryl, a current doctoral candidate in adult and higher education, a runner and a researcher, described three experiences being researched. The first experience that she had being the "subject" of academic inquiry was at a young age in elementary school. The second story shared was during her experience in higher education. The last experience happened during graduate school. During this conversation, Cheryl gave her opinions about what researchers need to do in order to appropriately and respectfully conduct research on AI/AN people. It is important to note that while Cheryl had provided information during several meetings, she and one of the coauthors were using the relationship that was through one of the other coauthors. This was done in an effort to establish the appropriate trust need in order to have this conversation.

By using alternative methods—informal, nonrecorded conversations— we believe the meanings of the stories, that are shared by or research collaborators, will take on the authenticity of the storyteller and the listeners through a dialogic spiral based on one's ability to reciprocate in being vulnerable and holding the vulnerability of another (Grande, San Pedro, & Windchief, 2015; San Pedro, 2013). In this way, personal meaning is coconstructed through the development of the relationship between the storytellers and the authors respectively.

RESULTS

Upon completion of the conversation analyses, several themes emerged that illuminated how AIANs experience research both as researchers and as "subjects" of research to include deficit model perspectives, ethical misconduct and trust, the importance of relationships, generative research, and exploitative research. We explain these themes and provide examples to clarify what they look like in the process of academic inquiry.

Deficit Model Discourse

One of our coresearchers, Kennedy, related her experience as a subject of a student led study that occurred a few years ago. She received an e-mail from a student she did not know, asking her to participate in a survey for the student's study about AIAN health issues. The student gave her name but very little other information. Kennedy was shocked at the questions being asked on the survey: How often do you drink alcohol? How has family dysfunction affected your life? Other questions that assumed the participant lived on a reservation and participated in cultural activities were included in the questionnaire. Kennedy was offended by these questions clearly based on stereotypes and responded to the student by explaining she should not ask these biased questions and that not all AIAN people have the same experiences and circumstances. After sending the survey back, she continued to feel bothered by it, and took action with the university Institutional Review Board to prevent it from being sent out to more AIAN students and eventually reported as valid and reliable research, serving to falsely substantiate deficit model perspectives as they relate to Indigenous peoples.

We assume that the student who sent out the survey had good intentions, but had not recognized the impact of their survey on the people who would be taking it. This was also brought up in all three of the examples that Cheryl used during her conversation with one of the authors.

Cheryl was asked questions during her undergraduate experience about nutrition, and the foundations of proper nutrition. Again, the researcher had made assumptions. This assumption had created frustration while answering questions that she was asked, because she was very knowledgeable about nutrition and exercise. Cheryl is a runner, and had been running for a long time, however, the researcher had made the assumption that all Native Americans would be deficient in the area of health and wellness.

Refraining from deficit model assumptions was important to the researchers during our study, (How AI/ANs have experienced research) as we recognized the lack of respect that such dialogue contains. Just because our AI/AN research collaborators had been researched in the past, did not mean that they were damaged or needed help because of their experience. In its place, it was important to recognize ways that in the future researchers could be more respectful in similar circumstances.

Ethical Misconduct and Trust

Examples of ethical misconduct were provided during the conversations with both Cheryl and John. Cheryl remembers asking the researchers (in the case of the health and wellness research) if they could provide the results of their study in the future, however, at the time of writing this chapter, she has yet to hear back from the researcher about their findings. Cheryl iterated the importance of reciprocity when doing all research, not just research on Native Americans. In this case, the researcher and the research collaborator, both saw the importance of making sure that research results make it back to the people that are being researched.

Ethical misconduct comes in multiple forms. John shares a story about water quality research, its effects and how ethical misconduct can have consequences that thwart important research that could be done in the future.

> One of our very sacred and historically important springs of water is now contaminated with dangerous e-coli bacteria from a septic system. Our own

scientific investigation points to a septic system installed, owned, and inadequately maintained by the State of Montana. The State is rejecting our results. They say they will have to have confirmation from scientists working for them. So, they created the problem, and then we used their science and technology to discover the problem. They say they can't, as of yet, correct the problem. They do not even admit their responsibility. Our community is left to suffer for who knows how long? Our people are feeling resentful and distrustful over this. A strong sentiment present at a recent Tribal IRB workshop was that the IRB approval process should be made so difficult that very little future research will be undertaken on reservations. That we also depend on and benefit from some of the systems (the ones that work properly and non-destructively) has been overshadowed.

John expressed his desire that this nonconstructive and adversarial situation be addressed in our current work, for the benefit of present and future generations, prompting us to ask an important question; what would happen if all Tribal Institutional Review Board requests were denied? The impact of this would affect not only researchers who had participated in research for their own gains, but also researchers who were well informed in their approach. It is important to recognize that distrust can happen during all aspects of a research study to include the intricacies of proper acknowledgement.

We contend that an Indigenous research paradigm considers, in an iterative way, what the individual and community thinks and feels before, during, and after the research. We assert that community input is vital to Indigenous research as a whole and is also indispensable to the process of evaluating and improving Indigenous community well-being. This is an active resistance to the deficit model discourse that is all too prevalent when educational research takes place within communities of color.

Relationship

Indigenous epistemologies often require an established, trusting relationship in order to transfer knowledge. For this reason, preestablished relationships are necessary when conducting culturally appropriate Indigenous research. This is accomplished through time spent with, and respect given to, Indigenous people(s) traditions, and communities. These relationships reveal the researcher's intentions, and are a natural phenomenon in the building of trust. The establishment of trust insures that participation in research is genuine, authentic and mutually beneficial to both the researcher and the community. The following is an example of how the lack of established relationships could lead to distrust between researchers and the people they wish to research.

In an attempt to help the non-Native researchers and staff understand how to work with AI/AN students, the program Kennedy worked for provided orientation sessions that gave pointers on what to expect from the students. While this was helpful to the researchers in some aspects, Kennedy noticed that much of the information was based on stereotypical information, promoted Indian "mysticism" and repeated deficit model thinking regarding Indigenous peoples. This served to misinform the researchers, as many did not seem to recognize that these students were highly intelligent teenagers from a variety of backgrounds, and savvy enough to realize when someone was there to exploit their heritage for personal or professional gain. The students, in response, would purposely provide misleading information to the staff, while privately sharing with each other their frustrations; often tolerating microaggressive and essentialist environments while being asked to share their personal lives and beliefs.

Had the staff of this program treated the students with respect and taken the time to develop relationships with the students, it is likely that the students might have been more genuine in their responses. Creating genuine relationships and developing trust are helpful in identifying needs within the Indigenous community, making sure that the researcher's intent and the subsequent impacts of their research are aligned. One way of accomplishing this would be to provide the research question to the students and have them provide feedback regarding the questions to be asked in the research protocol.

Relationship by Proxy

In the lived realities of researchers, relationships often cannot be directly established between a researcher and their collaborators. This phenomenon calls for the use of what we term as "relationship by proxy." Relationship by proxy is established when a person has established enough trust with an intermediary that they can be trusted to honor the relationship which allows for Indigenous research to occur in a culturally appropriate way. An example of how relationship by proxy can be utilized in practice is as follows: The researcher (who may be a member of the people(s) collaborating in the project) has previously established a strong relationship and trust with a tribal elder. This elder introduces the researcher to several people within the community who will be participating in the researcher's study, and because the researcher has this strong relationship with the tribal elder, they have the assumed trust of the collaborators allowing for results that better reflect lived realities. There is a fine line to be drawn here. To make friends with tribal elders and/or community members, for the sole purpose of research, is a good indicator that the research is exploitative as opposed to generative.

Generative/Exploitative Research

Research can be classified into two groups that represent the way in which research is utilized, (1) exploitative and (2) generative. Exploitative research is the utilization of knowledge without consideration for the sample, population, or community in which it is gathered or found. Generative research is the gathering of knowledge in a way that works to support the wellbeing of the sample, population, or community and is called for by that community. This was a topic discussed during the conversation conducted with John who iterates the damage that can come as a result of exploitative research:

> Many members of the community feel angry at research and researchers, which they regard as being detrimental to the community welfare, and they feel justified at being very distrustful and resentful of what they can see as a pattern of dishonesty and exploitation. Research which results in the erosion of community wellbeing is destructive research. It benefits somebody else, and is a kind of exploitation. It has happened a lot in our history.

As John helps us comprehend the dangers of exploitative and destructive research, we refer to its opposite, which is research that strengthens community well-being. We identify this as generative research. It is important to recognize that research almost always fall somewhere on a spectrum, with each of these terms, *generative* and *exploitative,* representing opposite sides of that spectrum. Below there are two hypothetical examples of similar research; the first example falls on the exploitative side and the second falls on the generative side of the continuum.

An example of research that is located on the exploitative side of the spectrum is a study on the cause of obesity in any given Indigenous community. The researcher goes into the community with the intention of determining obesity rates as they theorize that it might be an issue that should be tested and reported on. The researcher takes blood samples, gathers results, leaves, and publishes their article. A pharmaceutical firm notices the researcher's article and the researcher is invited to submit a proposal for a lucrative research grant from them as a result. The intention of this research was good, the researcher hoped that the knowledge gained could be utilized to further understand the causes of health problems within the community, however, this researcher failed to share the results of their study with the Indigenous community that they were working in, nor asked the community about their wishes regarding the knowledge gained, how it was shared or even if the results were provided in a useful way to the community. However from the perspective of the pharmaceutical firm, there is money to made as a result of community members sharing their experiences.

Conversely, a similar research study, which would be located on the generative side of the research spectrum, is shared. A researcher introduces themselves, revisits, or returns home, to an Indigenous community, they visit friends and relatives, and take time to reify their relationships within the community. The researcher asks the community if there is any way that the researcher's skills in biomedical research could be of use within the community. Research collaborators; the elders of the community, tribal leaders, and healthcare practitioners who are also community members, ask the researcher if they could look into the cause of obesity in their community and share the knowledge with the community as a whole. Upon getting permission through both appropriate community and academic avenues, the researcher gathers data, takes samples, articulates results, writes about their results, but before publishing those results they share with the community what they have discovered, and ask for permission to publish the findings. They consult the community, and share that the community has the right to refuse what is shared. The community collaborators (hopefully) give the researcher permission to proceed. Only then does the researcher publish the results in an academic peer-reviewed journal. In this iterative process, the research-related products must be delivered to the community and translated into pragmatic action. Once this is accomplished, chances are that other opportunities for research projects will be revealed.

When researching with and within Indigenous communities it is important to make sure that researchers are in constant and reliable communication with the collaborators. Reciprocal communication should occur at all stages of research, from before the research question is asked, through publication and pragmatic implementation. This ensures that the research being conducted is generative as opposed to exploitative, and serves the community well-being.

CONCLUSION

In conclusion, our research collaborators have communicated that the intricacies of Indigenous research are contextual, meaning that they are based upon where they and the researcher is located on an Indigenous identity continuum (Starnes, Swaney, & Bull, 2006). This continuum is defined in the literature as "American Indians are located on an identity continuum from being deeply immersed in Indigenous ontological space, to being deeply immersed in non-Indigenous ontological space" (Joseph & Windchief, 2015, p. 92). Importantly, it is noted that this is not a deficit perspective, rather it represents places of community contribution as a result of lived experiences. Furthermore, the relationship that has been developed between the researcher and the collaborator is of paramount importance (Wilson, 2008).

The practical implications of this chapter include; being mindful to not exploit the people who are willing to share knowledge. The goal is to listen, receive, and share in a responsible and trusting way. Doing this involves; making relationship a priority, working for the community and using community coconstructed definitions for success, giving control over the data and its dissemination to the collaborators, and challenge deficit based representations. When Indigenous people are reclaiming research there are generative ways of researching that serve to provide for the community while simultaneously protecting traditional knowledge from academic exploitation.

In reading and thinking about this chapter, our intention is that you will have a better understanding of how IRMs can be properly utilized in your own research involving Indigenous communities. In addition, this chapter serves as a call to action for the researchers, whose work will inform policy, curriculum, and practice in K–20 multicultural educational context. We advocate for the implementation of Indigenous values in research and its dissemination, community empowerment, reciprocal exchange, continual constructive development, tribal sovereignty, and self-determination. To communicate this in metaphor, Indigenous researchers and allies can be spokes in a much larger wheel. In order to contribute, researchers would do well to respect Indigenous peoples and communities in all settings, offer their contributions with mindful appropriate intention, and exhibit courage in finding ways to promote success from an Indigenous point-of-view. In the reclamation of Indigenous knowledge and process, there is substantive theory to draw from, Indigenous and decolonizing methodologies to employ, and practical applications to support "Our Knowledge, Our Way."

NOTE

1. This manuscript uses the terms Indigenous, American Indian, and Alaska Native, Native and Native American not interchangeably but in the terms that the literature uses or our research collaborators use them. Political connotation within the terminology is understood by these sources in multiple ways and without the authors' judgment.

REFERENCES

Archibald, J. A. (2008). *Indigenous storywork: Educating the heart, mind, body, and spirit.* British Colombia, CAN: UBC Press.

Baldwin, J. A. (1998). Conducting drug abuse prevention research in partnership with Native American communities: Meeting challenges through collaborative approaches. *Drugs and Society, 14*(1–2), 77–92. doi:10.1300/J023v14n01_07

Beauvais, F. (1998) Obtaining consent and other ethical issues in the conduct of research in American Indian communities. *Drugs & Society, 14*(1–2), 167–184. doi:10.1300/J023v14n01_13

Brayboy, B. M. J. (2005). Toward a tribal critical race theory in education. *The Urban Review, 37*(5), 425–446.

Buchwald, D., Mendoza-Jenkins, V., Croy, C., McGough, H., Bezdek, M., Spicer, P. (2006). Attitudes of urban American Indians and Alaska Natives regarding participation in research. *Journal of General Internal Medicine, 21,* 645–651. doi:10.1111/j.1525-1497.2006.00449.x

Chawla-Sahota, P. (2012). Critical contexts for biomedical research in a Native American community: Healthcare, history, and community survival. *American Indian Culture and Research Journal, 36,* 3–18.

Grande, S. (2004). Whitestream feminism and the colonialist project: Toward a theory of Indigenista. *Red Pedagogy: Native American Social and Political Thought,* 123–157.

Grande, S. (2015). *Red pedagogy: Native American social and political thought.* Lanham, MD: Rowman & Littlefield.

Grande, S., San Pedro, T., & Windchief, H. (2015). 21st century indigenous identity location: Remembrance, reclamation, and regeneration. In D. Koslow & L. Salett (Eds.), *Multiple perspectives on race, ethnicity and identity* (3rd ed., pp. 105–122). Washington, DC: NASW Press.

Guillemin, M., Gillam, L., Barnard, E., Stewart, P., Walker, H., & Rosenthal, D. (2016). "We're checking them out": Indigenous and non-Indigenous research participants' accounts of deciding to be involved in research. *International Journal for Equity in Health, 15*(8). doi:10.1186/s/2939-016-0301-4

Hiratsuka, V. Y., Brown, J. K., Hoeft, T. J., Dillard, D. A. (2012). Alaska Native people's perceptions, understandings, and expectations for research involving biological specimens. *International Journal of Circumpolar Health, 71.* doi:10.3402/ijch.v71i0.18642

Joseph, D. H., & Windchief, S. R. (2015). Nahongvita: A conceptual model to support rural American Indian youth in pursuit of higher education. *Journal of American Indian Education, 54*(3), 76–97.

Kirkness, V. J., & Barnhardt, R. (1991). First Nations and higher education: The Four R's-respect, relevance, reciprocity, responsibility. *Journal of American Indian Education, 30*(3), 1–15.

Kovach, M. (2010a). *Indigenous methodologies: Characteristics, conversations, and contexts.* Toronto, Canada: University of Toronto Press.

Kovach, M. (2010b). Conversation method in Indigenous research. *First Peoples Child & Family Review, 5*(1), 40–48.

LaVeaux, D., & Christopher, S. (2009). Contextualizing CBPR: Key principles of CBPR meet the Indigenous research context. *Pimatisiwin*, 7(1), 1.

Lomawaima, K. T., & McCarty, T. L. (2002). When tribal sovereignty challenges democracy: American Indian education and the democratic ideal. *American Educational Research Journal*, 39(2), 279–305.

Noe, T. D., Manson, S. M., Croy, C., McGough, H., Henderson, J. A., & Buchwald, D. S. (2007). The influence of community-based participatory research principles on the likelihood of participation in health research in American Indian communities. *Ethnicity & Disease*, 17(Suppl 1), S6–14.

Paris, D., & Winn, M. (2014). *Humanizing research: Decolonizing qualitative inquiry with youth and communities*. Los Angeles, CA: SAGE.

San Pedro, T. (2013). Understanding youth cultures, stories, and resistances in the urban Southwest: Innovations and implications of a Native American literature classroom. Available from ProQuest Dissertations and Theses database (UMI No. 3558673)

San Pedro, T., Carlos, E., & Mburu, J. (2016). Critical listening and storying fostering respect for difference and action within and beyond a Native American literature classroom. *Urban Education*. https://doi.org/10.1177/0042085915623346

Smith, L. T. (1999). *Decolonizing methodologies: Research and Indigenous peoples*. New York, NY: Zed Books.

Starnes, B. A., Swaney, E., & Bull, L. T. (2006). Montana's Indian education for all: Toward an education worthy of American ideals. *Phi Delta Kappan*, 88(3), 184.

Tom-Orme, L. (2015). Guidelines for conducting successful community-based participatory research in American Indian and Alaska Native communities. In T. G. Arambula Solomon & L. L. Randall (Eds.), *Conducting Health Research with Native American Communities* (pp. 145–156). Washington, DC: American Public Health Association.

Weber-Pillwax, C. (2001). What Is Indigenous Research? *Canadian Journal of Native Education*, 25(2), 166–174.

Wilson, S. (2008). *Research is ceremony: Indigenous research methods*. Halifax, NS, Canada: Fernwood.

ABOUT THE AUTHORS

EDITORS

Adriel A. Hilton, PhD, is dean of students and diversity officer at Seton Hill University in Greensburg, Pennsylvania. Recently, he served as director of the Webster University Myrtle Beach Metropolitan Extended Campus. As the chief administrative officer, he worked to implement programs and policies to achieve Webster University's overall goals and objectives at the extended campus. In the past, Dr. Hilton has served as chief of staff and executive assistant to the president at Grambling State University and assistant professor and director of the Higher Education Student Affairs program at Western Carolina University. A prolific author and researcher, Dr. Hilton's research is published in refereed journals, such as *Teachers College Record, Journal of College Student Development, Community College Review, Community College Journal of Research and Practice, Journal of Applied Research in the Community College,* and the *Journal of the Professoriate.* His numerous service commitments include membership on the editorial boards of the renowned *Journal of Negro Education* and the highly acclaimed *College Student Affairs Journal.* Dr. Hilton holds a Bachelor of Business Administration degree in finance from Morehouse College, Atlanta, Georgia; a Master of Applied Social Science degree, with a concentration in public administration from Florida A&M University, Tallahassee, Florida; a Master of Business Administration degree from Webster University, St. Louis, Missouri; and a PhD in higher education, with a concentration in administration, from Morgan State University, Baltimore, Maryland.

Brandi N. Hinnant-Crawford, PhD, is an Assistant Professor of Educational Research at Western Carolina University. As a mixed-methods methodologist, she believes in the complimentary nature of quantitative and qualitative research, and seeks to use quantitative research in transformative ways (such as with improvement science). Self-described as a womanist, liberation theologian, critical pedagogue, and aspiring scholar-activist, Dr. Hinnant-Crawford's work has been published in a diverse array of journals, including: *Journal for Multicultural Education, International Journal for Teacher Leadership,* and *Black Theology.* As a lifelong educator, she has experiences ranging from the classroom to the central office in settings from rural North Carolina to urban upstate New York. Employing an advocacy framework, Hinnant-Crawford's work seeks to expose policies and practices related to exploitation, domination, and marginalization—while simultaneously exploring remedies to alleviate impact of those policies and practices. Specifically, her multitiered research agenda explores environments that cultivate or encumber agents of change. In terms of cultivation, she examines spaces (such as religious and educational institutions) as well as curricula and pedagogical practices (such as multicultural education, youth participatory action research, and project-based learning) that lead to the development of agents of change. Brandi holds a doctorate in philosophy from Emory University in Educational Studies, a master's degree in Urban Education Policy from Brown University, and bachelor's degrees in English and Communication (media concentration) from North Carolina State University. While she loves research and teaching, her first priority is being the mother of her 6-year-old twins, Elizabeth Freedom and Elijah Justice Crawford.

Christopher B. Newman, PhD, is an Associate Professor at Azusa Pacific University in the School of Behavioral and Applied Sciences' Department of Higher Education. Formerly, he served as Chair of the American Educational Research Association (AERA) Multicultural/Multiethnic Education: Theory, Research and Practice Special Interest Group. His research focuses primarily on outcomes, inequities, and undergraduate student experiences in Science, Technology, Engineering and Mathematics (STEM). He also studies college readiness and pathways into postsecondary education for students of color. Additionally, he has interests in multicultural education in global contexts. Dr. Newman has served as a consultant to the National Science Foundation's Colloquy on Minority Males and has presented his scholarship at AERA, Association for the Study of Higher (ASHE), American Association for the Advancement of Science (AAAS), Understanding Interventions, National Society for Black Physicists (NSBP), and United Arab Emirates University Innovation and Research for Education Excellence conferences. He is coeditor (with Shaun R. Harper) of the volume,

Students of Color in STEM. His research has appeared in the *Journal of Multicultural Education, Journal of Women and Minorities in Science and Engineering, Journal of Research in Science Teaching, Teachers College Record,* the *Journal of Social Issues, The Journal of Negro Education,* and *Urban Education* among others. Dr. Newman earned his bachelor's degree in sociology from the University of California at Santa Barbara, his master's degree in leadership studies from the University of San Diego, and his master's and PhD in higher education and organization change from UCLA.

C. Spencer Platt, PhD, is an Assistant Professor of Higher Education Administration at the University of South Carolina. He earned his PhD from the University of Texas at Austin. His MS degree is from the University of Dayton, and he holds a bachelor's degree from the University of South Carolina. Dr. Platt has over 15 years of experience in student affairs, community engagement and academic affairs. His research interests include: Black males in higher education, access to higher education, critical race theory, mentoring relationships between faculty and students of color, and the socialization of doctoral students of color at predominantly White universities. Platt's research has been published in the *Journal of College Student Development,* the *Journal of Advanced Academics* and he has coedited a book titled *Boyhood to Manhood: Deconstructing Masculinity through a life Span Continuum.* He has presented his academic work at the *American Educational Research Association,* the *Association for the Study of Higher Education,* the *International Conference on Doctoral Education,* the *International Colloquium on Black Males in Education* and other national and international conferences. He is also married and the father of two sons.

AUTHORS

William David Aderholdt is a graduate student of the doctorate of philosophy in Adult and Higher Education program at Montana State University. David is currently working on a dissertation focused on the evaluation of federal education policy; specifically, Title IX of the Education Amendments of 1972. His research interests include: education law and policy, civil rights, student conduct, and behavioral intervention. His wife, Lana, and him live in Fargo, North Dakota with their dog, Rue.

Najja K. Baptist is a doctoral candidate and instructor in Political Science at Howard University. Bridging the gap between policy and populace, Najja's work seeks to expand the boundaries of politics by advocating for the disenfranchised through specificity and adaptive systems. His research interests include popular culture, political theory, political behavior, Black politics, political attitudes, African American politics, political psychology and public opinion.

Shamaine K. Bazemore-Bertrand, PhD, is an Assistant Professor of Elementary Education at Illinois State University. Shamaine's research focuses on exploring how to prepare preservice teachers for high-poverty schools in both rural and urban school districts. Her research interests include: university-school partnerships, teacher preparation, clinical practice, multicultural education, and action research.

Nathaniel Bryan, PhD, is Assistant Professor of Early Childhood Education at Miami University in Oxford, Ohio. He is a transdisciplinary urban education scholar whose research focuses on the recruitment and retention of Black male teachers in early childhood education and the school and childhood play experiences of Black boys.

James D. Cryer, EdD, Assistant Professor in the College of Education at the University of Northern Iowa, is a former elementary principal and current literacy professor. He has firsthand knowledge as a literacy leader and guiding teachers in creating literacy learning environments using the *Literacy as Access Framework*. His research interests include: literacy instruction, teacher education, and field-based clinical experiences.

James Coaxum, III, PhD, is an Associate Professor in the Educational Services and Leadership Department at Rowan University. His research agenda is focused on issues of equity and access that impacts students of color in the educational pipeline. He has received a number of awards in recognition for his contributions to higher education and student development fields. He spends a considerable amount of time as a practitioner organizing leadership development trainings and diversity workshops for paraprofessionals in higher education. Dr. Coaxum also has a strong interest in community engagement and so his work in this area is organized around programmatic initiatives that serve urban youth as well as their families. Dr. James Coaxum received his PhD from Vanderbilt University, his EdM from Harvard University, and his BS from Morehouse College.

James M. Del Duca (Chiluubé Akchiá) is the adopted child of Bachéewassee and Baaxpáa Íkaa of Crow Agency, Montana. A Big-Lodge clan member and a child of the Ties-the-Bundle clan, he is blessed with eight children and two grandchildren. He Sun Dances in both Lakota and Apsáalooge traditions. Currently a PhD student at MSU-Bozeman, he is examining Indigenous connections to Black music in the American South.

C. Vandyke Goings, PhD, was an exemplary math educator at the Westminster School in Atlanta, Georgia. Dr. Goings was beloved by all students and colleagues and known for making the people around him better. His scholarship focused on the dyadic relationships between teachers and students and how those relationships can cultivate or inhibit the development of positive mathematical self-concept in students of color.

Marjorie Hall Haley, PhD, is Professor of Education in the Graduate School of Education at George Mason University in Fairfax, Virginia (United States). Her research includes examining disproportionate representations of culturally, linguistically, and cognitively diverse learners in U.S. schools, providing culturally and linguistically responsive instruction for all learners, and brain-compatible teaching and learning. Her research and publication record is wide and includes numerous books, articles, and essays that have influenced national and international arenas.

Ted N. Ingram, PhD, is a Professor of General Counseling at Bronx Community College, CUNY. He earned a bachelor's degree in Spanish at University at Albany, a master's degree in higher education at Rowan University, and a PhD in higher education administration from Indiana University. Dr. Ingram's research focuses on how students of color thrive in college: the experiences of Black and Brown students in higher education, men of color persistence in community college, and persistence of first-generation students in graduate school.

Maya Kalyanpur, PhD, is Professor and Chair in the Department of Teaching and Learning at the University of San Diego. She worked as Inclusive Education Advisor to the Cambodian Ministry of Education under the World Bank-supported Global Partnership for Education program. Her research interests lie in the intersection of culture with special education, with a specific focus on international inclusive and special education policy and practice, and families of children with disabilities from culturally and linguistically diverse backgrounds.

LaGarrett J. King, PhD, is an Associate Professor of Social Studies Education at the University of Missouri. He is also the Founding Director of the CARTER Center for K–12 Black History Research, Teaching, and Curriculum. He received his PhD from the University of Texas at Austin after an 8-year teaching career in Georgia and Texas. His primary research interest is on the teaching and learning of Black history in schools and society. He also researches critical theories of race, teacher education, and curriculum history. His work has been published in *Urban Education, Journal of Negro Education, Teaching Education,* and *Race, Ethnicity, and Education.*

Deborah (Clairmont) LaVeaux, a first-generation descendant of the Confederated Salish and Kootenai Tribes in Montana, is a doctoral candidate in Adult and Higher Education at Montana State University. Her research interests include university-tribal community research, specifically the development, evaluation, and sustainability of these partnerships. She and her husband Thom have four children and two grandchildren who are a constant inspiration to persevere in this work.

Tiffany M. Mitchell, PhD, is an Assistant Professor of Secondary Social Studies at West Virginia University. Tiffany's work focuses on the analysis of social studies and civics curricula through Critical Race Theory and elevating teacher voices in education research and policy by exploring their instructional practices. Her research interests include antibias, social justice and multicultural education, examining curriculum policies through a critical lens, teacher and youth voice in activism, education research and policy, and utilizing archival research to uncover untold histories of people of color that can be incorporated in social studies classrooms.

James L. Moore III, PhD, is the Vice Provost For Diversity and Inclusion and Chief Diversity Officer at The Ohio State University. He is also the EHE Distinguished Professor of Urban Education in the College of Education, while also serving as the inaugural executive director for the Todd Anthony Bell National Resource on the African American Male. Dr. Moore is both nationally- and internationally-recognized for his research on Black males. He has obtained over $14 million of funding and accumulated over 130 publications, focusing on urban education, gifted education, STEM education, higher education, school counseling, and multicultural education/counseling.

Rhonda L. Sutton-Palmer, EdD, is the CEO/Founder, Michael J. Hawkins Transition Planning Services NJ Corporation. Utilizing servant, transformational, and symbolic leadership approaches, Rhonda's lifelong mission is to Pay It Forward by providing the necessary services for our young people to transition into adulthood. Ultimately, enabling them to make positive and productive decisions for their future. Her research interests include: multicultural education, youth and family empowerment, special education action research, activism, and educational policy.

Ashley N. Patterson, PhD, is an Assistant Professor of Language, Culture and Society in the College of Education at The Pennsylvania State University where she teaches a variety of courses addressing literacy issues through a social justice lens. In both her teaching and scholarship, Ashley seeks to identify and communicate ways in which equity can be achieved within the educational system and in particular those who are marginalized within the existing structure. Her research focuses on the intersection of identity and educational experiences as she considers the influence of race and other identity markers on both learners and learning spaces.

Gretchen G. Robinson, PhD, is an Associate Professor of Special Education at the University of North Carolina at Pembroke. Using an equity framework, Gretchen's work seeks to promote policies and practices to reduce disproportionality of minority students in special education, while investigating evidence-based instructional practices to solve this issue. Her research interests include: culturally responsive pedagogy, multitier systems of support, and language and literacy practices for students who are at-risk or who have disabilities.

Charmion B. Rush, PhD, is an Assistant Professor of Inclusive and Special Education at Western Carolina University. Dr. Rush's teaching, research, and service focuses on preparing educators to teach diverse populations; emphasizing the ethnic/minority students enrolled in special education. Her areas of research include culture responsive pedagogy, disproportionate representation, implicit bias, inclusion, and literacy practices.

Dwight C. Watson, EdD, is currently the Provost and Vice President of Academic and Student Affairs at Southwest Minnesota State University. He is the former Dean of the College of Education at the University of Northern Iowa. This article was written based on Dr. Watson's experiences as a literacy professor, elementary teacher, reading specialist, and district literacy administrator.

Sweeny Windchief (Tatanga Togahe), a member of the Fort Peck Tribes (Assiniboine) in Montana, serves as an Assistant Professor of Adult and Higher Education at Montana State University. His research interests include higher education specifically under the umbrella of Indigenous intellectualism. His teaching privileges include critical race theory, Indigenous methodologies in research, law and policy in higher education and institutional research. He and his wife Sara have two sons who help keep things in perspective.

Dorian L. Wingard, MPA, is a current doctoral student in Western Carolina University's Educational Leadership program, and also Principal & Chief Executive Officer at Midwest Strategies, LLC. Dorian's overall interest is in the application of progressive public policy on to systemic urban challenges as they relate to public higher education, human services and criminal justice system equity and alignment. His research interests include: public education policy, social injustice activism and the application of improvement science on to relevant public policies addressing inequity and inequality.

Brian L. Wright, PhD, is Assistant Professor of Early Childhood Education at the University of Memphis in Memphis, TN and author of *The Brilliance of Black Boys: Cultivating School Success in the Early Grades*. His research examines high-achieving African American males in urban pre-K–12 schools, racial-ethnic identity of boys and young men of color, and teacher identity development.